More
Safety and Security
at Sports Grounds

Jim Chalmers and Steve Frosdick

2

Published by Paragon Publishing, Rothersthorpe, UK
First published 2011
© Jim Chalmers and Steve Frosdick 2011

ISBN 978-1-907611-98-8

British Library Cataloguing-in-Publication Data
A catalogue record for this book is available from the British Library

Book design and layout by IWI Associates
Proof reading and copy editing by Sara Travis and Alison Frosdick
Production management by Into Print (www.intoprint.net)
Printed and bound in the UK and USA by Lightning Source

DEDICATIONS

Dedicated to my wife Pauline,
daughters Sue and Kim
and my grandchildren Kate, Mark and Sean
for all the love, joy and happiness
you bring into my life.

Jim (Husband, Dad and Grandad).

Dedicated to my wife Alison;
and to my children
John, Kat, Rachel and Andy.
With much love

Steve

TO BILL

A GOOD FRIEND, COLLEAGUE AND FELLOW

MEMBER OF ACPO. BEST WISHES FOR THE

FUTURE.

Jim Holmes

July 2011

Steve Lee

July 2011

CONTENTS

FOREWORD

We have both known Jim Chalmers and Steve Frosdick in a personal and professional capacity for over twenty years. They are well known names in the European safety and security at sports grounds industry and, on behalf of our members, we are delighted to have this opportunity to introduce their second book.

Safety and Security at Sports Grounds was published in 2005 and gathered together Steve Frosdick's magazine articles from 1994 to 2004. The articles were accompanied by commentaries by Jim Chalmers, critiquing them and bringing them up to date as necessary.

More Safety and Security at Sports Grounds is a similar work, covering the years 2005 to 2011. But there are some important differences. Most noticeable is Jim Chalmers' contribution to this second book. Free from the constraints of recent employment in the police and then the Football Licensing Authority, Jim has felt able to speak more plainly and in greater detail about his views. What he says is thought provoking. This is welcome, since his is perhaps the most experienced and well respected practitioner voice in the industry. There is also a more scholarly tone to the first two parts of the book, which include three of Steve Frosdick's recent academic journal articles as well as two previously unpublished dissertations. These are all authoritative reference documents which contain valuable arguments and insights.

We know that our members in the UK and Europe are looking forward to reading this new collection. We also believe it will be useful for students, practitioners and other readers interested in this field.

Both our organisations have the goal of seeing best practice shared. *More Safety and Security at Sports Grounds* makes an important contribution to that aim. Learn from the book – and enjoy it too!

John Newsham
Chairman
Football Safety Officers'
Association

John Beattie
President
European Stadium and Safety
Management Association

ABOUT THE AUTHORS

Jim Chalmers served in the Birmingham City and West Midlands police services between 1959 and 1991, retiring in the rank of Chief Superintendent. Most of his career was spent in uniform operational duties and at the time of his retirement he was the police commander at Aston Villa FC. He also had the unique distinction of being the police commander  responsible for the Birmingham Super Prix, when the streets of Birmingham City Centre were turned into a motor racing circuit.

From 1992 to 2003 he was a member of the Football Licensing Authority Inspectorate. He was also a member of the football authorities' safety management focus group. In these roles, he made a significant contribution to the development of safety management and stewarding practices at football grounds. He contributed to the football authorities' guidance documents on these subjects and to the multi-media stewards training packages developed by Steve Frosdick. He was also the author, co-author and contributor to various FLA guidance documents. These included spectator safety policies, contingency planning, exercise planning, briefing/debriefing, safety certification and the fourth edition of the Guide to Safety at Sports Grounds. Jim has been a regular speaker on safety management and stewarding both in the UK and across Europe. In 1996 he was appointed to assist the Guatemalan government to make recommendations to improve stadium safety after 82 football fans were crushed to death in their national stadium.

As a mature student he has obtained both a Certificate of Higher Education in Stadium and Arena Safety and a BSc degree in Risk and Security Management. He also holds two Level Four National Vocational Qualifications in Spectator Safety Management. For the latter award, he achieved the distinction of winning the City and Guilds 2008 gold medal prize for excellence in his Level Four standards. He was also honoured in the same year by being awarded the City and Guilds Lions Award for the Lifelong Learner of the Year. Jim is also a fellow of the Institute of Leadership and Management and a graduate of the City and Guilds Institute in Management.

Since 2004 he has been the Deputy Safety Officer with Kidderminster Harriers FC. In 2005, his lifelong achievements were recognized by his peers when he was unanimously elected as President of the Football Safety Officers' Association, a post he holds to the present day.

Steve Frosdick has been Director of IWI 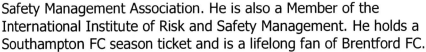 Associates Ltd since 1996. He has two postgraduate degrees (MSc and PhD) and is a Fellow of the Higher Education Academy. He was a Founder Member of the Football Safety Officers' Association and is a Faculty Member of both the International Association of Venue Managers and the European Stadium and Safety Management Association. He is also a Member of the International Institute of Risk and Safety Management. He holds a Southampton FC season ticket and is a lifelong fan of Brentford FC.

Through IWI Associates, Steve has completed a wide variety of consultancy, research and training projects. Clients have included various police and criminal justice organisations, European stadium companies, venue managers and their representative organisations, sporting bodies, conference organisers, universities and publishers. Steve has been involved in academia since 1991 and has developed an international reputation as an expert in safety and security at sports grounds. He has consulted for clients and taught at universities and conferences in the UK, US, Mauritius and throughout Europe. He has published four previous books and over 100 other papers.

In 2007 he was appointed as a Visiting Professor in the Centre for Applied Criminology at Birmingham City University. During 2008 he led the safety and security function for the inaugural season of the football-themed motor racing series, Superleague Formula. Since 2009 he has worked as a main contributor and content manager for SSET, the Safety and Security Expert Tool published by the European Union, Council of Europe and UEFA. During 2010 he designed, developed and delivered the Stewards Training Package for the UEFA Euro 2012 football championships in Poland and Ukraine.

From 1979 to 1995, Steve worked as a police officer in a wide variety of operational and support posts. He retired following a career break during which he developed a new consultancy and academic career.

ACKNOWLEDGEMENTS

Jim Chalmers would like to thank his wife Pauline for all her love and support during their marriage of over forty six years and yet again for her understanding and patience for all the hours he spent in his study working on this book project. She truly is the wind beneath his wings.

He would then like to thank Steve, his co-author, friend and academic mentor, for giving him the chance to share another book project and help prove that even a senior citizen can aspire to academic qualifications and literary ambitions once thought beyond his reach.

Jim would also like to thank Dave Preece, Safety Officer at Kidderminster Harriers, for the life they share at their club and for giving him the chance to continue to speak for safety officers at the grass roots football, where very often they do not have a voice.

Finally, Jim would like to thank his colleagues and friends in the Football Safety Officers' Association (FSOA) for allowing him the privilege of being part of a professional group of men and women who give so much of themselves to ensure the care, safety and well being of everyone who visits our football grounds, often without the thanks or recognition they deserve. In many ways, Jim's contributions in the book represent the personal and collective experiences he has learned from and shared with so many of his FSOA colleagues.

Steve Frosdick wishes to thank the many people who have supported his work over the last twenty years. They have not been named to avoid compromising their anonymity. Particular thanks are due to Jim Chalmers, Chris Conrad and Robert Newton, for the privilege of supervising the excellent dissertation research included in the book. Thanks also to Graham Joyce, who co-authored one of the articles.

Acknowledgements are due to Mark Webb at *Stadium and Arena Management* and Katie McIntyre at *Panstadia*, as well as to the journals *Soccer and Society* and the *International Journal of Police Science and Management*, which published the original versions of the papers in this collection. Thanks finally to Sara Travis and Alison Frosdick, who proof read and copy edited the manuscript.

INTRODUCTION

This book very much follows on from *Safety and Security at Sports Grounds*, which Frosdick and Chalmers published in 2005. This second book, *More Safety and Security at Sports Grounds*, stands alone because it covers the period 2005 to 2011. Nevertheless, readers who wish to gain an understanding of safety and security at sports grounds in the post-Hillsborough years should also read the first book – and perhaps read it first.

Once again, the intention behind this second volume has been to gather together into one place the work which Steve Frosdick has published, this time since 2005. Nothing in this book has been duplicated from the first. This second book also contains original research by Jim Chalmers and Chris Conrad, the latter co-authored with Steve Frosdick. Following the pattern of the first book, each of the articles has been reviewed and is accompanied by a commentary, making critical or reflective comments and bringing the articles up to date where appropriate.

The book is divided into six main parts. As before, each part has its own introduction, containing a short summary of the articles and commentaries within it. Previously published work is reprinted with its original citation and abstract or by-line. Each article, or in some cases a set of articles, is followed by the relevant commentary.

Part I of the book noted that most languages use the same word to translate the English terms 'safety' and 'security'. This can be problematic. Part I comprises two scholarly articles, a conference paper and accompanying commentaries which examine this important issue on both the conceptual and the practical levels.

Part II of the book contains one academic journal article, two previously unpublished dissertations and a magazine article. All four papers and their accompanying commentaries deal with a fundamental aspect of safety and security at sports grounds, namely the problem of bad behaviour by spectators. This is often referred to by the term 'football hooliganism'.

The third part of the book contains six UK and European case studies of different aspects of safety and security at sports grounds. The cases cover responses to violence in France, safe standing in Germany, non-league football in England, business continuity after floods and storm damage in football and horse racing, and preparations for the London 2012 Olympic Games.

Part IV comprises seven magazine articles by Steve Frosdick and a composite commentary by Jim Chalmers. The articles cover 'mystery spectator visits' between 2006 and 2010 to venues in the UK, Europe and the United States. The commentary notes the variety of venues and match day experiences and suggests that these demonstrate that UK lessons-learned are being applied internationally.

Part V comprises two short magazine features in which Steve Frosdick reports on venue security conferences, first in 2005 (prior to the July 7 bombings in London) and then in 2008. The accompanying commentaries note the change in the terrorist threat, outline the forthcoming demise of the Security Industry Authority and give a 2011 update on the preparations for the London 2012 Olympic Games.

Part VI focuses on the Football Safety Officers' Association of England and Wales (the FSOA). Jim Chalmers is the FSOA President and both he and Steve Frosdick are founder members from 1992. The two articles give an overview of the FSOA and its work. The extended commentary by Jim Chalmers then looks forward at likely developments in the run-up to the FSOA's 25th anniversary in 2017.

PART I – 'SAFETY' AND 'SECURITY'

Introduction

Most languages use the same word to translate the English terms 'safety' and 'security'. This can be problematic. This first part of the book comprises articles and commentaries which examine this important issue on both the conceptual and the practical levels.

1.1. Policing Safety and Security in Public Assembly Facilities

This *International Journal of Police Science and Management* article from 2010 explores how 'policing', in its widest sense, maintains public safety and security in the venues where people gather to view events. The long history of disasters and disorder in such facilities means that they have to be 'policed' and a wide range of bodies are involved in 'policing' them. The article discusses the terms 'safety' and 'security' and differentiates them with reference to four alternative models. There are serious practical consequences when policing overlooks safety, or else allows security and safety to get out of balance. Integrated safety and security is thus the best practice.

The accompanying commentary concurs with the arguments in the article and points out the importance of practitioners understanding these concepts.

1.2. Balancing 'Safety' and 'Security'

The first part of this *Stadium and Arena Management* article from 2008 was a precursor to the arguments in 1.1. above. The article goes on point out that stewards undertake both 'safety' and 'security' functions and highlights six important points for making a success of stewarding. The final part of the article deals with the 'friendly but firm' policing style which is the essential accompaniment to stewarding for delivering integrated safety, security and service.

The latest information on stewards' training and assessment in the UK and Europe is given in the commentary, which also supports the 'friendly but firm' policing style.

1.3. Safety and Security Risks in Superleague Formula

This second *International Journal of Police Science and Management* article from 2010 is a case study of Frosdick's work on safety and security in the football-themed motor racing series, Superleague Formula. After setting out the theoretical approach, the bulk of the paper gives an assessment of how the fans from 18 football clubs around the world might behave as spectators at six motor racing events in Europe. The research teased out eight key areas of threat, seven of which related to public order issues involving the fans. The eighth threat referred to fans as victims of indiscriminate policing. These threats were assessed for each of the 18 clubs at each of the six circuits — 864 risk assessments in all. Appropriate control measures, including police tactical deployments, were devised for each of the races. The paper then highlights the safety and security risks which became realities at the events. As well as having set out a rigorous analysis derived from applied theory, the paper concludes that the eight key threats form a good basis for others to hypothesise how football fans might behave in a new setting.

Jim Chalmers was involved in the work as a member of Frosdick's expert group. Chalmers' commentary concludes that Frosdick's theoretical ideas were successfully applied in practice, but has reservations about whether anyone else could deliver them in the same way.

1.1. POLICING SAFETY AND SECURITY IN PUBLIC ASSEMBLY FACILITIES

The original citation for this article is Frosdick, S. (2010) 'Policing Safety and Security in Public Assembly Facilities'. *International Journal of Police Science and Management*, 12(1): 81-89.

Reproduced with acknowledgements to Vathek Publishing.

Abstract

This article explores how 'policing', in its widest sense, seeks to maintain public safety and security in the places where people gather to view events. The paper begins by clarifying its setting in public assembly facilities and conceiving of 'policing' as 'almost anything done by anyone who controls other people' (Waddington, 2007). The paper goes on to show how the long history of disasters and disorder in such facilities means that they have to be 'policed' and outlines the various bodies involved in 'policing' them.

The paper then discusses the concepts of 'safety' and 'security'. 'Safety' starts with structural design and maintenance to prevent fire or collapse. It manages capacities, ingress and egress in complex space. It also deals with aspects of human behaviours, emergencies and evacuations. 'Security', on the other hand, addresses the prevention and detection of crime, the terrorist threat and the maintenance of public tranquillity. The paper seeks to differentiate the terms 'safety' and 'security' with reference to four alternative models. Two forms of the integrated whole in which 'security' is conceived as a subset of 'safety', or vice versa, are outlined and commended as best practice. However, the historical practice and current policy reasons why 'safety' and 'security' have been treated as either separate or overlapping concepts are also explored. The discussion refers to various facility disasters to illustrate the serious consequences when policing policy and practice overlooks 'safety' or allows 'security' and 'safety' to get out of balance.

Introduction

This is not another paper about soccer hooliganism. When I originally started researching safety and security in public assembly facilities, particularly in soccer grounds, I quickly discovered that 'it has become almost impossible to research into the regulation of football without being seen to be an integral part of the discourses about "football hooliganism"' (Redhead, 1991, p. 480). The debate about risk in public assembly facilities has historically been dominated by soccer hooliganism, the treatment of which bears all the hallmarks of the type of moral panic described by Cohen (1987). This moral panic has arisen for a combination of amplification factors, including over-reporting by the media (see Murphy, Williams, and Dunning, 1990, pp. 96–128), police overemphasis (see Bale, 1993, pp. 28–29) and excessive academic research (see Frosdick and Marsh 2005, pp. 78–79). This paper will not cover the same ground.

Neither is this paper a further addition to the growing social policy concern with terrorism (and to a lesser extent, natural disasters), reflected in the burgeoning 'homeland security' industry and associated guidance documents (e.g., see Homeland Security Council, 2007; National Counter Terrorism Security Office [NaCTSO], 2006). Indeed, the central thesis behind the paper is that the wrong kind of security can be bad for safety.

Nor is the history of disasters and disorder in public assembly facilities dealt with other than to justify the requirement for such venues to be 'policed'. There have been substantial changes in public safety and security management since the stadium disasters of the 1980s in England and Belgium. The multiplicity of changes, and the drivers behind them, have been well documented elsewhere (e.g., see Elliott and Smith 1993; Elliott, Frosdick, and Smith, 1997; Frosdick and Chalmers 2005; Frosdick and Walley, 1997).

What this paper will do is explore how 'policing', in its widest sense, seeks to maintain public safety and security in the places where people gather to view sporting events, pop concerts, arts productions, exhibitions and the like. The paper begins by clarifying its setting, giving a brief definition of 'policing', explaining why public assembly facilities have to be policed and clarifying who polices them. The bulk of the paper then discusses the concepts of 'safety' and 'security', seeks to differentiate these terms and then illustrates what goes wrong when 'security' and 'safety' get out of balance. The paper is primarily intended as a theoretical discussion with practical application. It seeks to explain in order to inform and so influence and improve the practice of safety and security management in public assembly facilities.

Public Assembly Facilities

The setting for this paper is in an international world of stadia, arenas, auditoria, amphitheatres, race tracks, performing arts venues, convention centres and exhibition halls. These may be collectively referred to as 'public assembly facilities', which have been comprehensively defined by Wootton and Stevens (1995, p. 6). Such facilities:

> have a number of characteristic features which require special consideration in their planning, design, management and operation. They
> – provide amenities for spectator viewing of sporting and non-sporting events;
> – must be accessible, comfortable and safe for a range of users and participants;
> – attract large number of spectators attending events of relatively short duration;
> – are managed to ensure the safe movement of people in a smooth, unimpeded, fashion in the time before, during and after the event;
> – provide pleasurable experiences in an enjoyable and safe way;
> – provide a range of ancillary services and amenities to meet the needs and demands of spectators, participants and promoters;
> – provide environments to encourage the highest standards for sporting participants within the criteria required by the regulations of that sport;
> – may be open to the elements, or may be covered or enclosed in total or in part;
> – involve an ensemble of features creating a sense of place and identity;

– contribute to the wider community, through economic, social and cultural benefits;
– adopt a responsible approach towards community aspirations and concerns;
– have the potential to be used for a range of sporting and non-sporting events on single or multiple use basis.

Examples of such venues could be a football stadium, baseball park, basketball arena, ice hockey rink, concert hall, convention centre, racetrack or speedway. All these facilities stage various kinds of events which attract larger or smaller crowds of people.

Why 'Police' Public Assembly Facilities?

The clear requirement for 'policing' arises from the long and continuing history of disaster and disorder in public assembly facilities throughout the world (see Elliott, Frosdick, and Smith, 1997, pp. 13–14; Frosdick and Marsh, 2005, pp. 10–23). We can go back as early as 1314 to find the English King Edward II banning the violent sport of soccer; and in 1888, one death and three injuries were reported as a result of collapsed railings at a rugby league ground in the north of England.

But these are not purely historical concerns. In terms of disorder, the phenomenon of hooliganism at sports events, particularly soccer, remains a global social problem. At the time of writing, English media had just reported crowd trouble inside the stadium at a soccer match between Stoke City and West Ham United (see 'Fears rise', 2009), whilst American media had recently carried footage of 11 arrests after a fight in the stands at a high school basketball game in Alabama (see 'Forfeit from fight', 2009). Turning to disaster, at the time of writing 19 fans had just died and over 130 had been injured in a stadium stampede just prior to an international soccer match between the Ivory Coast and Malawi in Abidjan (see 'Fifa orders inquiry', 2009). Disaster and disorder are thus both historical and contemporary concerns.

'Policing'

When we speak of 'policing' public assembly facilities, we are using the term 'policing' in its widest sense. As Alan Wright observes, 'policing can no longer simply be understood as the activity of the public policing institution' (Wright, 2002, p. xii). So we are looking beyond the sworn officers employed by the public sector. Indeed the range of people and activities involved in 'policing' grows ever wider. Waddington (2007, p. 14) commented that:

> In 1983, policing referred to the activities of public officials upon whom the law conferred special powers — the police. Now it refers to almost anything done by anyone who controls other people and enhances collective security.

Looking at both the need to 'police' public assembly facilities and at who actually 'polices' them, reveals a very highly regulated environment indeed. In the front line, we find public police officers both from local agencies, in the United States, for example, from the local Sheriff's Department, as well as from national agencies such as the Federal Bureau of Investigation (FBI), the Bureau of Alcohol, Tobacco, Firearms and Explosives (ATF) and the Secret Service. Also in the front line are the various designations of stewards or ushers employed to manage the crowds entering a facility, viewing an event and dispersing afterwards. These can include 'safety' stewards, 'security' stewards, car park stewards, hospitality stewards, fire stewards and liquor licensing stewards.

There are then a variety of other regulatory bodies which attend venues to 'police the police'. In the United Kingdom these include the local municipality, the governing bodies of sports and, in the case of soccer, the national Football Licensing Authority. The author attended one recent match in southern England where the 'police' personnel present included an inspector from the Football Licensing Authority, a crowd control advisor from the Football Association, representatives of the local certifying authority, various ranks from the local constabulary, the ground safety officer, his steward supervisors and various types of stewards.

The Policing of 'Safety' and 'Security'

In French, German, Spanish and Italian there is only one word — la sécurité, die Sicherheit, la securidad and la sicurezza respectively — to translate the twin concepts of 'safety' and 'security'. The same is true of various other languages. This raises some important issues. If there is only one word available in other languages, does this mean that the English words 'safety' and 'security' are synonymous? Or is one a subset of the other? Alternatively, are 'safety' and security' different concepts, and, if so, how? These are important questions because it may be that the linguistic differences prevent a full understanding of the concepts. This in turn may inhibit public assembly facilities from optimising the policing of both 'safety' and 'security'.

As a framework for the discussion, let us consider the logical possibilities depicted by the four different models shown in Figure One. Note that 'safety' is represented by the pale circle and 'security' by the dark one.

Figure One – Modelling 'Safety' and 'Security'

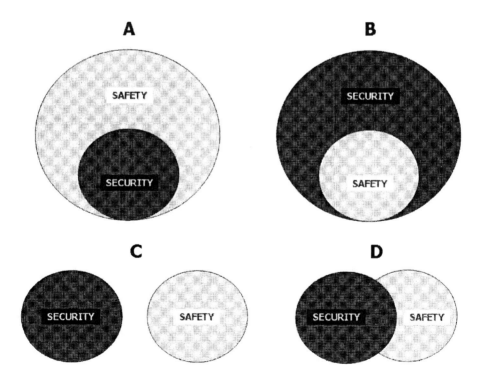

The first model (A) suggests that 'security' is a subset of 'safety'. This model is implied by the dictionary definitions. 'Safe' means 'free from risk or danger', whilst 'secure' means 'safe, especially against attack'. Thus 'safety' starts with the design, maintenance and integrity of the physical structures so that they do not collapse or catch fire. 'Safety' addresses the calculation and maintenance of capacities so as to know how many people can be safely accommodated in each part of the venue. 'Safety' refers to the management of crowd ingress and egress, i.e., getting people in and out of a complex space in a short period of time. It also refers to dealing with behaviours which put people at risk, such as climbing on structures, overcrowding, crowd surges and persistent standing in seated areas. 'Safety' means being ready to deal with emergencies, including those which may require a full or partial evacuation of the facility.

'Security', meanwhile, refers to the measures taken to prevent and deal with danger, i.e., the prevention and detection of crimes such as theft, damage or assault; the threat from terrorist bombs or attacks; and the maintenance of public tranquillity so that people are not frightened or hurt by disorder. In the event of a serious emergency or disaster, 'security' takes over from 'safety' to clear up the mess, investigate what went wrong and perhaps even enforce accountability. 'Security' is therefore a particular subset of overall 'safety'.

This model represents an almost utopian view. The overarching consideration of public assembly facilities management should be optimum freedom from risk, whatever the source of the hazard. Neither the terrorist explosion nor the crowd crush discriminate in killing and injuring people. However, the division of labour and organisation found at the policy and operational levels in the United Kingdom means that this utopian model is not always applied in practice. It is found in venues where there is a full-time professional safety officer with appropriate competencies, status and authority. Such persons will usually hold a professional qualification such as the UK Level Four National Vocational Qualification in Spectator Control. Such individuals lead and manage all the 'policing' resources deployed, which at the largest venues will exceed 1,000 staff per event.

This leadership includes the extent to which the public police intervene in crowd situations. Consider the following example from a UK soccer match between Wycombe Wanderers and Cardiff City (Frosdick and Marsh, 2005, p. 181):

> At one point, the Cardiff fans became fairly aggrieved by a refereeing decision and stood up, shouting aggressively. A Police Inspector quickly deployed a line of officers to stand in front of the fans. The Steward Supervisor said to the Police Inspector, 'I'm in charge here and there's no need for your officers. Withdraw them.' The Police Inspector (grudgingly) complied. In the post-match debrief, the Club Safety Officer told the stewards, 'I'm proud of you all. The Cardiff was hard work but we done it ourselves (*sic*).'

Such safety officers may be found at various grounds in the UK and in European countries which have adopted UK-style stewarding and safety management, for example France and Portugal. They represent the ideal, but probably not the norm.

The second model (B) is similarly utopian and represents the reverse, namely that in this case 'safety' is considered as a subset of 'security'. This does not fit with the UK dictionary definitions but, as George Bernard Shaw once commented, 'England and America are two countries divided by a common language'. Thus this may be seen as the United States model.

Job titles suggest that venues employ *security* managers. However, these people's jobs usually encompass not only prevention from attack, but also the management of overall facility and public safety. For example, in May 2009, the Atlanta Dome in Georgia advertised for an assistant security manager who understood 'the equal importance of customer-service and customer safety' ('Assistant Security Manager', 2009). Again, such security managers are very likely to hold professional qualifications, such as the emergency preparedness professional award for graduates from the International Association of Assembly Managers (IAAM) Academy for Venue Safety and Security (see 'Academy for Venue Safety', n.d.). One of the core courses within this programme is 'Security Operations', which covers both life safety and asset protection. There is potential for confusion in this different use of language, but best practice in Europe and the US is effectively the same: namely that 'safety' and 'security' — whichever word takes primacy — are understood as being part of an integrated whole.

In the third model (C), we see 'safety' and 'security' as completely different ideas. They have no connection with each other at all. If this is the case, and the focus of venue operations is on 'security', then the criticality of 'safety' may be altogether missed. This was the case in the United Kingdom up until the late 1980s, where the public police focused on 'security' issues and 'safety' got lost in a void. The Bradford fire in 1985 (see Home Office, 1985) resulted in 56 people burning to death, most of them at the back of a stand. The exit gates through which they sought to escape had been locked to stop people getting in without paying. The security was great — nobody could get in; but the safety had been utterly overlooked — no one could escape the fire.

The nadir for England was in 1989. The Hillsborough pitch perimeter fence did its security job very well — nobody could get onto the pitch. However, it was fatal for safety and 96 fans were crushed to death against it, unable to escape the crowd pressure behind them (see Home Office, 1989). Looking around the world, there are numerous other examples of fires or stampedes in leisure facilities where people have been crushed or burned to death because the exit doors were locked — venues so secure that they were fatally unsafe.

The experiences of travelling fans in parts of Europe and the developing world suggest that there are plenty of jurisdictions where the prevailing philosophy remains 'protection from the crowd' rather than 'protection of the crowd'. Oppressive measures such as high metal fences and aggressive officers in full body armour protect the structures, players, officials and police against attack, but the fans themselves face dangers from dilapidated buildings, overcrowding and stampedes resulting from the actions of the security forces. For example, the 1985 Heysel stadium disaster in Belgium resulted in 38 Italian fans being crushed to death when a wall collapsed in a badly managed stadium in poor physical condition (see Home Office, 1986). The security needs of segregation had been badly planned and were then ineptly policed without due consideration of the safety implications. In 2001, in the worst stadium disaster in Africa, at least

123 people died in a stampede after police fired tear gas into the stands (see 'Stadium Disaster', 2001). This was a quite disproportionate security response to fans who had thrown missiles onto the pitch, resulting in appalling consequences for people's safety.

Consider the experiences of Manchester United fans in the Champions League in February 2007. At the Stade Felix Bollaert in Lens, too many Manchester United fans were squashed into one corner even though there were available spaces nearby in the away zone. People were crushed, and those who tried to escape were beaten (see 'United and Lille Fined', 2007). This was overzealous security resulting in disgracefully bad safety. The scenes in Rome's Olympic Stadium in April 2007 represented the same story. The video footage on You-Tube showed the police officers using disproportionate and indiscriminate use of force on the fans (see 'Roma v Man U', 2007). Then in April 2008, Dutch supporters brought large quantities of toilet paper into the FC Groningen stadium. The fans then set the paper alight. When the fires got out of control, the continuous Plexiglas screen prevented most people from exiting onto the pitch to escape the smoke. Only a small number were able to climb over. As for the rest, there was uncontrolled crowd migration backwards to try and get away (see 'FC Groningen-Ajax', 2008). Fortunately, there were few injuries, but it seems clear that inadequate access control coupled with the security fences — both the wrong kind of security — were very nearly very bad for safety.

The principal lesson of such disasters and near misses is that the needs of 'safety' and 'security' must be kept in balance, with the former having precedence over the latter. This is emphasised in the 2006 *Counter Terrorism Protective Security Advice for Stadia and Arenas*, which says that, 'Safety must always have priority over security' (NaCTSO, 2006, p. 4). This makes a strong case for the safety-first integrated whole in model (A) being adopted as best practice across Europe. The US position is different because of the linguistic differences already discussed, but the principle of the integrated whole remains the best practice.

Yet it is the fourth model (D), which represents the position in many UK stadia today. In this model, the suggestion is that 'safety' and 'security' overlap. There are ways in which each is different from the other but there are elements which are the same. Since this model does not represent best practice, how is it that it is so prevalent, at least in the UK?

Whilst it is the stadium operator which carries the responsibility for both 'safety' and 'security', the basis for the overlapping model is revealed by examining the roles of various UK government agencies. Oversight of 'safety' in English football is led by the Football Licensing Authority (FLA), an independent public body which reports to the Department for Culture, Media and Sport. The FLA licenses each stadium to admit spectators and then monitors the work of the local municipalities, which issue the ground 'safety' certificate and take action if spectator safety is being prejudiced.

Meanwhile overall government monitoring of 'security' rests with a different government department — the Home Office (Interior Ministry). This oversees the work of the public police, who have agreed 'statements of intent' with venue management. The latter are responsible for 'safety' whilst the police take a 'security' role when deployed inside the facility. The Home Office also oversees the Security Industry Authority (SIA), an executive body which issues licences to 'security' operatives.

Where the two concepts overlap in the UK is seen clearly in the work of the stewards. It is the stewards who monitor all aspects of crowd safety in the ground and who deal with all aspects of crowd behaviour which affect safety. These 'safety' stewards are not caught by the SIA licensing requirements. However, 'security' stewards (for example search and eject personnel) are covered by the SIA legislation whilst operating in the areas of the stadium licensed for the sale of alcohol. Where the line falls between 'safety' and 'security' duties is not entirely clear. For example, what role is the steward performing when warning a spectator to stop standing on the seat or else face ejection?

The introduction of the SIA into the mix has worked against the best practice of an integrated whole. The need for stadium operators to avoid unnecessary regulation and licensing costs encourages the maintenance of a clear but artificial distinction between 'safety' and 'security' at the operational level. For example, the 'Conflict Management' module within the Training Package for Stewarding at

Football Grounds (see Frosdick and Joyce, 2005), explains the quite tortuous notion of a 'safety ejection', i.e. putting spectators out of the ground because their behaviour was affecting their own or another's safety. Such stewarding has always been regarded as a 'safety' function and was never intended to come under the SIA 'security' licensing requirements.

Conclusion

This paper has sought to demonstrate that 'safety' and 'security' in public assembly facilities is 'policed' by a wide range of public and private bodies. An attempt has been made to differentiate the terms and to model the logical relationships between them. The four models in Figure 1 have all been shown to exist in practice as well as in theory. The weaknesses of failing to see 'safety' and 'security' as interrelated within an integrated whole have been demonstrated, and the concept of the integrated whole has been commended as best practice.

The expressions 'safety', 'security' and indeed 'safety and security' are part of policing's daily language. The hope is that this paper will have helped the reader clarify the words in his or her own mind. It does not much matter what you call the concepts, but it can be a matter of life and death that both policy-makers and practitioners understand them both, apply them both and maintain an equitable balance between them.

References

Academy for Venue Safety and Security. (n.d.). Retrieved May 7 2009 from http://www. iaam.org/schools/AVSS/index.htm

Assistant Security Manager, GA Dome, Atlanta, GA. (2009). Retrieved May 7 2009 from http://www.iaam.org/IAAM_ News/Pages/NLcareerdetails.htm#01

Bale, J. (1993). *Sport, Space and the City*. London: Routledge.

Cohen, S. (1987). *Folk Devils and Moral Panics: The Creation of the Mods and Rockers*. Oxford: Basil Blackwell.

Elliott, D., Frosdick, S., and Smith, D. (1997). The Failure of 'Legislation by Crisis'. In S. Frosdick and L. Walley (Eds.), *Sport and Safety Management* (pp. 11–30). Oxford: Butterworth-Heinemann.

Elliott, D., and Smith, D. (1993). Football Stadia Disasters in the United Kingdom: Learning From Tragedy?. *Industrial and Environmental Crisis Quarterly,* 7(3), 205–229.

FC Groningen-Ajax. (2008). Retrieved May 7 2009 from http://www.youtube.com/ watch?v=Yzu6xhj9f5wandfeature=related

Fears rise over return of hooliganism as fans brawl at Stoke again. (2009). Retrieved May 7 2009 from http://www.dailymail. co.uk/sport/football/article-1176732/Fearsrise- return-hooliganism-fans-brawl-Stokeagain.html

Fifa orders inquiry over Ivory Coast deaths. (2009). Retrieved May 7 2009 from http: //www.guardian.co.uk/football/2009/mar/ 30/fifa-investigation-stadium-crush-abidjan

Forfeit from fight puts Talladega in Final Four. (2009). Retrieved May 7 2009 from http: //www.dailyhome.com/sports/2009/dhprepsports- 0219-hbaggett-9b18x2511.htm

Frosdick, S., and Chalmers, J. (2005). *Safety and Security at Sports Grounds.* Rothersthorpe: Paragon Publishing.

Frosdick, S., and Joyce, G. (2005, August). Conflict Managers. *Stadium and Arena Management,* 24–26.

Frosdick, S., and Marsh, P. (2005). *Football Hooliganism.* Cullompton: Willan.

Frosdick, S., and Walley, L. (Eds.). (1997). *Sport and Safety Management.* Oxford: Butterworth-Heinemann

Homeland Security Council. (2007). *National Strategy for Homeland Security.* Washington, DC: Executive Office of the President of the United States.

Home Office. (1985). *Committee of Inquiry into Crowd Safety and Control at Sports Grounds – Interim Report* (Chairman: Mr Justice Popplewell). London: HMSO.

Home Office. (1986). *Committee of Inquiry into Crowd Safety and Control at Sports Grounds – Final Report* (Chairman: Mr Justice Popplewell). London: HMSO.

Home Office. (1989). *The Hillsborough Stadium Disaster 15 April 1989 – Interim Report* (Inquiry by the Rt Hon Lord Justice Taylor). London: HMSO.

Murphy, P., Williams, J., and Dunning, E. (1990). *Football on Trial — Spectator Violence and Development in the Football World.* London: Routledge.

National Counter Terrorism Security Office. (2006). *Counter Terrorism Protective Security Advice for Stadia and Arenas.* London: NaCTSO.

Redhead, S. (1991). Some Reflections on Discourses on Football Hooliganism. *Sociological Review,* 39(3), 479–488.

Roma v Man U: police beating crowd. (2007). Retrieved May 7 2009 from http://www. youtube.com/watch?v=t5M7hv0W8eYand feature=related

Stadium Disaster. (2001). Retrieved May 7 2009 from http://www.ghanaweb.com/ GhanaHomePage/NewsArchive/dossier. php?ID=31

United and Lille Fined (2007). Retrieved May 7, 2009, from http://www.dailymail.co.uk/ sport/article-444067/United-Lille-fined. Html

Waddington, P. A. J. (2007, August 24). Who Got Rid of Our Guardian Angels? *Police Review*, p.14.

Wootton, G., and Stevens, T. (1995). *Into the Next Millennium: A Human Resource Development Strategy for the Stadia and Arena Industry in the United Kingdom*. Swansea: Swansea Institute of Higher Education, Stadium and Arena Management Unit.

Wright, A. (2002). *Policing: An Introduction to Concepts and Practice*. Cullompton: Willan.

1.1. COMMENTARY BY JIM CHALMERS – POLICING 'SAFETY' AND 'SECURITY'

If you were to ask a group of key players involved in events at sports grounds to define just what is meant by the terms, 'policing', 'safety' and 'security', I suggest you would get a wide variation in responses. Frosdick recognises this in his article and presents for the first time a cohesive and reasoned argument, which helps give an understanding on how an integrated approach to the management of sports grounds can be achieved. Whilst my particular skills and experience are in the management of football-related events, Frosdick's article encompasses any sporting event where people gather.

It could be argued that 'policing', 'safety' and 'security' are the main elements involved in staging any sports grounds event, and Frosdick rightly focuses on these in the article. In my experience whilst policing, safety and security are normally at the forefront in the planning for any sports grounds event, I am not certain that there is a commonality in understanding just what these concepts mean. This could have significant consequences for both the organisation staging the event and for those attending. Frosdick's article goes a long way towards improving our understanding of this commonly used terminology; something which has been long overdue, particularly in the safety officer's tool box.

I would suggest that if you asked anyone attending a sporting event at a sports ground what the term 'policing' means, they would probably respond by talking about the 'bobby on the beat', the police vans outside the event, perhaps the police horses who are present and the number of police in high visibility jackets deployed to keep football fans apart inside the ground. However, as Frosdick succinctly argues, the policing of safety and security at sports grounds extends well beyond the sight of traditional police officers at the event. In many respects, their presence represents only the tip of the 'policing' iceberg at the event. For example in the 2008/09 football season, 40% of games were 'police free', but this did not mean that the wider concept of policing identified by Frosdick was not taking place at these 'police free' games.

From personal experience as a police officer for 32 years, a member of the Football Licensing Authority (FLA) Inspectorate for 12 years and a safety officer and member of the Football Safety Officers Association (FSOA) for seven years, I can testify how the traditional style of policing football grounds has changed from 'high profile policing/low profile stewarding' to 'high profile stewarding/low profile policing'. In his article, Frosdick recognises the implications of this change, and how there needs to be a greater understanding of just what 'policing' 'safety' and 'security' means. The policing of an event encompasses a far wider spectrum than the sight of police officers, since it also involves the event staff such as the safety officer and stewards, security companies, local authorities and sports regulators. Each of these 'policing' bodies will bring to the event their own ideas on just what is meant by 'policing', 'safety' and 'security'.

Frosdick's arguments are essential for understanding the roles carried out by the extended policing family in the present day, compared to the single policing family that I was involved with in policing football matches for 32 years. Only by understanding this wider concept of the policing family can we fully understand the implications for policing safety and security at sports grounds. Such improved understanding makes it easier for sports ground management to plan for the 'policing' of their event.

I referred earlier to the problem of defining precisely what is meant by 'policing' in the context of safety and security at sports grounds. I would suggest the same problem exists in defining what is meant by the words 'safety' and 'security'. In all the legislation and guidance relating to safety at sports grounds, the term 'safety' has not been formally defined. Similarly, in all the far reaching inquiries into football-related problems and disasters, the term 'security' has not been defined either. One could perhaps infer from this that security has not been considered an issue by the legislators in the debate on safety at sports grounds, but without definitions, the baseline for both concepts will undoubtedly be vague. Frosdick addresses this issue and for the first time we have the opportunity to examine the precise distinctions between 'safety' and 'security', an opportunity that is long overdue. His conclusions and their importance are vital when contextualising safety and security in the management of sports grounds events.

Frosdick refers to the National Counter Terrorism Security Office (NaCTSO) guidance from 2006 which states that 'Safety must always have priority over security'. This argument was, however, made far earlier – in 1997 – when the Chief Executive of the FLA, in reference to the Hillsborough stadium disaster of 1989, said that the needs of safety and security must be kept in balance. Over the years, this imbalance has resulted in tragedy and Frosdick outlines just a few examples to illustrate the point. The historical approach of trying to make stadia safe by making them secure created the safety problems inherent in the Bradford and Hillsborough disasters. Measures included the erection of high fencing to contain the fans and locking exit gates to keep the grounds impregnable. All well intentioned at the time, but the imbalance between safety and security was always evident, remaining unresolved even after the 1985 Bradford fire.

Frosdick clearly explains how sports grounds safety cannot be delivered by looking at any part in isolation. Each part has to be examined, then the inter-relation between parts, and then the overall picture. Deficiencies in certain aspects may be offset in whole or in part by other aspects. This is important in achieving 'reasonable safety'. What is not explained in the article and should not be overlooked is that there is no requirement for 'absolute safety' or 'absolute security'. Such absolutes are unachievable. It could be argued that the only time a sports ground is 'absolutely safe' is when it is empty! All the legislation and guidance are therefore directed at ensuring 'reasonable safety'. This could perhaps explain why D represents the most achievable model in practice, whilst model A represents the almost utopian view which – although to be aspired to – would be unattainable at most sports grounds.

Frosdick refers to the role of the Security Industry Authority (SIA). It is disappointing that his article was not available in 2005 when the FSOA and the football authorities resisted vigorous efforts by the SIA to bring sports grounds stewards under their licensing remit. The SIA could not, or would not on economic grounds, accept the clear distinction between safety and security and how the principal role of stewards at sports grounds is to ensure safety, not to enforce security. Frosdick's article would have gone a long way in supporting the argument for sports grounds stewards to be exempt from the SIA licensing requirements, an argument which was eventually won.

If it is accepted that safety must always have primacy over security, then models B or C would undoubtedly represent the position at the time of the Hillsborough stadium disaster. Safety was different and disregarded or else so far subservient to security as to have been overlooked. Models B and C should therefore be discounted as unsound for managing a sports ground event. I mentioned earlier the difficulties in adopting model A, since this would require absolute integration, as distinct from normal reality in the way that safety and security operate at a sports ground. Having been involved for over 50 years in policing, regulating and managing safety and security at sports grounds, I agree that model D represents what actually happens in the planning and operations of sports grounds events, under the control and direction of professional safety officers.

Whilst Frosdick argues that the introduction of the SIA into the regulation of security has not helped, I would suggest that this has not created any significant operational problems either. With the hard-won exemption of in-house security stewards from SIA licensing, there has been no real barrier to implementing the needs of both safety and security. Whilst the distinction does exist, the event safety officer will always have customer care as their overriding principle. In my experience, safety officers will not let a line between safety and security cloud their judgment when it comes to implementing that service, and whether it is achieved by safety staff or security personnel will be immaterial in ensuring that the customer experience is always pleasant. That is why I would argue that, although Model D does represent what happens in reality, customer care sits across the top of the model. Focussing on customer care means it doesn't matter whether an activity is in either the safety or security box.

With the projected demise of the SIA announced in the Government spending review of October 2010, I hope we have finally seen the end of their interference in trying to licence and regulate sports ground stewards. Over many years, and long before the existence of the SIA, stewards have proven their capability to manage both safety and security at sports grounds under existing legislation. All that the SIA did was to confuse the issue, as Frosdick asserts in his article.

Whilst it is clear to me that safety officers will always put safety first, I am not so certain that the police will always have this as their priority. I suggest that many police officers would put security as having primacy at sports grounds events, particularly those classed as 'high risk'. With the current level of the terrorist threat, there is a danger that the police will want to return football to the dark days by making sports grounds impregnable fortresses as their answer to the terrorist hazard. If security begins to take primacy in place of safety, then we will have learned nothing from the legacy of disasters and the deaths of so many innocent fans.

This article is significant for the organisers of safety and security at the 2012 London Olympic Games. I would suggest that they would do well to consider which model which would best suit their planning and operations at the games venues. To reiterate earlier comments, this will be even more significant when considering how to respond to a terrorist threat, since in my opinion, the adoption of either model B or C will present an even greater risk to the spectator and venue safety than the terrorist threat itself.

I recommend this article to anyone involved in the management of sports grounds events, since for the first time, it explains the many facets of 'policing' sports grounds, and the concept of a totally integrated 'policing' approach as distinct from 'policing' in the narrower traditional context. It provides us with a clear understanding of what is meant by 'safety' and 'security'. Unless those charged with ensuring safety and security at sports grounds have a clear understanding of just what these terms mean, then they will have no clear understanding of just which model they operate or would best suit their event day operations. If it is accepted that the needs of safety and security should be kept in balance and that safety should have primacy, the likelihood of another disaster is extremely doubtful.

In all of this debate there are two words which should always be at the forefront of anyone involved in the policing of safety and security of a sports grounds event; 'customer care'. Whatever the needs of policing safety and security, there is a danger of forgetting who this is all done for: the fan, the spectator, the customer. This is something none of us involved in policing safety and security at sports grounds should ever lose sight of.

1.2. BALANCING 'SAFETY' AND 'SECURITY'

The original citation for this article is Frosdick, S. (2008) 'Striking a Balance', *Stadium and Arena Management*. August 2008, p. 28-31.

Steve Frosdick gave a paper on crowd control and safety at the 'Stadia and Arena 2008' conference in Rome.

To be in Rome is a thrill for any stadium enthusiast. The Colosseum is famous for the way its design and ticketing enabled the crowd to access, be accommodated and egress quickly and safely. Today's third and fourth generation stadia may be more sophisticated, but the basic principles of crowd management remain the same.

My overarching thesis in this paper is that *the wrong kind of security can be bad for safety*. I will deal first with the linguistic problem of understanding the difference between 'safety' and 'security' so that you can maintain the right balance between their different requirements. Second, I want to explain how UK-style stewarding works so you can think about how to adapt it for your own jurisdictions. Finally, I want to demonstrate the success of the 'friendly but firm' policing style, which is challengingly counter-intuitive for traditional public order approaches.

So let us begin by saying that there is a problem of language. La sicurezza; la sécurité; die Sicherheit; la securidad: in Italian, French, German and Spanish there is only one word to translate the two concepts of 'safety' and security'. The same is true of various other languages. This is important because it may be that the linguistic differences prevent a full understanding of the concepts. This in turn may inhibit stadium operations from optimising and maintaining a balance between both 'safety' and 'security'.

Let me try and summarise the differences between 'safety' and 'security'. I think 'safety' starts with the design and maintenance of the structures so that they don't collapse or catch fire. It's about knowing how many spectators can be safely accommodated in each part of the venue. 'Safety' involves getting people in and out of a complex space in a short period of time. It addresses aspects of behaviour such as over-crowding, surging and climbing on structures.

'Safety' means being ready to deal with emergencies, including those which may require an evacuation. The people who do the 'safety' work on the ground are of course the stewards.

'Security', on the other hand, refers to the 'policing' task, whether this is carried out by the public police or by private security staff. This addresses the prevention and detection of crime, the terrorist threat and the maintenance of public tranquillity. In the event of a serious emergency or disaster, 'security' takes over from 'safety' to clear up the mess and find out what went wrong. The agents of social control here are both the public police and those stewards with 'security' duties.

Referring back to my central thesis, let me illustrate what happens when there is a lack of balance between these two essential elements. In 1985, 56 people burned to death at Bradford trying to get out of the exit gates which had been locked to prevent people getting in without tickets. The security was great – nobody could get in; but the safety was appalling – no one could escape.

In the same year, 38 Juventus fans died when a wall collapsed. The Heysel stadium was dilapidated and unsafe, the segregation was badly planned and the policing was inept. Bad safety and security both.

The nadir for England was in 1989. The Hillsborough pitch perimeter fence did its security job very well – nobody could get onto the pitch. However, it was fatal for safety and 96 fans were crushed to death against it, unable to escape the crowd pressure behind them.

But let us not be under any illusion that these sorts of problems have gone away. Consider the experiences of Manchester United fans in the Champions League in 2007. At the Stade Felix Bollaert in Lens in February, too many Manchester United fans were squashed into one corner even though there were available spaces nearby in the away zone. People were crushed and those who tried to escape were beaten. This was overzealous security resulting in disgracefully bad safety.

The scenes in Rome's Olympic Stadium in April represented the same story. The video footage showed the police commander trying to get his officers to stop their disproportionate and indiscriminate use of force on the fans.

Finally, only a few weeks ago, Dutch supporters brought large quantities of toilet paper into the FC Groningen stadium. The fans then set the paper alight. When the fires got out of control, the continuous Plexiglas screen prevented most people from exiting onto the pitch to escape the smoke. Only a small number were able to climb over. As for the rest, there was uncontrolled crowd migration backwards to try and get away. Fortunately, there were few injuries, but it seems clear to me that inadequate access control coupled with the security fences – both the wrong kind of security – were very nearly very bad for safety.

There are plenty of other recent examples. In the April edition of *S&AM,* Ian Drury reported that at last year's *Stadium and Arena* event, delegates were discussing the inadequacies of both 'safety' and 'security' at the 2007 Champions League final in Athens.

This year, both the UEFA Cup and Champions League finals went well as far as the stadia were concerned, although there was an attempted pitch invasion by the Zenit fans in Manchester. But there were certainly problems with the crowd at the fan park in Manchester, and I shall say something more about this later on.

I mentioned that stewards can perform both 'safety' and 'security' tasks. Because the UK is widely regarded as having led the way, and because there are many *S&AM* readers in countries which would like to make a success of stewarding, I want to highlight six points which I think you could find helpful.

The first is this – make sure your stewards are smart and look the part. They need to provide a white shirt, black trousers and black shoes – not a t-shirt, jeans and trainers. You need to provide a good quality waterproof and reflective jacket and perhaps a clip on tie and protective cap – not just a shabby old tabard. If your stewards look professional, they will feel and perform better and be more likely to command the respect of the fans.

A professional appearance is an essential pre-requisite for moving from high profile policing to high profile stewarding, supported where appropriate by low profile policing. In the UK, we have seen the police and stewards change places. Most 'policing', inside and even around the stadium, is done by the stewards. This is true even for high risk local derby games, where the police presence inside the stadium is often comparatively low key. Many UK matches – and indeed several matches which I have seen in France – are 'police free', which means that there are no police at all in the stadium bowl, although they may be in the control room and at important points on the approaches to and from the venue.

My fourth point is that it is very helpful to have the support of stewards from the away club. Outside the ground, they can help with ticketing, customer care and access control. They know their fans and their fans should know them. Inside the ground, they can help supervise their own supporters. The French system is interesting because the away sector is treated as part of the away club's ground and is only stewarded by the away club. Any problems which arise are the responsibility of the away club and it is the away club who are punished by the League for any infractions.

There are various types of stewards. Some work in the car parks and others in the hospitality areas. Some have a fire prevention role and others look after the disabled. But the two main types of stewards cover the two main aspects of 'safety' and security'. In the UK, the security stewards usually wear a different coloured jacket, although there is no consistency in what the colours are. Rather obviously, the safety stewards do tasks like ticket checking and crowd monitoring, whilst the security stewards carry out searching and any necessary ejections from the stadium.

In order to do these important tasks well, stewards must be competent, that is they must have the knowledge, skills and experience to do the job. The 'learning platform' for the UK stewarding qualifications are the eight modules in the *Training Package for Stewarding at Football Grounds*, of which it is my privilege to be the editor. Essentially, this is a Powerpoint presentation of 336 slides, delivering 56 topics, each of which has learning outcomes, trainer's notes and sample assessments. The duration of the classroom and practical training should be at least 20 hours, although I know that people do deliver it more quickly.

Having completed the learning and practiced their skills, the novice stewards are individually assessed in the workplace. Clubs are free to choose one of the available stewarding qualifications at Level 2 in the UK National Qualifications Framework and their successful candidates are then qualified as safety stewards.

Regulatory requirements means that private security stewards also have to be both trained as 'door supervisors' – bouncers – and licensed by the Security Industry Authority. In-house security stewards are exempt, providing they have been trained in 'hands on' conflict management.

In summary then, the UK system comprises the learning package, formal assessment at work, national qualifications and – for private security stewards only – additional training and licensing. Let me turn now to the question of policing style and why this is so important.

If you are going to make a success of stewarding, I think that the fans' experience of social control needs to be consistent. If the police are harsh and arbitrary on the way to the ground, the fans will be unhappy and agitated when they arrive. It's now too late to try and steward them in a friendly and welcoming style. So we're back to my thesis again. Oppressive security just doesn't go with safety and customer care.

Let's look at how policing style has evolved over the years. It's certainly true that in the UK, the historical concern was with football hooliganism. As a police officer myself in London in the 1980s, I remember to my shame how badly we used to treat football fans. We treated them all as a security risk and used inappropriate levels of force on them. I will always remember escorting one group of fans, treating them as cattle. A middle-aged man walking with his young son turned to me in obvious distress and said, "Why are you treating us like this?" The truth is, his safety and comfort meant nothing to me – I only cared about security.

The 2000 European Championships in Belgium and the Netherlands saw two very different policing styles adopted. The Dutch set out to create a carnival atmosphere in which fans could enjoy themselves rather than to confront, contain and repress them. The police removed objects that might be thrown (such as tables and chairs) from town squares and arranged for local bars to serve low-alcohol beer in plastic glasses. They set up large sound systems to play popular music and, when fans became boisterous, they simply turned the volume up until people quietened down. The police presence was unobtrusive, friendly but firm if needed. This carefully planned approach resulted in no reports of serious problems.

The Dutch policing style contrasted markedly with the Belgian, where there were good examples of serious police over-reaction. In one notorious incident, Belgian police threw tear gas grenades into a crowded bar and indiscriminately arrested everyone inside. The deportees who arrived back in England included an American tourist and a Swiss businessman who just happened to be in the bar at the time.

What is significant here is that, of the two countries, it was Belgium and not Holland which experienced the public disorder. This led the Dutch police scientist, Otto Adang, to begin work with English colleagues such as Clifford Stott to develop the 'friendly but firm' approach. The Dutch experience suggested that it worked, but the hypothesis had not been scientifically evaluated.

Adang and Stott's work began to be noticed. For example, the UK authorities were able to point to the Dutch experience to persuade the Japanese and Koreans to soften their own policing style for the 2002 World Cup. The pair secured European funding and, by 2004, were able to carry out a large-scale scientific experiment at the European Championships in Portugal.

The police force covering the small towns and countryside – the GNR – adopted the traditional public order policing model – and experienced problems with public disorder. Meanwhile the urban police force – the PSP – policed the host cities using the 'friendly but firm' style – and had no incidents of any particular note.

The experiment concluded that it was the fans' perceptions of legitimacy which was the key determiner of whether there would be serious disorder. If the ordinary fans perceive policing as **targeted** and **proportionate**, then the fans marginalize the hooligans and even start to police them themselves. Conversely, where policing is perceived as **indiscriminate** and **excessive**, then the ordinary fans identify with the hooligans against the police. Those ordinary fans thus find themselves drawn into an escalating situation in which public order breaks down, property gets damaged and people get injured.

In summary, then, the wrong kind of security can be bad for safety. And remember, once the police have lost it on the way to the ground, you have no hope of stewarding successfully at the ground.

There is an excellent quote from a Portuguese riot squad Commander which so clearly shows his realisation that the wrong kind of police intervention could itself be the cause of violence.

> We had that kind of tension ... we were counting that the violence could actually happen at any moment. **But we have to be sure that we were not the cause, you see?** [*my emphasis*]. So the anti-riot unit was there but not in front of the football supporters. We placed it 100 metres away, they were around the corner, on the top of the stairs in the main square on the downtown.

It is extraordinary to see this change of mindset from someone who must have been brought up with the traditional model of public order policing. But he had found out what worked best.

So what are the elements of the 'friendly but firm' policing style? In brief, the seven elements first involve understanding the fans – how will the ordinary fans behave in your city? Whilst you want to keep a close eye on known hooligans, you must help the ordinary fans do what they legitimately came to do – not spoil their occasion with unnecessary controls. Officers in ordinary uniform should make friendly contacts with the fans. Such officers should be ready to intervene to communicate when behaviour is getting out of hand and to explain what the police are going to do.

Absolutely key is that fan groups should be policed on the basis of their actual behaviour and not on their reputation. If a particular fan group has a poor reputation, of course you will have the appropriate resources available. But that does not mean you deploy them. And if you do deploy, you focus on the people who are actually misbehaving and you use no more force than is reasonably necessary. The Portuguese PSP found that a four-level graded response for deployments worked very well indeed – in fact they never got to level four throughout the tournament.

Finally, you should make use of police officers from the visiting teams/countries as they will be able to tell you who the real hooligans are and whether the fans' behaviour really presents a risk. Visiting police can also make early interventions to advise fans about their conduct.

As a result of Euro 2004, the European Union handbook on policing football matches was amended to refer to dynamic risk assessment and police tactical performance. So why was there was still trouble at the 2006 World Cup in Germany? The underlying issue was political in that, for obvious historical reasons, the police forces from the Länder [States] were reluctant to be told how to police by the police forces from the Bund [Federation]. As a result, relatively little use was made of the visiting police from the participating nations.

Police in two cities – Frankfurt and Nuremberg – adopted elements of the 'friendly but firm' style but did not do enough to intervene in the early stages of problems. In two other cities – Stuttgart and Cologne – the police adopted a more traditional policing model and – surprise, surprise – experienced greater problems as a result.

Don't think that I am saying that there is no place for the deployment of the riot squad. Police in Manchester deployed riot police to deal with the violence at the fan park in Manchester at this year's UEFA Cup final. Even those politicians who initially criticised the police for over-reacting changed their minds after they had seen the CCTV pictures. The flashpoint may have been the large screen breaking down, but the subsequent violence was serious and had to be quelled –it was a 'level four' situation.

If you want to know more about the 'friendly but firm' policing style, I strongly recommend the recent book *Football Hooliganism: Policing and the War on the 'English Disease'* by Clifford Stott and Geoff Pearson (2007 Pennant Books – ISBN 978-1-909015-05-3).

To conclude, I've tried to share three lessons from European football: keeping 'safety' and 'security' in balance; making a success of stewarding; and adopting the 'friendly but firm' policing style. There are significant challenges ahead – particularly for Italy, South Africa, Poland, Ukraine and Brazil. I hope that these lessons will prove useful as these countries prepare for their tournaments.

1.2. COMMENTARY BY JIM CHALMERS – BALANCING 'SAFETY' AND 'SECURITY'

In the 2008 article, Frosdick outlines his presentation to a conference in Rome on the subject of crowd control and safety. In the article, he focuses on three key points which will surround any debate on this topic, namely;

- keeping 'safety' and 'security' in balance;
- making a success of stewarding;
- adopting a 'friendly but firm' policing style.

The 2008 article was very much a forerunner to his 2010 article 'Policing Safety and Security in Public Assembly Facilities' which features as article 1.1 of this book, together with my commentary. In the 2008 article, Frosdick addresses some of the fundamental issues relating to making a success of stewarding. In putting this subject into context the reader should refer to Part V of *Safety and Security at Sports Grounds*, where we go into detail on the history and development of stewarding, stewards training and assessment and the transition from 'high profile policing/low profile stewarding' to 'high profile stewarding/low profile policing'.

At the Rome conference, Frosdick only touches the surface of a subject which has been the cause of constant development since the 1989 Hillsborough stadium disaster. As someone who has been involved in the development of stewarding since those early days, what Frosdick outlines in his article can be regarded as very basic in the UK context, but since his primary audience was European, it is perhaps not quite so basic as first thought. For instance, he refers to the various types of stewards, their specific roles, conduct and appearance – all of which have developed and evolved over the years into the high standards seen throughout England and Wales. I would suggest that in the present day UK, untidy and undisciplined stewards with no understanding of their roles and responsibilities will be the exception, whereas they were once the norm.

Frosdick also refers to the key part he played in providing the first professional training package for stewards in England and Wales in 1996 (the detail of this can be found in Part V of *Safety and Security at Sports Grounds*). Having built a solid foundation, stewards training has continued to evolve. In October 2010, the football authorities, in partnership with the Football Safety Officers' Association (FSOA), introduced an updated stewards training package, *On the Ball*, for all football clubs in England and Wales. This new training package (mapped against the requirements for a Level Two qualification in Spectator Safety) has ensured the football authorities in England and Wales continue to set the standards and bench marks for training and assessing stewards at sports grounds.

Frosdick's expertise in the development of stewards training was recognised in 2010, when he was appointed to produce a stewards training and assessment package for use by the Polish and Ukrainian football authorities in readiness for UEFA EURO 2012. The training package comprises eight modules with over 300 slides with embedded photographs and videos. It is accompanied by a 210 page trainers' manual containing all the training, assessment and evaluation materials. The programme was launched at Arsenal football club, with trainers from both countries spending a week being taught how to use the package. That programme is now being rolled out at the venues to be used for the 2012 Championships. I am confident that UEFA will eventually see this European stewards training package spread across other countries in Europe.

Frosdick refers to policing agencies and the concept of adopting Cliff Stott and Otto Adang's 'friendly but firm' policing style as the way in which football matches should be policed. He makes specific reference to how European countries might benefit from the UK methods in this regard. Frosdick's objectivity in addressing an issue which could be viewed as controversial might even be regarded by some police agencies as confrontational. Yet Frosdick continues to speak his mind in addressing a topic which has a direct bearing on crowd reactions to policing styles, and gives reasonable explanations in support of his argument. Based on my own policing and safety management experience, I fully support his arguments, and as I suggest in my earlier commentary for article 1.1, many police agencies are still over concerned with security, using indiscriminate and aggressive force to the detriment of people's safety. The examples quoted by Frosdick support that viewpoint.

However, as Frosdick accepts, the aggressive style of policing football crowds in the 60s, 70s and 80s was very much aimed at containing the 'football hooligan' element. Unfortunately, the use of this policing style resulted in generations of football fans being alienated from the police. The Hillsborough stadium disaster was the catalyst for change in policing styles. After the disaster and during my time as the Police Commander at Villa Park in Birmingham, I can recall ordering the high pitch perimeter fences to be taken down. Many of my police colleagues thought I was mad, and feared being overrun by the fans. However, the opposite proved the case in that with the fences gone, the fans talked to my officers and they talked to them. I removed the physical barrier and in doing so, removed the psychological barrier between the fans and the police. For more comment on high pitch perimeter fences please see my commentaries on articles 4.1 and 4.2 in *Safety and Security at Sports Grounds*.

Perhaps the best example of how UK policing styles have changed from an aggressive style to the 'friendly but firm' style is the UEFA EURO 96 matches held at UK football grounds. Although they were held only seven years after Hillsborough, these matches proved that much had changed in that time, in that the police no longer considered every football supporter a 'hooligan', and the policing tactics reflected this. I was an FLA Inspector during the UEFA EURO 96 games held at Villa Park and witnessed first hand the transition to the 'friendly but firm' policing approach. Instead of having ranks of riot police to meet the fans from all countries, they were met by the traditional British bobby with a friendly and welcoming attitude. This policing style contributed greatly to the overall friendly atmosphere which prevailed throughout the competition both at the ground and in the city. There were riot police on standby should they be needed, but they were never deployed throughout the tournament in Birmingham. I remember writing to the Chief Constable after the event, praising their involvement in ensuring that football 'came home' to Villa Park in such a memorable way.

Without a doubt the 'friendly but firm' policing style endeared the West Midlands Police officers to the thousands of fans who attended the games. The police had indeed come a long way in recognising that policing styles and tactics would have a direct impact on the overall experience of those attending the games.

Whilst everything associated with crowd risk must be properly assessed, the majority of football supporters attending matches do so for two reasons; to enjoy a game of football, and to support their team. The majority are not remotely interested in creating disorder or engaging in acts of violence. However, there is still an attitude amongst some police agencies that this is precisely what a football fan wants to do. It is this attitude which will have a significant impact on how the police 'police' football crowds. During my time as Police Commander at Villa Park, I can recall an incident whereby a Police Inspector criticised my move towards the 'high profile stewarding/low profile policing' concept. He stated that all football fans were hooligans and that I was putting both himself and his officers in jeopardy. I replied by saying that my eldest daughter was standing on the Holte End terrace (a 23,000 standing terrace at Villa Park) with her boyfriend, and I did not consider either of them to be a football hooligan. This small example illustrates the changes which had to take place in altering a policing mind-set that all football fans were hooligans, to a mind-set that the majority were decent law abiding citizens who should not be penalised for the mindless actions of a minority. It is interesting that in 2004 (as explained in the article) a Portuguese riot squad commander went through the same process in questioning his policing style towards football supporters.

I agree with Frosdick that the 'friendly but firm' style of policing may not always be successful at certain games and with certain groups. However I would always advocate this style as the initial policing tactic, with the riot police held in reserve and out of sight until they are needed, which hopefully will rarely be the case. This approach will at least ensure the police cannot be criticised for 'over reacting' and giving fans an excuse to retaliate in confrontation with the police.

Frosdick gives European examples which would support this argument, but you do not need to travel into Europe or to major football competitions to experience this type of fan reaction to a policing style. At a game in the Blue Square Premier League (a lower league in the English football league structure) between Kettering Town and Luton Town in the 2009/10 season, there was a serious confrontation between the Luton Town fans and the local Northamptonshire police, with the police facing a barrage of bottles and other missiles thrown at them by visiting fans. My Club,

Kidderminster Harriers, were playing Luton Town a few weeks after this, and because of the violence displayed by the Luton Town fans at the Kettering game, I agreed with our own local police that our game should have a policing presence. This is unusual in our league since incidents of disorder and violence are very rare, proven by the fact that this was our first 'policed' game in over three seasons. In discussion with the local police, we did however agree that there would be a low profile style of policing both in the town and at the ground, with the riot squad police held in reserve, out of sight but ready to respond if needed.

As it turned out, there were no problems. Later, when I spoke to some of the Luton Town fans, they told me that the reason there was such disorder in Kettering was because they were met by riot police. These officers were, to use the fans' words, 'looking for trouble', and so the Luton Fans reacted by misbehaving. In our case, they were very complimentary about the way the local police and club stewards welcomed them to the game and the town, and this had a direct bearing on the fact that the event was incident free. No one is in any way excusing the irresponsible behaviour of a few of their fans in Kettering, but I use this as an example of how contrasting policing styles can impact on attitudes and behaviour towards the police.

Examples such as this serve to stress the importance of understanding the difference between safety and security, and how differing policing styles can have an impact on these concepts. There are still many policing agencies that see their role as providing 'protection **from** the crowd' as distinct from 'protection **of** the crowd'. I believe that the introduction of the 'friendly but firm' policing concept is now regarded as the way forward in Europe and various other countries in the policing of football crowds. This is not, however, universal, and the game of football will continue to be beset by tragedy until this concept is internationally recognised.

1.3. SAFETY AND SECURITY RISKS IN SUPERLEAGUE FORMULA

The original citation for this article is Frosdick, S. (2010) 'Superleague Formula 2008: A Case Study in Managing Safety and Security Risks in Soccer Themed Motor Racing'. *International Journal of Police Science and Management*, 12(3): 357-372.

Reproduced with acknowledgements to Vathek Publishing.

Abstract

This is a case study in five main sections. The introduction sets out the background as a commercial consultancy assignment involving the practical application of Grid Group Cultural Theory (GGCT). The second section outlines GGCT, a neo-Durkheimian theory which can be usefully applied for the assessment and management of risk. The paper then gives a brief overview of Superleague Formula, a new sporting series which combined motor racing and soccer.

The bulk of the paper details an assessment of how soccer fans from 18 clubs around the world might behave as spectators at six soccer-themed motor racing events in Europe. The research was problematic because of time constraints and because of the new risk setting. The application of GGCT teased out eight key areas of threat, seven of which related to public order issues involving the fans. The eighth threat referred to fans as victims of indiscriminate policing. These threats were risk assessed for each of the 18 clubs at each of the six circuits — 864 assessments in all. The risks were evaluated with reference to a defined risk appetite. Appropriate control measures, including police tactical deployments, were devised for each of the races. The paper then highlights the safety and security risks which became realities at the events.

As well as having set out a rigorous analysis derived from applied theory, the paper concludes that the eight key threats form a good basis for others to hypothesise how soccer fans might behave in a new setting.

Introduction

Background

> But can we know the risks we face, now or in the future? No, we cannot; but yes, we must act as if we do. Some dangers are unknown; others are known, but not by us, because no one person can know everything (Douglas and Wildavsky, 1982).

In June 2008, we took a phone call from the Chief Executive of Superleague Formula, a brand new sports event based in Spain, which described itself as 'the fusion of two of the world's most popular sports – capturing the passion of football [soccer] with the thrill and excitement of motor racing' (see http://www.superleaguefor mula.com/superleague/What-is-SF). The caller explained that his organisation had decided that it did not know how soccer fans would behave at motor racing circuits; it needed to know more about the safety and security risks such fans might pose. The first race was in eleven weeks time. Could we help?

Notwithstanding our expertise in safety and security at sports grounds, particularly soccer, our immediate thoughts were that we did not know how the fans would behave either. Yet, following Douglas and Wildavsky (1982), there were good reasons to act as if we could know. Although there was very little time to find out what could be known, this was a rare opportunity to demonstrate the commercial application of Grid Group Cultural Theory (GGCT) to the rapid identification, assessment and management of a real-life international policing situation. As well as helping our client, we would be able to build an empirical case study which could be useful for policy-makers and practitioners involved in safety, security and policing in international public assembly facilities.

Grid Group Cultural Theory

GGCT (see Thompson, Ellis, and Wildavsky, 1990) is rooted in neo-Durkheimian traditions of collective analysis and starts from the grid-group typology set out by Douglas (1978). This argues that there are two dimensions by which all cultures can be classified. The first is *grid*, which has been defined as 'the total body of rules and constraints which a culture imposes on its people in a particular context' (Mars and Nicod, 1983, p. 124), and as 'the degree to which an individual's life is circumscribed by externally imposed prescriptions' (Thompson et al., p. 5). The second dimension of *group* 'emphasises collectiveness among people who meet face to face' (Mars, 1994, p. 24). The group dimension also 'refers to the extent to which an individual is morally coerced by others, through being a member of a bounded face-to-face unit' (Mars and Nicod, p. 125) and describes, 'the experience of a bounded social unit' (Douglas, p. viii).

Considering the two dimensions together produces a fourfold typology of ways of life. The four archetypes – individualism, fatalism, hierarchy and egalitarianism – each reflect a cohesive and coherent cluster of attitudes, beliefs and styles of relationships. These ways of life determine the participants' behaviour and are used by them to justify the validity of their social situations. Fatalism represents a passive way of life whilst the other three are active. Tellingly, the ways of life also inform the perceptions of the participants, specifically in the present context, their perceptions of risk.

Tracing aspects of the theoretical development of GGCT demonstrates its value as an analytical tool for safety and security risks in Superleague Formula. First of all, in their review of rival theories of risk perception, Wildavsky and Dake (1990) concluded that GGCT offered more powerful elucidation than the traditional psychological explanations. Second, discussing the implications of GGCT for risk assessment, other cultural theorists argued that operationalising GGCT facilitated the capture of plurality and the negotiation of consensus (see Thompson and Rayner, 1998; Thompson, Rayner, and Ney, 1999). Third, when distinguishing between directly perceptible risks (cars), risks perceived through science (cholera) and 'virtual' risks where people do not know and cannot agree (mad cows), Adams (1999) and Adams and Thompson (2002) showed how GGCT provided the explanatory tool for those risks which were products of the imagination. Going on, Frosdick (2006, p. 1) argued that 'previous applications of GGCT have tended to be conceptual and retrospective'. He went on to demonstrate the practical application of GGCT to managing risk in two 'live' research settings, one of which involved public assembly facilities such as sports grounds. Pointing up useful future work, Frosdick suggested going back into the sports grounds setting to 'apply the consultancy methodology to a case study' (p. 265). Superleague Formula provided just such an opportunity.

The Superleague Formula Series

The series featured 18 single-seater race cars, each with a 750 brake horse power V12 engine. Each of the cars was liveried as a soccer team but the cars and components were otherwise identical. The cars had no technical aids, so the focus was on the skill of the drivers, each of whom wore his team's colours. There were two 45-minute races, the second being reverse grid, so the fastest driver from race one started from the back in race two. There were 18 participating clubs from various European countries as well as from Brazil, China and the Middle East.

The series attracted fans from both motor racing and soccer. The event format meant that during the day the fans moved around the circuit. For the 'penalty shoot out' qualifying competition on the Saturday and the two races on the Sunday, there were fans in the grandstands. For ancillary entertainments and to see the cars being worked on, the fans moved to the paddock, which was open to the public. To meet the drivers and see the cars close up, fans were permitted to walk in the pit lane at certain times during the weekend; the philosophy was one of open access.

The cars and drivers were run by various race teams, which did their best to keep the cars on the track. This was a competition, so winning and the traditional podium ceremony were also key parts of the event. Finally, Superleague Formula involved six different circuits, in six different countries, with six different legal systems, six different policing styles, six different approaches to stewarding and six different mixes of crowd size and nationalities. The six circuits were Donington Park, (England), Nürburgring (Germany), Zolder (Belgium), Estoril (Portugal), Vallelunga (Italy) and Jerez (Spain).

Methods

The three arms of the methodological approach – due diligence, special risk assessment and race oversight – are summarised in Figure One [on the next page].

Figure One – Summary of the Methodological Approach

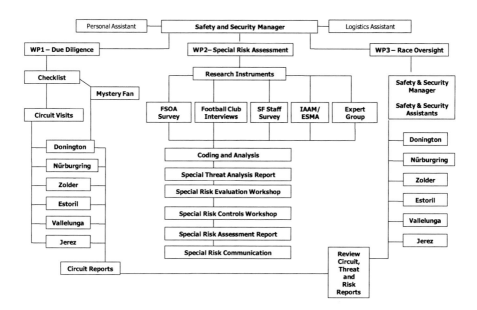

Due Diligence

From the very start, we conceptualised three main categories of safety and security risk. We designated these as the 'racing' risks, the 'normal' crowd risks and the 'special' crowd risks.

The 'racing' risks were rather obviously the risks associated with the motor racing itself, for example driver injuries from crashes, injuries to people struck by a car in the pit lane or on the grid, or injuries to race marshals from flying debris. However, the racing was taking place under the auspices of the Fédération Internationale de l'Automobile (FIA), the governing body of international motor racing, which provided a panoply of race direction, race stewards and scrutineers at each race. Like every series, Superleague Formula was entitled to assume that the six circuits were FIA licensed and considered competent to manage everything that happened inside the track perimeter fences. Accordingly, we took the policy decision to exclude this category of risk from our work, save where it impacted on the other categories, for example during the pit lane walk.

The next category was the 'normal' risks around crowd management at a motor racing event. Irrespective of any contractual terms, there were two compelling reasons why Superleague Formula needed to undertake 'due diligence' on the circuits' proposed arrangements. First, Superleague Formula had a moral and (depending on the jurisdiction) legal duty of care for its paying customers. In the event of a serious incident, there was every possibility that failings in exercising that duty could result in criminal charges and civil damages. This represented the contemporary notion of risk as blame (see Douglas, 1990, 1992).

The second reason was that, in order to understand the 'special' risks associated with the event, it was first necessary to be clear about what the 'normal' risks were and how the circuits proposed to manage them. We therefore visited each of the six circuits to establish and report on the local arrangements for managing the 'normal' risks. To support the visits, we put together a checklist of 138 points, cross-referenced to standards such as the UK 'Green Guide' to safety at sports grounds (Department of Culture, Media and Sport, 2008) and the UK counter terrorism advice for stadia and arenas (National Counter Terrorism Security Office [NaCTSO], 2006). The 138 points were organised under 15 main headings, namely: documentation, physical structures, traffic management, safety systems, safety personnel, safety procedures, fire safety, medical aid, local municipality, anti-terror, spectators, crime prevention, crime and public order, VIPs and hospitality, and press and television.

At each circuit, each point was assessed as 'red', 'amber' or 'green'. 'Green' meant that we were content that the proposed arrangements represented an appropriate local equivalent of the relevant UK standards. 'Amber' meant that some remedial action was recommended, for example repairs to broken seats. 'Red' meant that the matter required immediate action, for example securing an event permit from the local municipality.

Special Risk Assessment

The third and, for this paper, the most important category of safety and security risk, was the 'special' risks arising from the unique fusion of soccer and motor racing. The key point here is that what we were doing was completely new, i.e. there had never previously been a soccer-themed motor racing series. Superleague Formula did not know what the special risks might be, which is why it had brought us in. Despite our backgrounds, we did not know either – and we found that nobody else we asked was any the wiser.

Identifying the special threats

Using our privileged access as members, we commissioned a questionnaire survey of all the members of the UK Football Safety Officers' Association (FSOA). Because of their week-in, week-out expertise, we thought the FSOA members, particularly those with experience of European competitions, would be very well placed to hypothesise the threats. We were wrong. To encourage responses, we had offered the incentive of a £10 donation for each of the first 100 completed questionnaires. But from over 300 potential responses, we received only three, each of which effectively said 'we don't know'. Again using privileged access, we ran the same survey questions past the European Stadium Managers Association and the International Association of Assembly Managers in Europe. We had no replies at all. Chasing up, we were told that nobody felt able to say how the fans might behave. Finally, we asked the same questions of Superleague Formula staff. The collated responses were blank except for minor comments about the normal behaviour of supporters of five of the teams.

We mention these attempted surveys precisely because of the lack of response. This confirmed the status of the 'special' threats as the type of 'virtual' risks referred to by Adams (1999) as products of the imagination. However, our methodological approach had two other arms, both of which involved the application of GGCT.

The first additional arm involved the participating soccer clubs. Applying GGCT to this environment enabled us to identify the three active GGCT types to be found in this context (see Frosdick, 1995). These were: individualism, represented by the club's commercial manager or equivalent; egalitarianism, personified by a representative of an appropriate fan group; and hierarchy, exemplified by either the club's safety/security manager or by a senior police officer responsible for policing the club's matches. We sought contact with these persons and made efforts to interview them using a combination of briefing documentation circulated by email and telephone questionnaires. We used interpreters where necessary, for example when contacting clubs outside Europe. We also investigated relevant open source material from the Internet.

The second arm involved assembling an expert group which operationalised the three active ways of life within GGCT. Again, using our privileged access, we were able to convene very experienced safety officers from the Football Safety Officers' Association, together with police officers with extensive strategic and tactical soccer policing expertise. These represented hierarchy. The group also included national representatives from the Football Supporters Federation (egalitarianism); and the insurance brokers responsible for placing Superleague Formula's public liability risks with appropriate underwriters (individualism).

The analysis derived from the soccer club interviews and refined with the expert group revealed eight key 'special' threats.

Analysis of the Impacts if the Special Threats Became Realities

The estimates of impact were assessed with reference to the severities of impact set out in Table One [on the next page]. This was derived from the UK Central Computer and Telecommunications Agency[1] (CCTA) Risk Analysis and Management Method (CRAMM) which gives the benefit of allowing comparisons to be made between different types of impacts.

The estimates of impact were consensually agreed by the expert group through independent voting, discussion of differences in perceptions and, where necessary, aggregation. This represented the practical application of GGCT to risk estimation advocated by Frosdick (1998, 2006), who notes that the overarching experience for participants representing the different ways of life is that the exchange of views is very informative and very often results in changes in perception on the basis of new information received. It was here that the presence of the Football Supporters Federation

---

[1] Now the Office for Government Commerce

representatives added particular value, for example when debating the impact on fans of the indiscriminate policing tactics employed in certain jurisdictions.

Table One – Severity of Impact Table

Minor (1)	Minor distress to an individual
	Financial losses of up to £10,000
	Very minor disruption within the venue
	Minor loss of goodwill confined to the individual event

Moderate (2)	Minor illness/injury
	Minor distress to more than one person
	Civil damages/criminal penalty of up to £10,000
	Financial losses of £10,001 to £100,000
	Minor disruption or protest within the venue
	Loss of goodwill but with no effects beyond the individual event

Serious (3)	Serious illness/injury/threat to life, restricted to an individual
	Substantial distress to one or more persons
	Civil damages/criminal penalty of £10,001 to £250,000/up to 10 years prison
	Financial losses of £100,001 to £1,000,000
	Disruption or protest in the local community
	Damage to reputation/credibility extending beyond the individual event

Severe (4)	Serious illness/injury/threat to life, involving more than one person
	Financial losses above £1,000,000
	Unlimited civil damages/criminal penalty or imprisonment in excess of ten years
	Disruption or protest with nationally felt effects
	Significant damage to reputation/credibility resulting in widespread adverse publicity

Fatal (5)	Loss of life

Identification of the Probability Factors

The expert group drew out the factors which they considered would increase the probability of each threat becoming a reality. The group decided that the more that seven specific factors were present, the greater the probability that the special threat posed by the fans would become a reality. For the threats posed by the fans, the seven factors were: propensity of the fans to engage in that type of behaviour; geographical proximity of the club to the circuit; high numbers of fans expected; 'risk' fans associated with the club; local and historical rivalries with other participating clubs; absence of alcohol controls; no home game, attractive away game or other fixture clash and/or no participation in European competition.

The probability factors for the special threat of indiscriminate crowd management tactics were different, namely: reputation of the fans; 'risk' fans associated with the club; high numbers of fans expected; geographical proximity of the club to the circuit; public order style of the police force; public order reputation of the police force; likely police presence in or around the circuit.

The probabilities were assessed using a five-point scale: very low (1); low (2); medium (3); high (4) and very high (5). The initial probability assessments were reviewed and discussed by the expert group.

Risk Appetite and Evaluation

A risk appetite can be expressed as a cross-impact matrix which determines which risks are deemed to be 'high', which 'medium' and which 'low'. The boundaries between these three categories are contingent on an organisation's appetite for risk. The more risk averse the organisation is, the lower the thresholds will be set. The Superleague Formula risk appetite for each club and circuit was assessed on the basis of six factors: the acceptance by Superleague Formula of its moral and (depending on the jurisdiction) legal duty of care for its paying customers; the willingness of Superleague Formula to invest in specialist risk assessment consultancy; the contractual arrangements between Superleague Formula and the individual circuits; the results of the visits to report on the normal crowd management arrangements; commercial sensitivities involving particular clubs; and the commercial imperative for racing to take place.

On the basis of the impacts, probabilities and risk appetite, we then prepared 864 risk evaluations; each threat for each of the 18 sets of fans at each of the circuits.

Race Oversight and Risk Management

We communicated the risks to our client, their insurance brokers and the circuits during the course of the race oversight process. Race oversight involved arriving at the circuit in advance of the race, liaising regarding the risk management controls to be applied and being present throughout the race weekend in an operational role to monitor and respond to any actualisation of both the 'normal' and the 'special' risks.

The recommended special risk management controls for each race weekend took account of each circuit's proposals for managing the normal crowd-related risks at a motor racing event. The special risk management controls fell into the categories of risk transfer, probability reduction, impact reduction, response readiness and contingency plans. In recommending controls, careful consideration had to be given to the knock-on impacts. The question always had to be asked, would this control have disproportionate adverse impacts elsewhere?

Because the risk assessments were different, the recommended controls for each circuit varied. Taking the police attendance as an example, this ranged from no police presence at all at Donington, through six officers in normal uniform at Zolder, to officers in partial protective clothing with a unit of the National Guard on standby at Estoril.

Limitations

The methodological approach was constrained by five factors. First, the research was carried out at very short notice at the time of year when many of the potential respondents were on holiday. Second, several of the clubs were difficult to contact and, notwithstanding the use of interpreters, the researchers were simply unable to get through to an appropriate individual. These two factors were countered by using the expert group to review and validate the emerging identification of the special threats.

Third, there were no historical data on the behaviour of soccer fans in a motor racing environment. When safety and security experts, club representatives, circuit representatives and fans were asked to hypothesise, by far the most common response was 'We don't know'. This limitation confirmed the status of the 'special' threats as the type of 'virtual' risks referred to by Adams (1999) as products of the imagination, except that we had found that even the most likely 'experts' felt unable to exercise their imaginations about Superleague Formula.

Fourth, the known identities of the participating clubs changed during the research process. Each time a new club joined the competition, the crowd dynamics might change and the probability assessments had to be revisited. For example, Liverpool signed up just a few days before the first race and this required a review of the potential rivalries between Liverpool and Tottenham, Rangers and other clubs which Liverpool had met in European competition.

The fifth factor involved commercial sensitivities, which precluded contact with two clubs from outside Europe. It was very unlikely indeed that these fans would attend in any meaningful numbers and the two clubs were therefore deemed to be zero risk for the first race.

Results and Discussion

Identification of the Special Threats

The analysis revealed eight primary qualitative themes. Seven of these were threats posed *by* the fans, whilst the eighth theme was a threat *to* the fans. These threats whilst qualitatively different were symbiotic and should not therefore be seen as mutually exclusive. However, the expert group was content that they were jointly exhaustive.

Heavy drinking – several respondents mentioned this as a potential problem, noting how heavy drinking over the course of several hours could accentuate 'rowdy' and/or 'aggressive' behaviour (see Home Office, 1986).

Missiles – depending on the proximity of the fans to the track, anything from bottles to coins could be thrown at rival fans, the driver, the car or the race team.

Pyrotechnics – most participating clubs' fans bring flares and fireworks into their soccer stadia, and respondents suggested they might do the same for Superleague Formula. Pyrotechnics might be used as missiles. The fire risk was less of a concern because of the open air and the extensive fire safety arrangements at racing circuits.

The fourth and fifth factors concerned public disorder. As well as being related to the first three factors, local, international and historical soccer rivalries were quoted as a concern. Much of the research indicated a greater probability of problems if local rival fans attended the races. There were two types of public disorder that needed to be considered.

Minor public disorder – there was a potential for rival fans to use anti-social behaviour and be both verbally and physically aggressive in their interactions with each other and with stewards. A number of respondents mentioned that their fans exhibit 'passion' and 'noise' in the forms of flags, banners and musical instruments. In some countries, fans were not used to being given directions by stewards and might not recognise their authority.

Major public disorder – several respondents mentioned that most clubs have a small contingent of 'risk' supporters who could present serious problems. However, a number of clubs tended to downplay the 'hooligan' element. For example, one club suggested that two per cent of their fans were 'difficult to control'; however, our expert group considered this was more like 40 per cent. It should also be noted that minor public disorder could quickly escalate into serious disorder, especially if not dealt with effectively by either the police and/or stewards.

Hate – the most interesting theme to emerge was the potential problem with differing ideological belief systems between different sets of fans. For example, Rangers fans tend to sing and chant anti-Catholic sentiments. There had also been an incident at a Formula 1 grand prix in Spain where fans had racially insulted the English driver, Lewis Hamilton.

Protest – there was a potential for motor racing fans to protest. For example, one 'petrol head' fan blog was concerned about allowing 'hooligans' into motor racing. There was also potential for soccer fans to protest at the further commercialisation of their sport.

Disproportionate crowd management tactics – there was extensive research evidence (e.g. see Stott and Pearson, 2007), accepted by the Council of Europe, that the 'friendly but firm' policing style, which was both proportionate and targeted, was the correct tactic for crowd management. However, Superleague Formula races would be taking place in certain jurisdictions that did not practise this policing style. In such countries, *disproportionate* and *indiscriminate* crowd management tactics have regularly resulted in the escalation of minor disorder and serious injuries to fans caused by the police intervention.

The Impacts if the Special Threats Became Realities

If there were *heavy drinking*, then the most reasonably foreseeable impact would be *severe*, because of serious injury involving more than one person, and significant damage to reputation from widespread adverse publicity. If there were *missiles*, then the impact would be *serious*, because of serious injury to an individual, and damage to reputation extending beyond the event. If there were *pyrotechnics*, then the impact would be *moderate*, because of minor disruption within the venue.

If there were *minor public disorder*, then the most reasonably foreseeable impact would be *moderate*, because of minor distress to more than one person. However, if there were *major public disorder*, then the impact would be *severe*, because of serious injury involving more than one person and significant damage to reputation from widespread adverse publicity.

If there were *hate*, then the most reasonably foreseeable impact would be *serious*, because of substantial distress to one or more persons, and damage to reputation extending beyond the event. If there were *protest*, then the impact would be *serious*, because of damage to reputation extending beyond the event.

Finally, if there were *disproportionate crowd management tactics*, then the most reasonably foreseeable impact would be *severe*, because of serious injury to more than one person, and significant damage to reputation from widespread adverse publicity.

The Probabilities For Each Team at Each Circuit

The expert group considered that the eight threats and the impact estimates would be consistent across the six races. What would change the risk assessments were therefore the 864 individual probability assessments, derived from analysing the probability factors for each team at each circuit.

The probabilities were assessed as follows: probability factor score of three or less – very low (1); four or more — low (2); six or more — medium (3); eight or more — high (4); ten or more — very high (5). The examples in Tables Two and Three are offered to illustrate the analysis.

Table Two – [Team Name]: Flares and Fireworks

	Donington	Nürburgring	Zolder	Estoril	Vallelunga	Jerez
Propensity of the fans to engage in that type of behaviour	2	2	2	1	1	1
Geographical proximity of the club to the circuit	0	2	2	0	0	0
High numbers of fans expected	0	0	0	0	0	0
'Risk' fans associated with the club	2	2	2	1	1	1
Local and historical rivalries with other participating clubs	2	2	2	2	2	2
Absence of alcohol controls	2	2	2	2	2	2
No home game, attractive away game or other fixture clash; and/or no participation in European competition	0	0	0	0	0	0
Total	*8*	*10*	*10*	*6*	*6*	*6*
Probability Factor	4	5	5	3	3	3

Table Three – [Team Name]: Heavy Drinking

	Donington	Nürburgring	Zolder	Estoril	Vallelunga	Jerez
Propensity of the fans to engage in that type of behaviour	0	0	0	0	0	0
Geographical proximity of the club to the circuit	0	0	0	2	0	0
High numbers of fans expected	0	0	0	0	0	0
'Risk' fans associated with the club	0	0	0	0	0	0
Local and historical rivalries with other participating clubs	0	0	0	0	0	0
Absence of alcohol controls	1	1	1	1	1	1
No home game, attractive away game or other fixture clash; and/or no participation in European competition	0	0	0	0	0	0
Total	*1*	*1*	*1*	*3*	*1*	*1*
Probability Factor	1	1	1	1	1	1

The ongoing analysis was dynamic and the probabilities were amended as changes to the probability factors arose during the course of the season. For example, the addition of Athletico Madrid to the competition required a reassessment of the probability factors for Seville, their Spanish rivals. Again, for example, the last minute information that up to 20 coach loads of FC Porto fans would be attending the Estoril race in Lisbon required a wholesale reassessment of the probability factors, particularly since the intelligence suggested that one of the coaches contained a group of 'risk' supporters.

The Superleague Formula risk appetite

The Superleague Formula risk appetite is shown in Figure Two [on the next page], which shows the bands of high, medium and low risk.

Figure Two – Superleague Formula Risk Appetite.

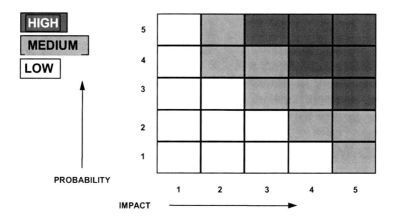

Evaluation of the special risks for each circuit

Each of the eight threats was evaluated for each club at each circuit in the light of the risk appetite. The initial evaluation report ran to 74 pages and formed the base document from which interim and then final circuit specific risk assessments were produced in the run-up to each of the race weekends. The interim assessments were prepared to inform the discussions with the circuit and local police about risk management controls, for example, the tactical options to be employed by the police. The final assessments were then prepared to reflect the decisions taken, which had the effect of 'treating' the risks and so reducing them.

The base document went through six version changes during the course of the season. The probability assessments in the initial report were revised for the Nürburgring race in Germany following faceto-face discussions with the head of security at Borussia Dortmund and with the security staff at the circuit. The next version took account of revised intelligence about the behaviour of FC Basel fans and the addition of the AS Roma and Liverpool teams to the series. The document was then updated to reflect changes in the policing arrangements for the Zolder race in Belgium and then again to add Athletico Madrid to the competition. The very good behaviour of the large numbers of Anderlecht and PSV Eindhoven fans who attended the Zolder race resulted in the probability assessments for their subsequent behaviour being revised downwards. Finally, changes in the policing arrangements for Jerez and the anticipated attendance of many thousands of Seville fans resulted in the final revision.

Because of the dynamic nature of the risk assessment process, the evolving season of six races and the experienced gained along the way, it is necessary to be careful about making comparisons between the circuits. However, one comparable indicator of the relative riskiness of each of the race weekends was the number of high risks communicated to the circuits in the final risk assessments prepared for each race weekend. This showed that, prior to the race weekend, Circuit Zolder was perceived as the highest risk event. So we shall refer to Zolder for the discussion of risk management controls which follows.

Special Risk Management Controls

The ten high risks in the Zolder analysis are set out in Table Four. Note that the names of the clubs have been replaced with identifying letters.

Table Four – Circuit Zolder High Risks

Club	Threat	Prob.	Impact	Multiplier
A	Heavy Drinking	5	4	20
B	Heavy Drinking	5	4	20
A	Disproportionate Crowd Tactics	4	4	16
C	Disproportionate Crowd Tactics	4	4	16
D	Heavy Drinking	4	4	16
C	Heavy Drinking	4	4	16
A	Major Public Order	4	4	16
B	Major Public Order	4	4	16
B	Hate	5	3	15
B	Missiles	5	3	15

Risk Transfer

The Superleague Formula insurance brokers had been involved in the normal and special risk assessment processes, received copies of all the reports produced and fed back that they were content that no additional risk transfer controls were needed for any of the races.

Additional Probability Reduction Controls – Zolder

Three of the ten high risks and four of the medium risks referred to heavy drinking. This was unlikely to be a big problem with VIPs, for whom there were no alcohol restrictions. For the general public, only beer was available at the circuit. The question, then, was whether the event should be dry. The answer was 'no' because the knock-on impacts of any such decision would be to spoil the enjoyment of the vast majority of fans and to undermine the commercial viability of the event. The staff in the Zolder beer kiosks were very experienced and able to give early warning of any emerging tensions or problems to the control room.

Notwithstanding that the threat of missiles appeared once as a high risk and four times in the medium risk category, the wide variety of objects which could be used as missiles means that there was no point searching spectators prior to entry. Which objects would one seek to confiscate as potential missiles? In any event, the knock-on impacts would be disproportionate. First, motor racing fans are not used to being searched and would take umbrage at a blanket searching policy. Second, flow rates would be reduced and queue times extended, thus considerable additional staff would be needed for access control. So, it was not recommended that spectators were searched prior to entry to the circuit. Pyrotechnics appeared four times in the medium risk category. The impact of this risk was only moderate because of the large number of race marshals. Irrespective of any probabilities, this risk did not therefore justify additional searches of spectators prior to entry to the circuit.

There were only four mentions of minor public disorder in the medium risk category; however, minor public disorder which is not addressed can quickly escalate into major public disorder. This was mentioned twice in the high risk category – in respect of clubs A and B – and eleven times in the medium risk category. Although there was no police intelligence to suggest that known 'risk' fans would attend the event, the public order risk remained a concern. The overt presence of suitable and sufficient stewarding staff in the main grandstand, viewing areas and paddock would provide a visible reminder to spectators of the presence of social control. The attendance of police officers in ordinary uniform to provide a visible patrol and communicate in a friendly manner with the fans would also be useful.

The local police took as their starting point a requirement that the fans of clubs Anderlecht and PSV Eindhoven should be segregated from each other throughout the race weekend, which was clearly impracticable in a motor racing circuit. They also felt they might require riot squad units of the federal police to be available for deployment. After some lively debate, the local police were persuaded to take account of the risk assessment and intelligence reports received from the Belgian and Dutch police to agree the final tactic that they would deploy just six local officers to carry out security duties at the event. There would also be two motorcycle police officers deployed on traffic duties and available to support a response to any incidents in the circuit.

There was one occurrence of hate as a high risk and four in the medium risk category. The most effective measure here was to screen the fans on the way in and so a copy of the Football Against Racism in Europe handbook (Football Against Racism in Europe [FARE], 2008), on racist and extremist symbols, was provided to the circuit and to the police. This point was also covered in the briefings. The protest threat appeared four times in the medium risk category. The recommended probability reduction controls for public order and hate would also address this risk.

The threat of disproportionate crowd tactics appeared twice in the high risk category and nine times as a medium risk. The threat would only be likely to arise in the event of inappropriate police first response to any incidents. Such response was more to be feared from the federal police (ie, the former gendarmerie) than from the local police who would now be attending.

Additional Impact Reduction Controls – Zolder

The first aid and medical arrangements appeared adequate to deal with the personal illness aspect of heavy drinking. However, if problems did occur, for example a rowdy group of fans gathering at a particular beer stand, there would be a requirement for a response capability, which was available.

If missiles, flares or fireworks were thrown, the impact was a matter of chance. The presence of the race marshals served as the impact reduction control for the cars and drivers. The availability of medical aid served as the impact reduction control for the spectators.

Early and proportionate intervention in minor public order situations would usually prevent their escalation. Access control, crowd monitoring and the police presence would reduce the impact here. However, the outbreak of major public disorder would require a police response to quell the situation and this would be coordinated by the police already on site.

Crowd monitoring should allow hate instances of racist or homophobic chanting to be noted and an appropriate response deployed. Any display of offensive flags or banners would be similarly noted and dealt with. In the case of peaceful protest, the impact reduction tactic would usually be to contain rather than to quell and the stewards should be able to deal with such matters. Larger scale and more violent protest would become a major public disorder situation requiring a police response.

The impact of disproportionate crowd tactics towards the fans could be serious and the fans could be badly hurt if the police lose their self-control and apply disproportionate and indiscriminate force. In the unlikely event that this did happen, the police would have to answer for their actions.

Additional Response Readiness Controls

The control rooms used by Zolder and the emergency services were located in the same building. This arrangement provided sufficient capability for response readiness.

Additional contingency planning controls

Zolder already had an internal disaster plan in place. This plan included the setting up of an internal coordination centre to coordinate any incident for which the disaster plan had been activated.

Risks at the Races

There was only one occurrence of one of our special risks – hate – at one of the races. This was at Donington Park, where there were small groups of Liverpool, Rangers and Flamenco fans amongst the crowd. On the Sunday afternoon, a group of three or four Rangers fans in kilts started chanting 'Fuck the Pope' whilst walking through the tunnel from the paddock to the infield. They were heard by one of our number and given suitable advice about their future conduct.

Nürburgring saw only a few small groups of Borussia Dortmund and PSV Eindhoven fans and no special risk incidents. At Zolder, our potentially highest risk event, about 6,000 fans attended the Sunday races. There were large groups of PSV Eindhoven and Anderlecht supporters and a small but noisy group of expatriate Galatasaray fans, but again no special risk incidents.

The Estoril race saw about 20,000 fans – including 17 coach loads of FC Porto supporters, whose attendance had only been notified at the last minute. One of these coaches contained about 50 so-called 'risk' fans. We convened a 'crisis management' meeting with the circuit and the police and agreed on five main tactical changes: the clearing of debris (potential missiles) from the entrances to the circuit; the replacement of beer glasses with plastic; a coach management plan, an increased police presence and a police reserve on standby at the nearby barracks. Pleasingly, the fans were well behaved and there were no special risk incidents.

The Vallelunga crowd included small groups of AS Roma and AC Milan supporters. There were no special risk incidents. Finally, Jerez saw a large crowd of about 30,000 fans, many (including four coach loads) from Seville, which was only a 30-minute drive away. There was also a coach load of FC Porto fans who had travelled for 11 hours and a coach load of fans from the home town of the Liverpool driver, who was a Spaniard. There were no special risk incidents.

However, the relative absence of special risks did not mean that we were idle, for we found that there were several aspects of the normal crowd risks which required our attention. There were five recurring themes.

Structures – the stands had trip hazards arising from unexpected changes in levels on the terraces and from uneven riser heights and tread depths on stairways and gangways. There was at least one accident involving an elderly person who fell on a stairway.

Emergency exit capacities – safe capacities depend on the access control arrangements and their impact on emergency exits. At two of the circuits, additional exits had to be opened to maintain the capacities.

Incidents of crowding – there were two such incidents, one on a staircase overlooking the podium at the end of the first race, and the other in a main stand at another circuit at the start of the second race.

Stewarding style – the stewards at all the venues provided access control for tickets, gates and accredited zones but there was no supervision at all of the crowds in the stands. People stood on seats, stood and sat in gangways, blocked the heads of staircases and even climbed on walls, and were clearly quite unaccustomed to being stewarded.

Cabling trip hazards – throughout the sites, particularly at two of the circuits. Things improved as the TV contractors got used to us asking them to cover trip hazards and so began covering them properly in the first place.

Conclusion

We have set out here a case study of how we sought to apply GGCT to enrich a short notice and complex risk assessment process for an area of virtual risk which had to be a product of stakeholders' imaginations. We have described our methodological approach, acknowledging its limitations. The results of our research reveal eight key areas of threat which we suggest are robust enough to form a good starting point for anyone else faced with the question of hypothesising how soccer fans might behave in a new setting.

We have explained how we assessed the impacts of those threats becoming realities, how we assessed the probabilities for each of the eight threats for each of the 18 participating clubs at each of the six circuits, and how we then evaluated the 864 risks with reference to Superleague Formula's risk appetite. Finally, we have outlined how we used the risk assessments to inform the design of appropriate risk management controls, including police tactical options, at each of the circuits.

Of course it is impossible to say whether the relative absence of special risks becoming realities was because of our risk assessment work, or indeed in spite of it. Nevertheless, as researchers and practitioners it was a privilege and a pleasure to protect people and to protect the Superleague Formula brand during its inaugural 2008 season.

Acknowledgements

The author wishes to acknowledge the considerable help and support provided by Mark Canning, Jim Chalmers, Simon Clayton, Bryan Drew, Nathan Hall, Kevin Jones, John Newsham, Andy Williams, Superleague Formula staff and members of the Football Supporters Federation.

References

Adams, J. (1999). *Cars, Cholera and Cows*. Washington: CATO Institute.

Adams, J., and Thompson, M. (2002). *Taking Account of Societal Concerns About Risk: Framing the Problem* (Research Report 305). Sudbury: HSE Books.

Department of Culture, Media and Sport. (2008). *Guide to Safety at Sports Grounds* (5th ed.). Norwich: The Stationery Office.

Douglas, M. (1978). 'Cultural Bias' (Royal Anthropological Institute, Occasional Paper 35). Reprinted in M. Douglas (Ed.). (1982). *In the Active Voice* (pp. 183–254). London: Routledge and Kegan Paul.

Douglas, M. (1990). Risk as a Forensic Resource. *Daedalus, 119*(4), 1–16.

Douglas, M. (1992). Risk and Blame. In M. Douglas, *Risk and Blame: Essays in Cultural Theory* (pp. 3–21). London: Routledge.

Douglas, M., and Wildavsky, A. (1982). Can we Know the Risks we Face? Why Risk Selection is a Social Process. *Risk Analysis, 2*(2), 49–51.

Football Against Racism in Europe. (2008). *Racist and Neo-Nazi Symbols in Football: a Training Manual for Stewards and Security Staff*. Football Against Racism in Europe.

Frosdick, S. (1995). Organisational Structure, Culture and Attitudes to Risk in the British Stadia Safety Industry. *Journal of Contingencies and Crisis Management, 3*(1), 115–129.

Frosdick, S. (1998). Strategic Risk Management in Public Assembly Facilities. In P. Thompson, J. Tolloczko, and J. Clarke (Eds.), *Stadia, Arena and Grandstands: Design, Construction and Operation* (pp. 65–76). London: EandFN Spon.

Frosdick, S. (2006). *Risk and Cultural Theory: a Management Consultancy Approach.* Rothersthorpe: Paragon Publishing.

Home Office. (1986). *Committee of Inquiry into Crowd Safety and Control at Sports Grounds* (Final Report). London: HMSO.

Mars, G. (1994). *Cheats at Work: an Anthropology of Workplace Crime* (2nd ed.). Aldershot: Dartmouth.

Mars, G., and Nicod, M. (1983). *The World of Waiters.* London: Allen and Unwin.

National Counter Terrorism Security Office. (2006). *Counter Terrorism Protective Security Advice for Stadia and Arenas.* London: NaCTSO.

Stott, C., and Pearson, G. (2007). *Football Hooliganism: Policing and the War on the 'English Disease'.* London: Pennant Books.

Thompson, M., Ellis, R., and Wildavsky, A. (1990). *Cultural Theory.* Boulder, CO: Westview Press.

Thompson, M., and Rayner, S. (1998). Risk and Governance Part I: the Discourses of Climatic Change. *Government and Opposition, 33*(2), 139–166.

Thompson, M., Rayner, S., and Ney, S. (1999). Risk and Governance Part II: Policy in a Complex and Plurally Rerceived World. *Government and Opposition, 33*(3), 330–354.

Wildavsky, A., and Dake, K. (1990). Theories of Risk Perception: Who Fears What and Why. *Daedalus, 119*(4), 41–60.

Website

http://www.superleagueformula.com/ superleague/What-is-SF What is Superleague Formula? Accessed 13 May 2009.

1.3. COMMENTARY BY JIM CHALMERS – SUPERLEAGUE FORMULA

In his 1997 book *Sport and Safety Management*, written with Lynne Walley, Frosdick describes how,

> Managing Public Assembly Facilities (PAFs), particularly sports stadia so as to provide spectators with an environment in which they can watch events safely is a highly complex problem. It includes questions of architectural and engineering design, operations management, technological sophistication, health and safety, public order, customer care and an understanding of how people behave in a crowd.

This would be put to the test when Frosdick accepted the challenge of assessing the safety and security risks associated with the combining of motor racing and football at six motor racing circuits in six different European countries. Since 1996, Frosdick has written much about risk and Grid Group Cultural Theory (GGCT) in PAFs, but his academic theories had not previously been given the opportunity to be tested at a real sporting event in a real sports venue. Superleague Formula 2008 presented him with this opportunity and he eloquently summarises the results in this article.

As a non-academic member of the Superleague Formula expert group, I had some doubts that the GGCT approach was necessarily the most appropriate path for assessing the hazards and risks associated with the Superleague Formula events. However as the project developed, I was reassured how Frosdick did not get bogged down in academic jargon, but instead was able to present a series of analytical tools which the expert group could all relate and work to.

As the project expanded, I was not conscious of how GGCT was being used as the basis for the discussion and conclusions which the expert group determined. Nor did I realise how the archetypes of individualism, fatalism, hierarchy and egalitarianism were operating in the expert group; but the simple facts were that Frosdick's theories actually worked in practice. Without wrapping it all up in academic jargon, the data and analysis showed that GGCT can be applied as a practical methodology for risk assessment.

Did GGCT work? In a word 'Yes', but that would be too simple a critique. The unique nature of the events meant that traditional methods of hazard identification and risk assessments would have been difficult to apply in any analysis of the safety and security implications for all the venues. There is no doubt that Frosdick validated the use of GGCT in both theoretical and operational contexts. In this regard, Frosdick was able to make the transition from the academic mode to the operational safety practitioner and back again with all the interim learning stages along that path.

Could GGCT be used in a practical commercial application for the rapid identification, assessment and management of a sports ground real-life risk situation? Frosdick has proved that it can be, but there is a caveat which I would apply. Frosdick is a well known and respected academic with a foot in both the academic and practitioner camps. He is also an acknowledged consultancy expert in the management of risk. Without his knowledge and expertise, GGCT could not have been applied in this project. With him leading the project, applying GGCT would undoubtedly be successful and therein lies the weakness. Without his expert involvement I suspect efforts to apply GGCT would founder and fail.

PART II – SPECTATOR BEHAVIOUR

Introduction

Part II of the book contains one academic journal article, two previously unpublished dissertations and a magazine article. All four papers deal with a fundamental aspect of safety and security at sports grounds, namely the problem of bad behaviour by spectators. This is often referred to by the term 'football hooliganism'.

2.1. The Nature and Extent of Football Hooliganism in England and Wales

This article in the journal *Soccer and Society* was published by Steve Frosdick and Robert Newton in 2006. It demonstrates the difficulties in defining 'football hooliganism' and the shortcomings in the available statistical data. Using privileged access to alternative empirical data sources, the study concludes that hooliganism is associated with about one match in 20 and that only 0.011% of spectators are arrested for a football-related offence. Over half of reported incidents take place away from the ground, and just under half take place after the match. One in five incidents involves fans of teams that have not played each other that day. Football hooliganism involves public disorder, sometimes with the use of missiles, but it does not generally result in injuries. It is thus not a particularly violent phenomenon.

In the commentary, Chalmers notes the volume of other academic work on football hooliganism. He affirms the difficulties with definition and with interpreting the statistical data which does exist, adding some more recent data and critiquing its meaning.

2.2. Spectator Ejections

This previously unpublished research by Jim Chalmers examines spectator ejections at Premier and Football League grounds in England and Wales. There has been a lack of consideration of spectator ejection statistics, partly because official publication of the figures ceased in 1992. The research questions whether the lack of published spectator ejection statistics affects our understanding of spectator behaviour and how spectators are being managed inside football grounds.

The accompanying commentary commends Chalmers research and outlines four reasons why the work is worthy of publication. The research is original and well done; it is valid and reliable; it adds to knowledge; and it has proved to be ahead of its time.

2.3. Who are the Hooligans?

This previously unpublished 2005 research by Chris Conrad was supervised by Steve Frosdick. Using privileged access to data involving one major club's supporters, the study showed that the group of individuals engaged in criminality at football matches was male, white and predominantly working class. This was in line with previous demographic studies. However the results also showed that football hooligans were some ten to twenty years older than previous studies had suggested.

The commentary notes that this was a well researched and important finding well worthy of publication. Not since 1988 has there been an empirical study of who the hooligans are as opposed to why they behave as they do. The commentary also reports emerging evidence in 2010 of a new generation of younger football hooligans.

2.4. Conflict Management

In this *Stadium and Arena Management* article from 2005, Steve Frosdick and Graham Joyce explain how stewards in the UK are receiving additional training on how to deal with conflict in the stadium.

The commentary brings the topic up to date by referring to the conflict management training incorporated in the brand new stewards training package, *On the Ball*, introduced by the English and Welsh football authorities in October 2010. Chalmers also comments on how stewards enjoy conflict management training and find it useful in their daily lives. He also refers to the absence of misuse of force by stewards and the rising number of 'police free' matches as evidence of the success of stewards' conflict management training.

2.1. THE NATURE AND EXTENT OF FOOTBALL HOOLIGANISM IN ENGLAND WALES

The original citation for this article is Frosdick, S. and Newton, R. (2006) 'The Nature and Extent of Football Hooliganism in England and Wales'. *Soccer and Society*, 7(4): 403-422.

Reproduced with acknowledgements to Routledge and with grateful thanks to Robert Newton.

Summary

This paper demonstrates the difficulties in defining 'football hooliganism' and the shortcomings in the available statistical data. Using privileged access to alternative empirical data sources, the study concludes that hooliganism is associated with about one match in 20 and that only 0.011% of spectators are arrested for a football-related offence. Over half of reported incidents take place away from the ground, and just under half take place after the match. One in five incidents involves fans of teams that have not played each other that day. Football hooliganism involves public disorder, sometimes with the use of missiles, but it does not generally result in injuries. It is thus not a particularly violent phenomenon.

Acknowledgements

The authors would like to thank their colleagues Carol Hayden, Les Johnston and Steve Savage for helpful comments on earlier drafts of the paper.

Introduction

Spectator violence is generally referred to as 'football hooliganism', or sometimes as the 'English disease'. These populist terms have been used by the media and by politicians (see Dunning 2000) to label the deviant behaviours which became associated with English football from the 1960s onwards. Whilst spectator violence has not been confined to football, or indeed to England and Wales, the phenomenon of 'football hooliganism' has received considerable academic scrutiny. By 1996, commentators were noting that, 'It is generally agreed that British football hooliganism has probably been over-researched. Despite a general decline in violence at British football matches, the phenomenon still attracts a disproportionate amount of research activity' (Carnibella *et al.* 1996, p. 6). Moorhouse later argued that, 'By any estimation of its social significance violence around football has been overstudied, as well as being poorly studied. ... The debate on hooliganism has lost all power to generate any new social insights' (2000, p. 1464).

These criticisms might appear to work against new research in this area. However the criticisms are directed at previous academic work on rival theories of causation about who the hooligans are and why they behave as they do. The various theories have been thoroughly reviewed elsewhere (for example see Canter *et al.* 1989; Hobbs and Robins 1991; Williams 1991; Giulianotti 1994; Carnibella *et al.* 1996 and Dunning *et al.* 2002). This paper will not cover the same ground.

The previous academic research has far less to say on other salient questions, for example on the definition of the phenomenon or on questions about its nature or extent. What is football hooliganism? How much of it is there? What kinds of behaviours are we talking about? There is therefore good scope for further useful research on the phenomenon of football hooliganism. This paper examines a particular aspect of that phenomenon; namely the nature and extent of football hooliganism in England and Wales.

Problems of Definition

Football hooliganism can be traced back to the Middle Ages (see Elias and Dunning 1971). Notwithstanding its long history, there are real difficulties in defining the phenomenon itself. In the first place, what do we call it? The particular association with football caused the media to invent the label 'football hooliganism'. However, the fact that violence occurs in other sports, albeit less often, suggests that 'spectator violence' could be a more accurate name. This implies something done whilst watching an event. Yet much of the violence takes place away from the stadium. So we might say 'sports-related violence' instead, only this could then include violence committed by the players.

Since the literature deals entirely with football, the academic discussions of definition deal only with 'football hooliganism'. Taking four samples in chronological order, we find that Canter *et al.* (1989) described 'football hooliganism' as 'a term which covers many behaviours, both simple and complex' (p. 108). Carnibella *et al.* 1996 (p. 13) argue that 'The question of what, precisely, is meant by football hooliganism …. remains to be fully answered.'Dunning (2000, p.142) noted that, 'the label 'football hooliganism' …. lacks precision and is used to cover a variety of forms of behaviour which take place in more or less directly football-related contexts.' Whilst Williams (2002, p. 45) argues that 'there is no useful precise definition of 'football hooliganism' available'.

The second problem of definition is that there are so many variables around the phenomenon.

Criminal offence categories – the main categories of Home Office Recordable Offences are offences against the person (e.g. assaults), offences against property (e.g. vandalism), or offences against the State (e.g. disorder). 'Football hooliganism' straddles all three categories.

Extent of criminalisation of behaviours – should the definition be limited to acts which are recorded as crimes, or do we include 'misdemeanours' (non-recordable offences such as drunkenness) or even plain anti-social behaviour, e.g. urinating in someone's front garden?

Location – where do the behaviours take place? Is it inside, outside or even well away from the venue?

Extent of organisation – are we only counting organised violence, e.g. a pre-planned fight between two 'crews'? Or do we include the spontaneous, e.g. a pitch incursion to celebrate a goal?

Whether arrests were made or not – do we only count incidents for which arrests are made? There are several offences, e.g. unlawful pitch incursion, which are only counted in the official statistics when they are detected as a result of a person being arrested by the police.

Extent of injuries sustained and/or extent of damage caused – should we use the outcomes of the violence as a means of categorisation? On the one hand, a relatively minor incident may result in a few broken windows. On the other hand, a fairly serious affray may result in no actual injury or damage but in considerable numbers of people being afraid for their personal safety.

There are many other possible variables, for example when the violence took place, whether alcohol was involved or whether the behaviour was provoked by the actions of the players or the decisions of the match officials. A considerable number of variables are involved in this further quote from Dunning (2000);

> '.... the politicians and media personnel who employ the term are liable to use 'football hooliganism' in a 'cover-all' sense which includes *inter alia*: forms of verbal as well as physical violence; the throwing of missiles at players, match and club officials and other fans; the vandalising of club and private property; fist fights, fights involving kicking, and fights involving weapons such as knives and even guns. It is also important to realise that such behaviour takes place, not only at or in the immediate vicinity of football grounds, but also involves fights between groups of males who share a claimed allegiance to opposing football clubs and which take place on days other than as well as on match days and in contexts, e.g. pubs, clubs, railway and bus stations, which are sometimes far removed from football stadia *per se*. In terms of these political and media usages, the label 'football hooliganism' is also sometimes loosely used to cover politically orientated behaviour, e.g. that of groups on the political right. It is also used in relation to protests against the owners and managers of clubs and in the condemnation of racist behaviour in football-related contexts as well as of more or less directly football-related fighting. As one can see, 'football hooliganism' is a complex and many-sided phenomenon.' (Dunning 2000, pp. 142-143)

It is also difficult to consider 'football hooliganism' in isolation from other social phenomena. In 2001 a Home Office Working Group on Football Disorder commented that, 'English football disorder cannot be removed from its wider social context. In many ways it is a manifestation of a wider social problem of alienated young males demonstrating their frustration in an anti-social and violent way. It occurs in high streets up and down the country every weekend. Mediterranean holiday resorts are equally at risk' (Home Office 2001, p. 15).

Thus no succinct definition of 'football hooliganism', 'spectator violence' (or whatever we choose to call it) is practicable. We have seen how difficult it is to name, let alone define, the phenomenon. There is a wide range of behavioural and other variables involved and it is difficult to divorce the phenomenon (whatever it is) from the wider social context in which it takes place. Nevertheless, a working definition is required to form the basis for our investigation and we have chosen to adopt the quote from Dunning (2000) above as the most comprehensive available.

Troublesome Statistics

Football intelligence has been part of the remit of the National Criminal Intelligence Service (NCIS) since its inception in 1992. Prior to that date, there was no accessible statistical data on football hooliganism (see Trivizas 1980). Up until 2000/2001, statistics on what were described as 'football-related' arrests were published annually by the NCIS. Since 2001/2002, the Home Office have published the figures. These NCIS and Home Office statistics provide us with the only 'official' statistics on the nature and extent of football hooliganism.

For 2003/04 the statistics are set out in eleven tables covering numbers of banning orders, international arrests and various combinations of arrests by club supported, place of arrest and type of offence. As were the NCIS before them, the Home Office are careful to emphasise the caveat that, 'Statistics for football-related arrests tell only part of the story and need to be placed in context' (Home Office 2004). This caveat is frequently ignored by the media, including the broadsheets, who are content to take the figures as a league table of the extent of football hooliganism (for example see Hopkins 2002).

Our discussion of the statistics will be confined to illustrating the importance of this Home Office caveat, thus our analysis in this section is limited to extracts from the figures for the four seasons from 2000/2001. Table One (extracted from Home Office 2004) shows arrests in League matches only for arrestable offences that are football offences under Schedule 1 of the Football Spectators Act 1989 (as amended).

Table One: Arrests in League Matches for Football Offences

	NCIS 2000/2001		Home Office 2001/2002		Home Office 2002/2003		Home Office 2003/2004	
	No.	%	No.	%	No.	%	No.	%
Total Attendances	26,030,167	-	27,756,977	-	28,346,386	-	29,197,510	-
Total Arrests	3,391	100	2,977	100	3,355	100	3,010	100
1.1 Premiership	1,623	48	1,192	40	1,460	44	1,137	38
1.2 Division One	816	24	929	31	945	28	849	28
1.3 Division Two	601	18	595	20	641	19	616	20
1.4 Division Three	351	10	261	9	309	9	408	14
Arrest Rate	1 in 7,676	-	1 in 9,324	-	1 in 8,449	-	1 in 9,700	-

To illustrate the problems in interpreting the figures, look at the arrests by division. We see that the Premiership accounts for between 38% and 48% of arrests across all four divisions. For each of the four seasons, the percentage share of the arrests decreases as we go down the divisions. The correlation is clear, but what does this tell us? Are the spectators in the Premiership the worst behaved? Or is it simply that there are more spectators at these matches? Perhaps there are more police in attendance? Or the policing is more stringent? It is salient to note that the Home Office (2004) report that '25% of matches [are] completely police free'. These are generally lower division matches where there are simply no police present to make any arrests.

Turning to banning orders, the Home Office (2004) figures show that these have increased dramatically from 1,794 on 14 August 2003 to 2,596 on 18 October 2004. Does this mean that more football violence is occurring? Or is it that a different policing approach is being applied – particularly given that in 2003 an extra £5 million was provided for intelligence-led policing operations to obtain more banning orders (Home Office 2003)?

Delving into the statistics for individual clubs, all sorts of problems of interpretation arise. Two examples will serve to illustrate the issues. First, Kidderminster Harriers in Division Three had no arrests at all for the two seasons 2002/03 and 2003/04. Does this mean they have the best-behaved fans? Or are there no police in attendance? Second, for the two seasons 2002/03 and 2003/04, Sunderland had the highest numbers of arrests in Division One. Does this tell us that Sunderland have the most hooliganism in that Division? Or does it demonstrate the impact of the Sunderland Ground Safety Officer's zero tolerance policy on spectator misconduct?

Difficulties in interpreting these arrest and banning order statistics add considerably to the problems of definition. Further problems arise from the fact that, as with other crime statistics (see for example Coleman and Moynihan 1996 pp. 32-39), the figures are socially constructed. Not all the offences committed will get discovered or reported to the police, who are then selective about what they record. Of those recorded only a small percentage will result in an arrest. Even fewer will result in a clear-up or conviction at Court. From the authors' considerable experience in and around football grounds, we can say with confidence that many offences are either ignored, result in a word of warning or at worst in ejection from the ground. So we can be fairly sure that only a small proportion of offences make it into the arrest statistics.

In addition to this 'attrition rate', there is a problem with what then does get counted. The NCIS figures previously included 'ticket touting', 'drugs offences', 'theft' and a range of other non-violent offences. The Home Office figures now cover defined 'football offences' but these include 'ticket touting', breach of banning order' and 'miscellaneous'. So if we read that 'City' had 50 fans arrested, 'United' had 20 and 'Rovers' had ten, we might be tempted to conclude that 'City' had the most hooligan fans. However if most of the 'City' arrests were for ticket touting, most of the 'United' arrests for a pitch incursion to celebrate a goal and most of the 'Rovers' arrests for violent disorder, then we might draw rather different conclusions.

The statistics are also more a reflection of police tactics than of the extent of spectator violence. Both the NCIS and Home Office have acknowledged that the figures are an unreliable indicator of extent. Sometimes the police will make large numbers of arrests to intervene and prevent disorder, whilst at other times they will disperse a disorderly crowd and make few or no arrests (see NCIS 2000 and Home Office 2004).

In short, it needs to be made quite clear that the published figures on arrests and banning orders do not provide more than a small part of the overall picture. Additional data sources are required if we are to discover more about the nature and extent of football hooliganism in England and Wales.

Methodology

In addition to analysing the official statistics, this study used privileged access to four data sources relating to the four football seasons 1999/2000 to 2002/2003. Data was obtained from the Football Disorder Logs compiled by the NCIS from the post-match reports submitted by Police Football Intelligence Officers[1]. Data was also obtained from the post match reports recorded by Ground Safety Officers in a private database held by the Football Safety Officers Association (FSOA 2004)[2]. Finally, data was taken from a database of football-related disorder incidents compiled by the BBC (2002) and published on the Internet.

These data sources have their own shortcomings. The BBC investigation does not purport to be a full census and can thus only be regarded as an accidental sample. Not all Ground Safety Officers file their post match reports thus the FSOA database is also incomplete. Only those incidents which the Police Football Intelligence Officers chose to report are included in the NCIS disorder logs. Thus the data sources, whilst adding to the story, have limitations in themselves.

---

[1] For 1999 to 2001, the NCIS Football Disorder Logs were published on the Internet (see NCIS 2000b, 2001a). Since 2001/2002, however, the logs have been restricted and not released into the public domain (NCIS 2002, 2003). We therefore gratefully acknowledge the access granted by the NCIS for this research.
[2] Access to the FSOA Post Match Reports database is restricted to members of the FSOA. We are again grateful for the privileged access granted.

The data was analysed and coded into tables using variables which focused on temporal and spatial aspects, indicators of violence and the type of competition. Because of the varying quality of the data, no attempt was made to weight the incidents for seriousness. A descriptive approach was then used to seek to interpret the tables. Note that the totals numbers in the tables vary, depending on whether there was more than one incident, weapon or injury per match, or whether the incident was even connected to a match.

The Extent of Football Hooliganism

The numbers of matches with reported incidents of hooliganism associated with them is shown in Table Two. To facilitate comparison of the three data sources, the data are set out in source order rather than year order.

Table Two: Numbers of Matches with Incidents

NCIS Log 1999/2000	NCIS Log 2000/2001	NCIS Log 2001/2002	NCIS Log 2002/2003	BBC Investigation 2001/2002	FSOA Database 2001/2002
No.	No.	No.	No.	No.	No.
73	131	107	95	80	329

Considering this data together with the arrest rates set out in Table One, the phenomenon of football hooliganism does not appear to be very extensive. The average arrest rate over the four seasons in Table One was one in 8,787 or 0.011%. There are a vast number of matches played each season – 2,036 in the four divisions alone – yet the number of matches with incidents appears small. The FSOA database reports a larger number, however Safety Officers may record less serious matters such as breaches of ground regulations resulting in an ejection which would not make it into the arrest figures or disorder logs.

Including cup matches, we conclude that there would appear to be incidents of football hooliganism associated with only about one match in 20.

Where Does Football Hooliganism Take Place?

To understand more about its nature, we first need to establish where football hooliganism takes place. Table Three shows the coded data on the location of the behaviours recorded in the data sources.

Table Three: Location of Incidents of Football Hooliganism

	NCIS 99/00		NCIS 00/01		NCIS 01/02		NCIS 02/03		BBC 01/02		FSOA 01/02	
	No.	%	No.	%	No.	%	No.	%	No.	%	No.	%
Total Incidents Coded	110	100	232	100	181	100	162	100	121	100	412	100
Inside Ground	22	20	30	13	37	20	29	18	17	14	335	81
Near/Outside Ground	21	19	36	15	43	24	32	20	25	20	30	7
Away from Ground	52	47	148	64	96	53	98	60	72	60	17	4
Town/City Centre	*22*	*20*	*43*	*19*	*27*	*15*	*23*	*14*	*17*	*14*	*9*	*2*
Railway Station	*4*	*3*	*32*	*14*	*16*	*9*	*15*	*9*	*31*	*26*	*0*	*0*
Unlinked Town/City	*12*	*11*	*23*	*10*	*7*	*4*	*6*	*4*	*7*	*6*	*1*	*0*
Other	*14*	*13*	*50*	*21*	*46*	*25*	*54*	*33*	*17*	*14*	*7*	*2*
Not Known	15	14	18	8	5	3	3	2	7	6	30	7

One might expect football hooliganism to be found largely at or near a football ground. However, with the exception of the FSOA (which has an understandable focus on the inside and vicinity of the ground), the sources show that some 50% to 60% of incidents took place away from the ground, i.e. not inside, near or outside it. This is supported by the Home Office (2004) statistics which report that '57% of the total arrests were made outside of grounds'. Recorded problems near or outside the grounds account for only between 7% and 24% of incidents, whilst (again with the exception of the FSOA) only one in five or fewer incidents took place inside the ground.

There is good supporting evidence from other sources for a low level of football hooliganism inside grounds. Following an upwards trend in media interest in reporting incidents in January 2002, the Premier League undertook a snapshot survey which showed that, 'Of the 306,595 people who attended the ten elite matches, only 20 were arrested and 58 ejected' (Winter 2002). This represents an arrest rate on the day of 0.007% – extremely low – and we should note that, of the 20 arrests, 15 were for drunkenness, two were for ticket touting, one was for criminal damage and one for running onto the pitch.

Fan surveys also support the point, with seven out of ten fans reporting that they never see fighting or missile throwing (see Winter 2002; Williams 2002). Whilst Williams concludes that, 'the *routine* place of the serious hooligan encounter, as an obvious and intrusive part of the main football event, on a near-weekly basis at larger football grounds in England 20 years ago, now seems ruptured, possibly for good' (2002, pp. 40-41).

NCIS (2001b) suggests that 'Dealing with football hooliganism within and in the close vicinity of stadiums has been increasingly successful but it has displaced the problem'. This idea of displacement is a key point. The stadiums may be more peaceful, but police resources are stretched dealing with 'increasingly mobile 'football gangs' who more frequently engage in violence at pubs, railway stations and on the streets before and after matches' (Evans 2001). Certainly the British Transport Police (BTP) reports an increase in displaced football-related violence. Their Annual Report for 2002, 'highlights an increase in disorder amongst travelling football fans. ... BTP spends around 8% of its total budget and a third of the overtime budget on football policing' (BTP 2002).

Developing the displacement theme, Garland and Rowe (2000) suggest that the experience of watching football has also been displaced from the stadium. Given the rising admission prices and more muted atmosphere, many people now choose to watch live football on large-screen televisions in public houses and clubs – and incidents of more spontaneous disorder do break out in such establishments. So the problem is changing because its traditional nature has been displaced from inside the stadium to the public transport network and to other locations.

When Does Football Hooliganism Take Place?

Having dealt with the question of 'where', the logical next step is to examine 'when' football hooliganism takes place. The coded data are set out in Table Four [on the next page].

Table Four: Timing of Incidents of Football Hooliganism

	NCIS 99/00		NCIS 00/01		NCIS 01/02		NCIS 02/03		BBC 01/02		FSOA 01/02	
	No.	%	No.	%	No.	%	No.	%	No.	%	No.	%
Total Incidents Coded	110	100	232	100	181	100	162	100	108	100	412	100
Before Match	33	31	59	25	46	26	51	31	24	22	23	6
During Match	21	19	38	16	38	21	32	20	20	19	324	79
After Match	48	44	125	54	84	46	70	43	50	46	20	4
Unconnected Day	4	3	3	1	2	1	6	4	2	2	0	0
Not Known	4	3	7	3	11	6	3	2	12	11	45	11

With the again understandable exception of the FSOA, the data consistently show that most incidents – between 43% and 54% – happen after the match. Between 22% and 31% of recorded trouble took place before the match. The fewest incidents happen during the match. This all supports the displacement theme identified above.

The key finding is that the majority of football hooliganism takes place after the match. This is significant for policy. The focus of most current police and stewarding activity is on the build up to the match and the arrival of the crowd. There are good safety management reasons for this given the sorry history of overcrowding disasters in English grounds (see Elliot *et al.* 1999). After the match, the tendency is to get the crowd away as quickly as possible and then stand down. However this finding suggests that the period after the match merits at least the same level of attention as the period before. It may be that, following Harrison (1974), the build up of tensions during a match through gesturing, chanting and tribalism, together with the general atmosphere of the game and crowd in a tightly controlled area, are given freedom to erupt into violence in the period after the match when controls and policing are reduced.

What Divisions Do the Hooligans' Teams Come From?

Table Five [on the next page] shows the coded data on whether the reported incidents could be specifically linked to the followers of teams in a particular division.

Table Five: Incidents Associated With Particular Divisions

	NCIS 99/00		NCIS 00/01		NCIS 01/02		NCIS 02/03		BBC 01/02		FSOA 01/02	
	No.	%	No.	%	No.	%	No.	%	No.	%	No.	%
Total Incidents Coded	69	100	120	100	95	100	85	100	68	100	287	100
Premiership	14	20	26	22	9	9	15	18	15	22	130	45
Division One	18	26	29	24	35	37	22	26	21	31	89	31
Division Two	17	25	23	19	28	30	24	28	12	18	43	15
Division Three	6	9	19	16	14	15	17	20	4	6	24	8
Conference	1	1	0	0	0	0	0	0	1	1	0	0
Unlinked	13	19	23	19	9	9	7	8	13	19	1	1
Not Known	0	0	0	0	0	0	0	0	2	3	0	0

Football violence appears most prevalent in Division One (renamed 'The Championship' from 2004/05). Division One has the highest percentage of incidents in four out of the six sources used in this research, and the second highest in the remaining two sources. It is perhaps surprising that the Premiership does not have the most incidents given its larger crowds and highly valued matches. However the atmosphere at Premiership matches is perhaps more consumerist and less tribal, as noted by Inglis (2001). There has been a change in the culture of football, primarily in the Premiership, through commercialism, family-orientated entertainment, the removal of terracing and the introduction of plastic seating.

It is interesting that three of the sources indicate that 19% of incidents were not specifically linked to a particular division. It is thus not uncommon for hooligan fighting to occur between fans from clubs in different divisions, such as when Huddersfield fans returning from Sheffield clashed with Barnsley supporters in Barnsley train station and town centre. Also in this context, Harrison (1974) comments on the notion that the 'enemy of your enemy is your friend'. This is exemplified by a fight between Chesterfield and Mansfield hooligans. During the fight, Leicester City and Derby County fans joined up with the Chesterfield group, while Nottingham Forest supporters joined the Mansfield group.

Hooliganism in Cup Competitions

Table Six shows the coded data for reported incidents at matches in various cup competitions.

Table Six: Incidents Associated With Cup Competitions

	NCIS 99/00		NCIS 00/01		NCIS 01/02		NCIS 02/03		BBC 01/02		FSOA 01/02	
	No.	%	No.	%	No.	%	No.	%	No.	%	No.	%
Total Incidents Coded	4	100	11	100	12	100	10	100	12	100	42	100
F.A.Cup	3	75	9	82	3	25	3	30	4	33	22	52
League Cup	1	25	0	0	4	33	5	50	1	8	10	24
LDV Trophy	0	0	1	9	2	17	1	10	0	0	2	5
Play-offs	0	0	0	0	2	17	0	0	3	25	2	5
Welsh F.A.Cup	0	0	1	9	1	8	1	10	1	8	0	0
Not Known	0	0	0	0	0	0	0	0	3	25	6	14

There appear to be relatively few incidents at cup matches. The NCIS and BBC sources suggest that a mere ten to twelve cup matches per season involved hooliganism, although considerably more incidents were recorded by the Ground Safety Officers. However the vast majority of cup matches pass without serious hooligan occurrence. For example, for the season 2000/2001, the NCIS disorder log records 232 incidents, of which only eleven involved cup matches.

Though there are fewer incidents in cup competitions than league matches, the ratio of arrests to attendances in cup matches is much greater. For example, for the season 2002/2003, arrests at league and cup matches were 3,695 and 653 respectively, whilst attendances were 28,346,386 and 3,655,397. Thus one person in 8449 was arrested at a league match, whilst one in 5598 was arrested at a cup game. This variation may be explained by the additional competitive edge of such one-off matches. In the latter stages of a cup or in the league play-offs, the intensity and 'knife-edge' of the atmosphere may contribute to certain behaviours. Hobbs and Robins (1991) point out how a 'euphoric hyped-up sensation' in such a tense environment can lead to scenes of hostility.

Does Football Hooliganism Result in Injuries?

If football hooliganism involves violence, it seems worthwhile examining the extent to which such incidents result in reports of injuries. The coded data are set out in Table Seven.

Table Seven: Incidents Involving Reported Injuries

	NCIS 99/00		NCIS 00/01		NCIS 01/02		NCIS 02/03		BBC 01/02		FSOA 01/02	
	No.	%	No.	%	No.	%	No.	%	No.	%	No.	%
Total Incidents Coded	118	100	269	100	252	100	177	100	172	100	343	100
Fans	18	15	48	18	20	8	15	9	15	9	5	2
Police Officers	18	15	19	7	77	31	13	7	94	55	1	0
Stewards	2	2	0	0	1	0.5	2	1	2	1	11	3
Other Public	5	4	21	8	6	2	1	1	4	2	0	0
None/Unknown	75	64	181	67	148	59	146	82	57	33	326	95

The data suggests that football hooliganism does not generally result in injuries. Considering the attendance figures in Table One, the number of injuries reportedly suffered by fans is very small indeed. There are only 121 reports of fan injuries in 1331 incidents in Table Seven, which equates to only one report of injuries in every ten incidents of disorder. The low level of fan injuries is particularly marked inside the ground.

The NCIS and BBC 2001/2002 sources show larger numbers of injuries sustained by police officers, however both data sources show that most of these injuries (NCIS 61 and BBC 45) were suffered at just one match. This was a Millwall v Birmingham City play-off semi-final which had very serious post match disorder outside the ground and must be considered an exceptional event.

Issues in reporting are important. With the exception of the BBC, the data sources show that the vast proportion of incidents involve no report of an injury. 'Victims' of football violence are however difficult to locate, particularly since they are unlikely to make a complaint to the police if they have been involved in the fighting themselves (see Williams 1986).

To What Extent Are Weapons Used In Football Hooliganism?

To continue the analysis of indicators of violence in football hooliganism, we looked next at the extent to which the data sources reported that weapons had been used in the incidents. The coded data are set out in Table Eight.

Table Eight: Incidents Involving Use of Weapons

	NCIS 99/00		NCIS 00/01		NCIS 01/02		NCIS 02/03		BBC 01/02		FSOA 01/02	
	No.	%	No.	%	No.	%	No.	%	No.	%	No.	%
Total Incidents Coded	141	100	296	100	211	100	194	100	108	100	333	100
Bottles	23	16	40	13	22	10	26	13	14	13	4	1
Knives	4	3	2	1	3	1	3	2	2	2	3	1
Stones/Bricks	9	6	12	4	12	6	5	3	9	8	0	0
Glasses	10	7	18	6	10	5	14	7	5	5	0	0
Pool Balls	2	2	5	2	2	1	2	1	1	1	1	0.3
Gas Canisters	4	3	5	2	5	2	5	3	1	1	1	0.3
Other	31	22	71	24	52	25	32	16	31	29	19	6
Not Known	58	41	143	48	105	50	107	55	45	41	305	92

Hobbs and Robins (1991) argued that, especially during the 1980's, scalpels, machetes, Stanley knives, ammonia and CS Gas were commonly used in hooligan fights. The implication is of serious injury, however knives and gas canisters receive very little mention in our data sources. Weapons are mentioned in between 50% and 59% of the NCIS and BBC incidents, but the largest category in all the sources is of weapons or missiles of an unspecified kind. Thus we cannot discover from the data very much about the types of weapons used by hooligans, although the weapon mentioned most is the bottle, in an average 11% of incidents.

Tying these findings in with the previous finding about the low level of injuries, we conclude that, although weapons or missiles do feature in more than half or reported hooligan incidents, they do not necessarily cause injuries. The most likely use of weapons would seem to be the throwing of missiles such as bottles in the general direction of opposing fans or the police. Such missiles generally land on the ground and so are unlikely to result in injury.

Numbers Involved in Incidents of Football Hooliganism

The next variable examines the extent to which football hooliganism involves lone offenders or different sizes of groups of offenders. The coded data are shown in Table Nine.

Table Nine: Sizes of Groups Involved in Incidents

	NCIS 99/00		NCIS 00/01		NCIS 01/02		NCIS 02/03		BBC 01/02		FSOA 01/02	
	No.	%	No.	%	No.	%	No.	%	No.	%	No.	%
Total Incidents Coded	110	100	228	100	180	100	162	100	88	100	362	100
0 to 20	12	11	9	4	12	7	8	5	9	10	317	88
21 to 40	5	5	27	12	11	6	8	5	5	6	9	2
41 to 60	5	5	19	8	10	6	11	7	7	8	0	0
61 to 80	6	6	9	4	4	2	3	2	2	2	1	0
81 to 100	1	1	4	2	4	2	6	4	1	1	1	0
Over 100	25	23	37	16	23	13	33	20	14	16	3	1
Not Known	54	49	123	54	116	64	93	57	50	57	31	9

The high percentage of incidents for which the numbers involved could not be determined makes the interpretation of this table problematic. However the results do show a clear distinction between the FSOA database and the remaining data sources. The vast majority of incidents reported by the FSOA (i.e. largely inside the ground – see Table Three) involve small numbers of people, perhaps reflecting the greater number of minor incidents recorded. For the NCIS and BBC, known incidents involve over one hundred participants in between 13% and 23% of cases. Smith (1978 p.124) suggests that individual or small-scale unrest can snowball into large-scale trouble. Whilst Dunning, Murphy and Williams (1986 p.170) show that incidents of disorder can attract numbers well into three figures. For example, the exceptional incident after the play-off game between Millwall and Birmingham in May 2002 involved some 1,000 hooligans attacking Birmingham supporters and police (see Peachey 2003).

Summary and Conclusions

Previous academic work has focused on theories of football hooliganism. However its nature and extent has received little if any academic scrutiny. There are difficulties in defining 'football hooliganism' and it is difficult to divorce it from its wider social context. Official arrest statistics are difficult to interpret and afford only a glimpse of the overall picture. This study has drawn on additional data sources to reveal a little more about the nature and extent of football hooliganism in England and Wales. The geographic limitations of the study must be emphasised, since the findings are not generalisable to other countries. As Carnibella *et al.* (1996, p. 82) conclude, 'Different historical, social, political and cultural traditions have affected the nature and scale of football-related violence in different European countries'.

Football hooliganism in England and Wales does not appear to be a very extensive social phenomenon. Hooligan incidents recorded by the police are associated with about one match in 20 and only 0.011% of spectators are arrested for a football-related offence. Ground safety officers report more incidents than the police but these tend to involve minor disorder and sanctions short of arrest. Between 50% and 60% of reported incidents of football hooliganism take place away from the ground, and between 43% and 50% of incidents take place after the match. These findings support the notion that intensive social controls during the pre-match period and at the stadium have displaced the phenomenon to town centres, licensed premises and public transport systems.

The more passive consumerist fans of Premiership teams engage in less hooliganism than those of Division One. Cup matches have a higher arrest rate than league matches. However some 19% of football hooliganism involves encounters between fans of teams that have not played each other that day. Football hooliganism involves public disorder, sometimes with the use of missiles, but it does not generally result in injuries. It is thus not a particularly violent phenomenon.

This study does not purport to have revealed the full picture of football hooliganism in England and Wales. There is ample scope for further more detailed work. Future studies could seek to define 'seriousness' and code incidents accordingly. Coding and statistical testing using factor analysis might also yield further insights. We will continue our research in this area and would encourage others to join in this new and alternative avenue of research into football hooliganism.

References

British Broadcasting Corporation (2002) 'Hooligans: Troublespots'. Retrieved 03/06/04 from *http://news.bbc.co.uk/hi/english/static/in_depth/ programmes/2002/hooligans/diary*

BTP (2002*)* 'Press Release 22 July 2002'. Retrieved 13/08/02 from *http://www.btp.police.uk/press_july02.htm#annualreport*

Canter, D., Comber, M. and Uzzell, D. (1989) *Football in its Place: An Environmental Psychology of Football Grounds*. London: Routledge.

Carnibella, G, Fox, A., Fox, K., McCann, J., Marsh, J. and Marsh, P. (1996) *Football Violence in Europe*. Oxford: The Social Issues Research Centre.

Coleman, C. and Moynihan, J. (1996) *Understanding Crime Data: Haunted By The Dark Figure*. Buckingham: Open University Press.

Dunning, E. (2000) 'Towards a Sociological Understanding of Football Hooliganism as a World Phenomenon', *European Journal on Criminal Policy and Research*, 8(2): 141-162.

Dunning, E., Murphy, P. and Waddington, I. (2002) 'Towards a Sociological Understanding of Football Hooliganism as a World Phenomenon'. In E. Dunning, P. Murphy, I. Waddington and A. Astrinakis (Eds.) *Fighting Fans: Football Hooliganism as a World Phenomenon*. pp. 1-22. Dublin: University College Dublin Press.

Dunning, E., Murphy, P. and Williams, J. (1986) *Casuals, Terrace Crews and Fighting Firms: Towards a Sociological Explanation of Football Hooligan Behaviour.* Leicester: University of Leicester.

Elias, N. and Dunning, E. (1971) 'Folk Football in Medieval and Early Modern Britain'. In E. Dunning (Ed.) *The Sociology of Sport: a Selection of Readings*, pp 116-132. London: Frank Cass.

Elliott, D., Frosdick, S. and Smith, D. (1999) 'The Failure of Legislation By Crisis'. In S. Frosdick and L. Walley (Eds.) *Sport and Safety Management*, pp. 11-30. Oxford: Butterworth-Heinemann.

Evans, R. (2001) 'Call for Contribution to Costs of Policing Football Games'. *Police Review*, 24 August, p. 9.

Football Safety Officers Association (2004) 'Match Reports'. Retrieved 26/03/04 from *http://www.fsoa.org.uk*

Garland, J. and Rowe, M. (2000) 'The Hooligan's Fear of the Penalty', *Soccer and Society*, 1(1): 144-157.

Giulianotti, R. (1994) 'Social Identity and Public Order: Political and Academic Discourses on Football Violence'. In R. Guilianotti, N. Bonney and M. Hepworth (Eds.) *Football, Violence and Social Identity*, pp.9-36. London: Routledge.

Harrison, P. (1974) 'Soccer's Tribal Wars'. *New Society*, 5 September, pp. 602-604.

Hobbs, D. and Robins, D. (1991) 'The Boy Done Good: Football Violence, Changes and Continuities'. *The Sociological Review*. 39(3): 551-579.

Home Office (2001) 'Working Group on Football Disorder Chaired By Lord Bassam: Report and Recommendations'. Retrieved on 12/01/05 from *http://www.homeoffice.gov.uk/docs/ftblwgrp.pdf*

Home Office (2003) *Targeted Help To Tackle Football Hooliganism.* Home Office Press Release: 222/2003, 18 August. London: Home Office.

Home Office (2004) 'Home Office Statistics on Football-Related Arrests and Banning Orders: Season 2003/2004'. Retrieved 12/01/05 from *http://www.homeoffice.gov.uk/docs3/football_stats2004.pdf*

Hopkins, N. (2002) 'Hooliganism on Increase in First Division Football'. *The Guardian*, 9 August, p. 6.

Inglis, S. (2001) 'All Gone Quiet Over Here'. In M. Perryman (Ed.) *Hooligan Wars: Causes and Effects of Football Violence*, pp. 87-94. Edinburgh: Mainstream Publishing.

Moorhouse, H. (2000) Book Review of G. Armstrong (1998) 'Football Hooligans: Knowing the Score', *Urban Studies*, 37(8): 1463-1464.

NCIS (2000a) 'NCIS Press Release 26/00'. Retrieved 18/02/02 from *http://www.ncis.gov.uk/press/26_00.html*

NCIS (2000b) *Football Disorder Log for Season 1999/2000.* London: NCIS.

NCIS (2001a) *Football Disorder Log for Season 2000/2001.* London: NCIS.

NCIS (2001b) 'NCIS Press Release 29/01'. Retrieved 18/02/02 from *http://www.ncis.gov.uk/press/29_01.html*

NCIS (2002) *Football Disorder Log for Season 2001/2002.* Restricted document.

NCIS (2003) *Football Disorder Log for Season 2002/2003.* Restricted document.

Peachey, P. (2003) 'Violence Cut By Away Fans Ban'. *The Independent*, 19 August, p.6.

Smith, M. (1978) 'Participants of Crowd Violence', *Sociological Inquiry*, 48(2): 121-131.

Trivizas, E. (1980) 'Offences and Offenders in Football Crowd Disorder', *British Journal of Criminology*, 20(3): 281-283.

Williams, J. (1986) 'Football Hooliganism: Offences, Arrests and Violence – A Critical Note', *British Journal of Law and Society*, 7 (1): 104-111.

Williams, J. (1991) 'Having An Away Day: English Football Fans and The Hooligan Debate'. In J. Williams and S. Wagg (Eds.) *British Football and Social Change: Getting Into Europe*, pp. 160-184. Leicester: Leicester University Press.

Williams, J. (2002) 'Who Are You Calling A Hooligan?' In M. Perryman (ed.) *Hooligan Wars: Causes and Effects of Football Violence*, pp. 37-53. Edinburgh: Mainstream Publishing.

Winter, H. (2002) 'Premiership Safe From Hooliganism, Says Scudamore'. *The Daily Telegraph*, 16 January, p. S1.

2.1. COMMENTARY BY JIM CHALMERS – THE NATURE AND EXTENT OF FOOTBALL HOOLIGANISM

The 2006 article by Frosdick and Newton joins the volumes of inquiries, books, articles and other publications written the world over on the subject of 'football hooliganism'. The phenomenon has provided a rich source of material for research by academics across the globe, with some making a lifetime career out of researching and writing on the topic. This article therefore provides only a small piece of the academic thousand-piece jigsaw which tries to explain the causes and consequences of the phenomenon.

In 2005, Frosdick and Marsh made reference to Frosdick and Newton's research in Chapter Three of their book, *Football Hooliganism*. I was privileged to write the foreword to the book and believe that what I wrote then will help others understand the difficulties in interpreting and understanding what is meant by 'football hooliganism'.

> *When I was approached to write the foreword to this book, my first reaction was, 'Oh no, not another academic study of football hooliganism.' As a former senior police officer, an Inspector with the Football Licensing Authority and currently as a Safety Manager at Kidderminster Harriers FC, I have experienced at first hand the growth and decline of the phenomenon in the UK from the 1960s to the present day. As a very mature student who has recently completed a BSc in Risk and Security Management, a good part of my studies, including my dissertation focused on the topic of football related violence and disorder.*

> *In my studies I soon discovered how over the years there has been a plethora of books, articles, studies, judicial and Government inquiries with numerous diverse opinions on the causes and cures of football hooliganism. It is a topic that everyone seems to have an opinion on. So it was with a sense of foreboding that I started to read the book. How wrong I found I was. My concerns were soon allayed since as each chapter unfolds, so does another dimension of the subject to grip the readers' attention.*

One of the aims of the book is to provide a 'course reader' to support the teaching of the subject in schools, colleges and universities. As members of the Football Safety Officers Association we regularly receive questionnaires or requests for interviews from students of all ages who are studying the topic of football hooliganism, which confirms the popularity of the subject as a field of study. I wish this book had been available to me during my own studies since for the first time all the threads of the debate have been pulled together in a concise yet comprehensive publication. The book is structured in a logical and readable style, with personal and practical experiences included to support and explain the academic theories.

The strength of the book lies in the balanced, unbiased yet critical review of all that has been written about the subject from the very early days of the sport to the present time. It is not another study where academics try to score points off each other merely because they disagree on the causes and cures of football hooliganism. Instead the authors present the arguments, the debates, the evidence and opinions from the widest of sources without judging who is right or wrong. Having presented the theories and the facts they leave the final judgment to the reader.

The authors suggest that this book is aimed principally at the world of education. Yet having viewed the book from both a practical and an academic perspective, I find there is much to commend it to a far wider audience. It will interest members of my Association, the police, regulatory bodies and the genuine fan concerned with the harm which hooliganism does to what Pele described as 'The Beautiful Game'.

I hope this helps explain why it is important not to view the 2006 article in isolation but instead to view it as a further piece of academic research which adds to overall knowledge and understanding of the phenomenon which is football hooliganism. This is a view shared by the authors when they say that their study does not purport to reveal the full picture of football hooliganism in England and Wales. Their honesty is refreshing in this regard.

What the article does is identify some of the common problems related to any research into football hooliganism. It also focuses on perceived realities about the nature and extent of the phenomenon.

One of the main problems is that of definition since the phenomenon can mean all things to all people, as I found during my degree studies and in particular during the course of preparing my dissertation (see Part 2.2. – Spectator Ejections). To this day there is no commonly agreed definition of what 'football hooliganism' means and I doubt there ever will be unless everyone starts to recognise the problem for what it is – anti-social behaviour associated with football. However I doubt this will ever occur since 'football hooliganism' has more of an appeal to the media than 'anti-social behaviour associated with football' ever will. Whilst Dunning's definition used by Frosdick and Newton may have resonance with academics, it will mean little to the media, football authorities, police or government. I am sure that academics will argue whether Frosdick and Newton have chosen the right definition. So the research and debate will rage on with no agreement on what is being researched or talked about.

In the article Frosdick and Newton also explain another major problem with regard to definition, and that is in interpreting the many variables associated with the phenomenon. This is particularly so in any attempt to analyse and interpret the only official statistics which are available relating to football hooliganism, namely the annual Home Office statistics on football related arrests and banning orders. Despite the lack of definition, despite the problems of interpreting the variables associated with the phenomenon (and despite the widely held view that there are three kinds of lies: lies, damned lies and statistics), nevertheless the Home Office statistics are regarded by everybody – by Government, the police, football authorities and clubs – as a barometer of the state of crowd-related problems associated with football, season in and season out.

Many clubs also view the statistics as league tables and when they are published each year use them as an indicator of how well or otherwise their fans are behaving at home and away. In other words those with the highest number of arrests and banning orders in their particular league will be considered to have the worst behaved fans. Those with the lowest recorded arrests and banning orders will be considered as having the best behaved fans in their league. I know from personal experience that this is certainly the view shared by Safety Advisory Groups up and down the country without any consideration of the variables which directly affect the statistical data.

As an example of the difficulties in interpreting the statistics, consider the arrest figures I have extracted for five clubs in the Premier League, both home (H) and away (A), over the four seasons to 2009/10.

Table One – Arrest Figures For Five Premier League Clubs

Club	2006/07	2007/08	2008/09	2009/10
Aston Villa	Total 80 H.64 A.16	Total 97 H.45 A.52	Total 77 H.35 A.42	Total 89 H.41 A.48
Chelsea	Total 135 H.77 A.58	Total 106 H.58 A.48	Total 102 H.41 A.61	Total 126 H.101 A.25
Manchester City	Total 91 H.64 A.27	Total 101 H.35 A.66	Total 82 H.43 A.39	Total 118 H.50 A.68
Manchester United	Total 192 H.117 A.75	Total 248 H.65 A.183	Total 185 H.91 A.94	Total 165 H.76 A.89
West Ham United	Total 111 H.94 A.17	Total 94 H.53 A.41	Total 65 H.36 A.29	Total 145 H.126 A.19

In the 2008/09 season I am sure West Ham United will have been pleased with only 65 arrests. However they will not have been so pleased with the total of 145 in the following season – but why the increase? Were there more police officers inside the ground? Were crowd attendances up? We don't know about these variables. What is also of interest is the increase from 36 to 126 home arrests for this club in these seasons. But why was this? In the season 2007/08, why should there have been 183 away arrests for Manchester United compared to the other seasons when the number of arrests was below 100? At Manchester City, why should the number of away arrests have been so much higher in the seasons 2007/08 and 2009/10? These are just some of the questions for which there is no explanation unless the statistics are analysed and interpreted in a much more sophisticated way, as advocated by Frosdick and Newton.

Another variable will be the attitude of the police and/or the safety officer to any anti-social behaviour associated with their games. I know from experience how some police commanders and safety officers have a high tolerance level to anti-social behaviour at matches, whilst others adopt a zero tolerance policy. So the arrest statistics can and do owe as much to attitude as to actual incidents.

As another example of unexplained seasonal variations, let's look at the Home Office statistics I have extracted on attendances, arrests and the ratio of non-policed games over the same four seasons.

Table Two – Attendances, Arrests and Police-Free Matches

Season	2006/07	2007/08	2008/09	2009/10
Attendances	29,578,141	29,914,212	29,881,966	30,057,892
Total arrests	2,833	2,893	3,394	2,507
Premier League	999	1,263	1,931	1,225
Championship	1,103	836	753	699
League One	428	602	458	393
League Two	303	192	252	190
Police Free	43%	41%	40%	47%

Taking total arrests related to attendances and the percentage of police free games, it will be noted that it was the 2008/09 season which had the lowest level of police free games. This was also the season which had the highest number of arrests, despite there being a higher attendance in the 2009/10 season. So it could be argued that increased attendances does not necessarily result in increased arrests.

It will also be noted that the 2009/10 season had the highest percentage of non-policed games and that this coincided with the lowest number of arrests recorded. Some might argue that this rather obviously shows that no police presence will have an influence on the arrest statistics. However closer analysis shows that the majority of police free games are in Leagues One and Two and that the arrest levels in those leagues show little variation. The most notable variation is in the Premier and Championship Leagues where most games are policed and yet the number of arrests by season shows a wide variation.

Also what the statistics do not show is that at police free games there may well have been numerous ejections as an alternative to arrest. As argued in Part 2.2. – Spectator Ejections, this is a hidden statistic. Also absent from the annual published statistics is the number of people banned by their club as distinct from Court imposed banning orders. The Home Office and police place great emphasis on the beneficial effects of banning orders in excluding risk fans. I do not disagree with this, but no account at all is taken of bans imposed by Clubs without any police or Court intervention. At my club, with practically all games classed as police free, we very often impose club bans for anti-social behaviour by our home fans. This proactive action precludes the need for arrests or prosecutions.

There is also the variable of what is meant by 'police free' games. At some fixtures there will indeed be a total absence of police. However at many games classed as 'police free' the police will still be in attendance for the purposes of intelligence gathering. I also know of games where the police provide a presence of several officers in a police van sitting outside the ground for the entire game. Should this therefore be classed as 'police free'? Probably not. So the percentage of 'police free' games quoted in the Home Office statistics will include fixtures which are only partly 'police free'.

This absence of constant variables makes it very difficult indeed to make any correlation between arrest numbers and police presence at matches. This strengthens the argument for the next significant problem identified in the article, namely the use of statistics. The article eloquently summarises the difficulties in the use of any statistical data. I had exactly the same dilemma in researching for my own dissertation (see Part 2.2. – Spectator Ejections). However I consider Frosdick and Newton's research achieved its objectives by looking beyond the headlines and probing the meaning of the Home Office figures. Statistics are only a tool for the collection, organisation and analysis of numerical facts. But the facts do not speak for themselves and raw data will never answer research questions. It is up to the researcher to give the statistics meaning and Frosdick and Newton have done just that in this piece of research. This is unlike the Home Office statistics which in my opinion raise more questions than they provide answers and cry out for more meaningful analysis.

The authors' wider analysis – of the numbers of matches with incidents, location, timing, competition, reported injuries, use of weapons and sizes of groups – goes much further than the Home Office statistics and provides much more valuable information on the nature and extent of football hooliganism than the Home Office figures do at present.

Sadly, despite the research conclusions, neither the football authorities, police nor Home Office have chosen to take any action to refine the published data to provide a more meaningful overview of what the statistics mean. Combined with a lack of definition, erratic variables and issues with interpretation, this means that the Home Office will continue to publish statistics which tell us very little about football-related anti-social behaviour. The statistics will also continue to be used as the barometer for football hooliganism in this country despite the many shortcomings identified by Frosdick, Newton and others.

In their conclusions Frosdick and Newton argue that there is ample scope for more detailed work. When I read this I was minded of my own conclusion into my research on spectator ejections (see Part 2.2.). I said that every long journey starts with the first step and that my dissertation could be the first step in what might be a long journey through the murky waters of spectator ejections. It is disappointing that neither the football authorities, the police nor the Home Office have so far considered more detailed analytical work to be worthwhile.

Perhaps we have reached a stage of accepting that, since there will always be an element of anti-social behaviour in society, then that element of anti-social behaviour known as football hooliganism will always be part of football. If that is so then perhaps there is little point in any further research. But to take this view would be to admit defeat. We need people like Frosdick and Newton to continue to push the boundaries of research into football hooliganism if we want to keep trying to find some sort of an explanation of and solution to the phenomenon. We also need those in authority to take account of research findings such as those in this article as they seek to understand and address the national and international problem which is football hooliganism.

2.2. SPECTATOR EJECTIONS

This paper is an edited version of Jim Chalmers' previously unpublished 2005 dissertation *What impact does the lack of published statistical data of spectator ejections at Premier and Football League Clubs in England and Wales have on our current understanding of spectator behaviour inside football stadia?*

Summary

This paper describes the first piece of empirical research into spectator ejections at Premier and Football League grounds in England and Wales. It is not a further discourse on football-related violence or hooliganism since the focus on this phenomenon has put other research into football-related spectator behaviour into the shade. In particular, there has been a lack of consideration or discussion of spectator ejection statistics and how they could be utilised in both analysing spectator behaviour inside football grounds and the way football fans are being managed on a match day. Part of the current problem lies in the secrecy which surrounds spectator ejection statistics with official publication of the figures ceasing at the end of the 1991/92 football season. This paper questions whether the lack of published spectator ejection statistics affects our understanding of spectator behaviour and how spectators are being managed inside football grounds.

The paper offers some clarity and openness on the subject based on the views of the majority of Premier and Football League Safety Officers and representatives of the football authorities, academics, authors and the police. The paper draws on some elements of empirical research to outline alternatives in our current understanding of spectator ejections and their meaning.

Introduction

Background

It is the Home Office, through the UK Football Policing Unit, which has the responsibility of collating and publishing football-related arrest statistics in England and Wales. Up until the end of the 1991/92 football season their predecessors in the National Criminal Intelligence

Service also published ejection statistics. This was because at that time it was the police rather than club stewards who were mainly responsible for ejecting fans from stadia. Following a change in policing policy, the police no longer ejected spectators from grounds saying that this was, and still is, a club responsibility through their stewards. Thus since 1992 there have been no published ejection statistics, even though over the years stewards have frequently ejected spectators for breaches of both ground regulations and the criminal law.

In 2000, the Football Safety Officers' Association (FSOA) established their own website with a system of post-match reporting by their members, including the provision of information on spectator ejections. The system of reporting was not compulsory and the number of clubs choosing to submit reports varied from year to year. Moreover these reports were held on a secure website and were not in the public domain.

The situation remained therefore that the only published statistics relating to spectator behaviour at our football grounds were the arrest statistics published by the Home Office. It could be argued that the absence of published ejection statistics was a missing piece of valuable data in analysing crowd behaviour and did not give a true indicator of stewarding performance in the control and management of football crowds. This led to the author deciding to undertake research to test the hypothesis that '*the lack of published spectator ejection statistics at Premier League and Football League Clubs in England and Wales gives a false impression of spectator behaviour inside football stadia.*'

Methodology

The research design sought to follow best practice in social science and enhance the validity of the findings by combining both quantitative and qualitative survey methods. The quantitative element comprised a postal questionnaire survey and the qualitative element a telephone interview survey.

A postal questionnaire was considered the most appropriate main research instrument since it enabled a census of all 92 Premier and

Football League club safety officers. The questionnaire used closed questions of fact, which left little opportunity for interpretation. An opportunity was however given for the respondent to include qualitative comment. The questionnaire was piloted by sending it to four safety officers and following up with a personal interview. The views obtained were incorporated in the final questionnaire design.

For the telephone interview survey, ten representatives drawn from the Football Association, Football League, Football Licensing Authority, academics involved in football research, football authors and the police were interviewed to ascertain whether there was any discrepancy between the views of the safety officer questionnaire respondents and those of key individuals associated with football safety and security. The interview comprised a schedule of 'open ended' questions, the responses to which were recorded in writing.

Respondent anonymity was preserved by using code numbers to identify the questionnaire respondents and code letters for those involved in the telephone interviews.

Findings

The Postal Questionnaire

This section examines and discusses the data from the questionnaires distributed to the 92 Premier and Football League Safety Officers.

High Response Rate

Non-response is a very serious issue when using postal self-completion surveys. Academics contend that a typical first-rate response, without follow up, will normally be between 20% and 40%. In a postal survey conducted in 2004 by the FSOA Administrator of the same respondents on the subject of stewards pay the response rate was n35 or 38%. For this research, 76 questionnaires were returned, a response rate of 82.6%. The initial response rate, without follow up, was 60 or 65%. The Premier League response was 90%, Division One (now the Championship), 87.5%, Division Two (now League One), 66% and Division Three (now League Two) also 87.5%.

It is difficult to judge why the Division Two response was lower than the other three Divisions. A possible explanation is that safety officers in the Premier League and Division One are generally full time employees and may have received the questionnaire more promptly and had the time to complete them more quickly compared to safety officers in Division Two, many of whom are part time employees. The same argument could be made for Division Three safety officers, the majority of whom are employed on a part time basis, but since the author is an assistant safety officer in the same Division this could have been an influencing factor.

Respondents' Position in the Club

Moving onto the questionnaire, Question One asked, 'What is your position in the Club?' The responses showed that 67 or 88% of the respondents were safety officers. The remainder were six deputy safety officers, two stadium managers and one operations manager.

One disadvantage of a postal survey is that the researcher has no control over who fills in the questionnaire. Since the research guaranteed the anonymity of the respondent there was no expectation for the questionnaire to be signed or for personal details to be included. However many of the respondents included a personal note with their response, indicating that the intended recipient had indeed completed it. In addition, the detail in the responses, including comments, indicated a high level of knowledge of the subject by the respondents.

Another disadvantage of postal surveys is that the respondents might not treat the exercise seriously. However the response rate and senior level of the Club respondents would tend to indicate this was not the case. All of these factors lend weight to the validity of the findings.

Recording of Ejections

Question Two asked, 'Do you record ejections from your stadium?' 75 respondents did record ejections whilst only one did not.

In the additional qualitative comments made, reasons given for recording ejections were: to identify problem areas in the stadium; to identify troublemakers; and to enable action to be taken. Views were expressed that such recording indicated a pro-active club approach in preventing anti-social behaviour with one safety officer describing ejection statistics as being as valuable as arrest statistics.

The safety officer who did not record ejections argued that ejections for minor breaches of ground regulations could give a misleading picture of crowd behaviour problems, an argument to be discussed in more detail later on.

The high number of clubs recording ejections and the reasons given for doing so both support the notion that the FSOA database should be a useful source of empirical data.

Number of Ejections

Question Three asked, 'During the 2003/2004 football season how many persons were ejected from your stadium?'

Table 3.1 shows a summary of the arrest and ejection statistics for the 2003/04 season compiled from three sources: the ejection statistics reported by the respondents for this research; FSOA database ejection statistics and Home Office (HO) statistics on football related arrests and banning orders.

Table 3.1 – Arrest and Ejection Statistics

Division	Respondents	FSOA Database	HO Arrests
Premier	2,047	1,807	1,137
Division One	1,135	974	849
Division Two	453	364	616
Division Three	435	190	408

The discrepancies in Table 3.1 between the FSOA database and the respondent statistics are explained by the fact that, to a small extent, some safety officers who report in to the FSOA database did not respond to the questionnaire and, to a much greater extent, that more safety officers who did respond do not report in to the FSOA database.

It is therefore considered that the respondent statistics provide a better database for discussion than the FSOA figures. There are several reasons for viewing the FSOA figures with some scepticism. First, there are some duplicate entries and thus some double-counting. Second, the FSOA figures report on 120 Clubs listed in alphabetical order, including European, Irish, Scottish and Conference Clubs, and so comparison between leagues and seasons is difficult. However the main reason for scepticism is that the FSOA figures are based on club reports, which are partial and sporadic, whilst a fuller sample of safety officers provided the respondent figures. For the purposes of the remaining discussion, only the respondent statistics will be referred to.

Ejection statistics are therefore available but what, if anything, can they tell us about spectator behaviour inside football stadia? One thing they do tell us is that ejections in the Premier and First Divisions far exceed the number of arrests. With 57% of arrests taking place outside of stadia this comparison is even more extreme.

There is a problem of definition by what is meant by 'spectator ejection'. The Oxford Illustrated Dictionary (1962) describes ejection as to 'expel (from place, office), evict from property, and throw out from within'. One safety officer queried whether, 'If fans are refused entry, should this be recorded as an ejection?' Whilst another offered the view that, unless an ejection was clearly defined, then accurate statistics would be impossible. The data therefore only indicates an action as distinct from defining the conduct leading to the action.

Another problem of definition is the number of variables surrounding the ejection figures (see Frosdick and Newton's article earlier in Part II). Some of these include the sport involved (some football stadia also host rugby matches), the ground regulations being enforced, the extent of penalising spectator behaviour, the location, the Division, whether alcohol was involved or whether the behaviour was provoked by player or officials behaviour. Unlike arrest statistics, ejections are not categorised and this will be discussed more fully at Question Six.

Ejection figures will also be influenced by the way the safety officer or individual stewards enforce ground regulations or the criminal law in 'police free' games. Club policy is another variable or as one safety officer put it 'We eject for smoking in a no-smoking area and how can this be compared with a club that does not have a no-smoking policy?' Another said 'We eject for persistent standing in a seated area whilst other clubs ignore this'.

The attitude of the safety officer will have a bearing as one said, 'Ejections are for us a last resort. I feel ejecting them admits defeat. The fewer we get the better it shows we are managing our fans'. Another safety officer said, 'Low ejection figures could be the result of good behaviour or lax stewarding whilst high numbers could indicate bad behaviour or an attempt to enforce ground regulations'. This sums up the difficulties in using numbers as an indicator of spectator behaviour.

So do the figures in themselves tell us anything? Compare the following most and fewest club ejection figures by division in Table 3.2.

Table 3.2 – Most and Fewest Club Ejections

Division	Most	Fewest
Premier	443	36
Division One	196	16
Division Two	60	13
Division Three	92	0

Does this mean that the clubs with the highest number are those with a history of poor crowd behaviour and those with a low number a history of good crowd behaviour? Or does it mean that those with the highest number have a good pro-active safety management and stewarding operation and those with a low number a poor and lax stewarding operation? Could it also mean, as one safety officer put it, 'The more stewards you have the more ejections there will be.'?

In 2002, whilst the author was a member of the Joint Football Authorities Safety Management Focus Group, the safety officer of club PL 16 raised a similar argument. In respect of a high number of arrests for racist behaviour, did this mean his club had a racist problem or did it mean his club had an affirmative action programme to deal positively with incidents of racist conduct?

During the season club PL 11 had a total of 144 ejections of which only 13 were home fans. Club D1 20 had a total of 196 ejections of which 174 were home fans. What does this tell us about the conduct of the home and away fans at these clubs? In the absence of any analysis the answer is very little.

What, if any, lessons can be drawn from the published annual arrest statistics? For the 2003/04 season, the Home Office described the 10% reduction in arrests, from 4,413 to 3,982 as painting a very encouraging picture. The police said they were pleased with the statistics but this was due to more rigorous controls and police investigations having a positive deterrent effect rather than a massive reformation of troublemakers. The Home Office and police were therefore using the statistics as a barometer of worsening or improving crowd behaviour.

However could the reduction be due to 25% of fixtures being non-policed? Could it be that crowd management by clubs resulting in over 4,000 ejections had been an influencing factor? Both the Home Office and police in their considerations ignored ejections. The arrest figures also included categories such as alcohol offences, ticket touting, breach of banning orders, offences against property and a miscellaneous section (1,404 offences out of 3,982). It is difficult to sustain a strong defence for using arrest statistics as a measure of crowd behaviour when non-violence and disorder figures are included in the same collective statistics as violent disorder and racist conduct. Neither the Home Office nor the police made any attempt to provide a meaning for the data other then saying that a 10% reduction in arrests is encouraging. This lack of analysis is argued as a fundamental flaw in the arrest statistics and is a lesson to be learned in any presentation of ejection statistics. As various academics have argued, statistics need to be interpreted before they are of any real use. Even the Home Office advises that football related arrests only tell part of the story and need to be placed in context.

Recording the Ejected Person's Details

Question 4 asked, 'Do you record details of the person ejected?' The responses showed that 57 or 75% recorded details whilst 19 or 25% did not.

Generally the reasons given for recording details were to help clubs identify persons causing trouble and to enable further action, such as sending warning letters or issuing a club ban from the stadium. The main reason given for not recording details was that there was no legal right to require this information and fans were aware of this. This was overcome where a membership scheme was in existence or where the offender was a season ticket holder and thus could be identified from Club records. Other reasons for not recording details were that very often false information was given and in what might already be a highly charged and volatile atmosphere pursuing the provision of personal details could exacerbate the situation.

In the absence of any legal requirement for a person being ejected to provide personal details it could be argued this weakens the system in preventing further sanctions against the individual. Whether there should be such a legal requirement is a matter for further debate.

Recording Reasons

Question Five asked, 'Do you record the reasons for the ejection?' The responses showed that 74 or 97% of Safety Officers recorded the reasons, whilst only two did not.

In many respects the reasons given repeat the responses to Questions Two and Four. The reasons provided information on particular issues such as breaches of specific ground regulations; identifying areas where things were going wrong; providing information to the police and other safety officers on particular anti-social behaviour; assisting in planning for specific visiting team fans; and justifying banning a fan from the Club.

Interestingly there was no specific comment on protecting the club or a steward from a civil action for damages should a fan be injured in the course of an ejection, yet the author knows of at least three instances where this has occurred.

From this almost unanimous response it could be argued that an awareness of the reasons for ejections could be more important than recording the details of the person ejected.

Categories of Ejections

Question Six asked, 'Of the total number of persons ejected, can you provide the numbers ejected in the following categories? (a) Breaches of Ground Regulations. (b) Criminal Offences'. Not all safety officers were able to supply a breakdown between ground regulation and criminal offence ejections. This explains the discrepancy between the research project total (4070) and the responses to this question (2906).

The standard ground regulations issued by the Premier and Football Leagues in 2003 indicated a total of twenty-seven ground regulations. Of the 2906 persons ejected, 2455 or 84.4% were for breaches of ground regulations with the remaining 451 or 15.6% being criminal offence ejections. It could be argued that the statistics indicate one of the primary roles of Club stewards is in enforcing ground regulations as distinct from enforcing the criminal law inside football stadia.

It could also be argued that a weakness in the research questionnaire was that it did not include a more detailed question on the reasons for ejections. The Interview Survey therefore sought to address this weakness in the next stage of the research.

The FSOA match report form provides the opportunity for the safety officer to record the number of arrests and ejections. There is no opportunity, other than in the narrative section, to include the reasons for any arrests or ejections. It could be argued that the issues identified in Question Three could equally apply to Question Six, principally 'What do the figures tell us?' They would appear to tell us simply that either as a result of spectator behaviour, a club policy, the policy of a safety officer or the actions of an individual steward, 2455 fans were ejected for ground regulation infringements and 451 for breaches of the criminal law.

It could however be argued that the responses to Question Six do tell something more since this is the first piece of research which has sought to distinguish between ground regulation and criminal offence ejections by stewards. The author was a member of the Football Licensing Authority Inspectorate from 1991 to 2003 and in that time attended 506 Premier and Football League fixtures. During each visit details of arrests and ejections were recorded together with the reasons. From personal experience, stewards generally ejected for breaches of just nine of the 27 ground regulations.

In addition to the issue of which categories of ground regulations lead to ejections, there are important questions to ask about how individual breaches are counted. For example a fan could be in possession of a can, be standing in a seated area, be abusive to a steward and be smoking in a no-smoking area. Would this be counted as one ejection for one breach or four breaches? Since it is argued that many politicians and journalists treat statistics as an accurate barometer of crime, note that the 451 criminal offence ejections are not included in the Home Office football arrest statistics, which brings into question the validity and reliability of the football-related arrest statistics.

Should the FSOA Collate the Statistics on Ejections?

Question Seven asked, 'Should the FSOA collate the statistics on ejections from stadia?' The responses showed that 70 respondents or 92% agreed with the question whilst six or 8% disagreed.

The views of the respondents support the provision of an accurate and uniform system of recording statistics to enable a better level of information to be available to them. Those who commented were in general agreement that if all safety officers contributed to the FSOA website, this would enable a better national picture of problems to be developed. One safety officer said, 'Ejection statistics are just as important as arrest statistics because they give a more accurate picture of the extent of football trouble. The FSOA is the obvious choice for collating the information since the system is already set up for this'. The only safety officer who voiced a negative opinion said the Football Licensing Authority already did this but this assertion was inaccurate.

Can a parallel be drawn with the views of Government and police on intelligence-led policing and the FSOA intelligence obtained from collating, analysing and disseminating information from FSOA post-match reports. If, as Her Majesty's Inspectorate of Constabulary have asserted, quality intelligence is the life blood of modern policing, should not good quality information be of equal value to the world of football? In 2003, the Home Office provided £5 million, over three years, to the 43 police services in England and Wales for use in intelligence-led operations aimed at gaining banning orders on known and emerging trouble makers. Based on this, is there not a case for Government funding to assist the FSOA in the development of its information and intelligence systems, since Clubs themselves ban fans without the need for a Court banning order. Given the importance placed on banning orders by the Home Office and police in tackling football hooliganism, why is no consideration given to the impact club banning orders could have in a similar context?

Should the Ejection Statistics be Coded for Reasons?

Question Eight asked, 'Should the statistics be coded to show the reason for the ejection? (i.e. the breach of a particular ground regulation or the commission of a criminal offence)?'

The responses showed that 66 or 87% of the respondents agreed the statistics should be coded whilst ten or 13% disagreed but did not give a reason for this disagreement. This question continues the debate about the difficulties experienced in understanding the reasons for spectator ejections and, without some form of analysis of the statistics, their usefulness in assessing spectator behaviour.

Of the 29 who provided comment, the majority supported a coding system based on the ground regulation number or criminal offence identification. Concerns were expressed of including too many classifications since this would confuse the recording system and would deter safety officers from keeping statistics. It was also argued that if the codes were too complicated the system would collapse.

Since 66 of the respondents favoured a system of ejection coding it is argued this would benefit from further research if the statistics are to form any part in the ongoing debate about football spectator behaviour.

FSOA Publication of the Statistics

Question Nine asked, 'Should the FSOA publish the statistics on ejections?'

The responses showed that 68 or 89% agreed the statistics should be published with eight or 11% disagreeing with the proposal. Of the 23 respondents who expressed an opinion, the majority took the view that publication would assist with intelligence gathering and the provision of information on spectator behaviour, particularly with regard to identifying specific trends or behavioural patterns. As one Safety Officer said in agreeing with the proposal, 'This would present a more accurate picture regarding problems with visiting fans, i.e. at one game 17 visitors were ejected from the home area having gone there to engage with home hooligans. Since the police do not record ejections the full intelligence picture is not being presented.'

Concern was expressed at the validity of ejections statistics with some safety officers saying statistics on their own may be misread or could lead to league tables, which prove nothing. A contrary view was however expressed by other safety officers saying the statistics must be in the public domain, as in the case of the police arrests, to show the football industry is committed to eradicating bad fan behaviour.

What however should be published? Is it right for the Home Office to publish football related arrests and to ignore spectator ejections? Is it right for the police, through intelligence, to identify and comment on what they perceive to be football-related problems and yet ignore information from ejection statistics? It could be argued that the way forward at a national level is to share the database information in much the same way that local information on known troublemakers is shared between police and clubs under a formal agreement.

Extent of Publication

Question Ten asked respondents who had answered 'Yes' to Question Nine to say whether the publication of the statistics should be:

(a) Restricted to FSOA members?
(b) Restricted to FSOA members and the football authorities?
(c) Restricted to FSOA members, football authorities and the police?
(d) Restricted to FSOA members, football authorities, the police and members of the Safety Advisory Group?
(e) Accessible to anyone including the media?
(f) No opinion.

The responses were:

(a) 11 or 14.4%.
(b) 2 or 2.6%.
(c) 10 or 13.1%.
(d) 25 or 32.8%.
(e) 20 or 26.3%.
(f) 8 or 10.5%.

The majority of respondents (a) to(d) (58 or 76.3%) favoured a limited level of publication with 20 or 26% indicating a willingness for general accessibility to the data.

The author is aware of the grave concern expressed by many safety officers about the interpretation made by the media and others of the football-related arrest statistics. The police no longer publish football disorder logs as a result of media misrepresentation of the data. Safety officers view with equal concern such misrepresentation of ejection statistics, with what they described as 'league tables' being drawn up by the media and others. Claims could then be made that clubs with the greatest number of arrests and/or ejections had the worst crowd behavioural problems.

This concern over the media amplification of football-related problems stems from the 1960s when journalists were sent to football matches to report on crowd behaviour rather than just the game. The reporting was often sensationalist and various academic commentators have noted how such reporting helped shape public opinion about misbehaviour at football matches.

The problem continues to the present day when the day after the publication of the 2003/04 arrest statistics the Daily Mirror had the headline 'League of Thuggery, a league of football shame'. They then put Portsmouth FC at the top of the league based solely on the number of arrests for violent disorder. Cardiff City FC was also singled out as the most violent club in the non-Premiership leagues despite having only 15 arrests for violent disorder compared to West Ham United FC with 107 arrests in the same category. Concerns about league tables are very real and unless statistics are given meaning by those publishing them this concern is not likely to ever go away.

Whilst concerns over unrestricted access to the ejection statistics are valid, a dilemma exists with unrestricted access to football arrest statistics. Could it be argued that if the FSOA continue to hold the ejection data on a secure website this in itself could be misinterpreted as having something to hide?

Response to the Research Hypothesis

Question Eleven used a Likert scale to ask, 'Do you agree or disagree with the following statement? The lack of published spectator ejection statistics gives a false impression of spectator behaviour inside football stadia'.

The responses were:

Strongly agree – 32 or 42.1%
Agree – 20 or 26.3%
No opinion – 6 or 7.8%
Disagree – 7 or 9.2%
Strongly disagree – 1 or 1.3%

A majority of 52 or 68.4% agree with the statement with 10.5% disagreeing and 7.8% with no opinion either way. Given this majority view about the effect of ejection statistics on our understanding of spectator behaviour this will have to be reconciled with the concern expressed over the extent to which the data should be published.

Additional Information

Question Twelve was an invitation to respondents to include any additional information, which might assist the research project. Relevant responses are incorporated into the preceding discussion.

Telephone Interview Survey

This section of the research examines the views of other disciplines associated with the world of football. Telephone interviews were conducted with ten respondents selected from the Football Association (one), Football League (one), Football Licensing Authority (one), academics (three), authors (two) and police (two). All have considerable knowledge of the world of football, football stadia and football fans. Although the questions asked were slightly different to those in the questionnaire the same theme was used since it was hoped this would underpin the safety officer responses or show any significant discrepancies.

The interviews were conducted in an 'open-discussion' format and although semi-structured were done in a deliberately conversational manner to obtain the most useful results. As with the questionnaire respondents, the interview respondents were guaranteed anonymity. The researcher considered that by identifying the football authorities' personnel interviewed this might have prejudiced their anonymity but the Football Association, Football League and Football Licensing Authority agreed to their organisations being referred to by name.

Recording Ejections

Question One asked, 'The majority of clubs that took part in the postal survey record the names and addresses of persons ejected and the reasons for the ejection. Is this what you would have expected and why?'

Seven of the respondents said this is what they would have expected explaining the main reasons for doing so was to protect the club and stewards from any complaints, particularly against any civil law suit resulting from the ejection, an opinion not expressed by the safety officers. Contrary views were expressed by RE (police) who said he had doubts with the truth of the safety officers' response since, with no legal power to require details to be provided, he would be surprised either if the fans provided their details or if any information provided was accurate. RG (academic) expressed surprise with the club actions since with no criminal offence having been committed there was no legal basis for the club to require personal details to be given. This legal issue confirmed views expressed by safety officers of the main weakness in the ejection process.

Total Number of Ejections?

Question Two asked, 'Using your skill, knowledge and judgement, what do you think was the total number of spectators ejected from the 92 Premier and Football League grounds during the 2003/04 season?'

In the absence of any public knowledge of the ejection figures this question was intended to judge the respondents' perceptions of the scale. The numbers given varied between 900 (Football Licensing Authority) and 40,000 (police). The Football Association and Football League views varied between 4,000 and 1,200 respectively. Such a variation of opinion arguably justifies a need for accurate statistics to be available if only to negate such widely varying views on club sanctions relating to spectator behaviour inside stadia.

Reasons for Ejections

Question Three asked, 'Within your knowledge, what would you describe as the main reasons why spectators are ejected?'

All of the respondents regularly attend fixtures in either an official or fan capacity. Their general consensus was for conduct such as drunkenness, breaches of ground regulations, pitch encroachments, general bad behaviour and failure to comply with the instructions of a steward. RA (Football Association) said that because the police deal with the more serious offences, ejections would be for minor misconduct by the fans. The respondents also said that the Division and club policies would also be an influencing factor. RD (police) said the introduction of a total ban on smoking at his club had resulted in increased ejections. RE (police) and RG (academic) both identified persistent standing in seated areas in the Premier League and Division One as a major factor in spectator ejections.

Whilst the respondent opinions are valid, in the absence of an ejection coding system, the precise reasons for spectator ejections are, at present, difficult to quantify.

Central Point for Analysis?

Question Four asked, 'Do you consider there should be a central point for collating and analysing spectator ejection statistics and, if so, who should be responsible for this?'

Everyone with the exception of RD (police) agreed there should be a central point for the collation and analysis of the statistics. In opposing this RD said that ejections from nightclubs, pubs and other licensed premises are not recorded so why should football fans be treated differently? Only RA (Football Association), RC (Football Licensing Authority) and RF (academic) supported the safety officers who argued for the FSOA to have this responsibility. The other respondents considered there should be an independent element introduced into the system. The organisations mentioned included the Football Licensing Authority, the University of Leicester, Home Office and the [then] National Criminal Intelligence Service. RJ (author) was opposed to any of the football authorities performing this function saying they were more likely to use the statistics for 'spin' purposes as distinct from providing information.

Publication?

Question Five asked, 'Do you believe spectator ejection statistics should be published and, if so, how wide a publication should there be?'

In common with the safety officers, there were conflicting views on the publication of the statistics. Some respondents favoured widespread publication but others such as RD (police) argued that the general public would have no interest in statistics of this nature. RC (Football Licensing Authority) also questioned their publication arguing that neither arrest nor ejection statistics should be regarded as any measurement of crowd trouble inside stadia. In arguing for publication RF and RG (academics) said the information should be widely available so as to give a full picture of spectator conduct with RK (author) advocating transparency in the provision of the information. RJ (author) summed it up saying 'If records are kept secret this could be misinterpreted in much the same way as the media can misinterpret them if published. It is a case of damned if you do and damned if you don't'.

Question Six then asked, 'What would you describe as the possible positive and negative aspects of publishing spectator ejection statistics?' RF and RH (academics) said on the positive side that publication would present a fuller picture of spectator behaviour at football grounds. Others giving a positive viewpoint included RG (academic), RD and RE (police) who said that publication would indicate clubs were adopting a pro-active approach to crowd problems by not tolerating anti-social behaviour in the grounds.

On the negative side RB (Football League), RF (academic) and RK (author) spoke of media misrepresentation of the statistics arguing they would be unlikely to be presented in a way beneficial to football. Like the safety officers, concern was expressed that the statistics would be presented in league tables as an indicator of clubs with crowd problems. RC (Football Licensing Authority) argued how one ejection for racist conduct could be compared with 3,000 fans using racist language where action would be impossible. He used the same argument for how one ejection for persistent standing in a seated area could be used to measure conduct when several thousands were standing and action was impossible. The comments very much echoed those of the safety officers.

Response to the Research Hypothesis

Question Seven asked, 'Do you believe the lack of published ejection statistics gives a false impression of spectator behaviour inside football stadia?'

Unlike the safety officers, where the majority agreed with the statement, the majority of the interview respondents disagreed. One who did agree, RF (academic), referred to the attrition rate down from 100% of incidents; with W% resulting in arrests, X% resulting in ejections, Y% resulting in a warning by stewards and Z% where no action was taken? He described the dark figure between incidents that happen and those which result in ejections and how publication of the statistics would throw some light on this dark figure of attrition.

RA (Football Association), RB (Football League) and RC (Football Licensing Authority) all said that since ejections were for minor matters they did not in themselves indicate poor spectator behaviour. RJ (author) said that the statistics say more about club attitudes to fans than they do about crowd behaviour.

RD and RE (police) supported by RG (academic) said that the lack of published statistics does not necessarily give a false impression of spectator behaviour but does contribute to an incomplete picture of spectator behaviour. This was described as a hidden variable, missing in any debate or discussion about current spectator behaviour at football grounds.

Additional Information

Question Eight invited any other comments. The value of the research was supported by RB (Football League), RF and RH (academics), RD and RE (police) and RJ (author) who all agreed the research raised interesting issues which would benefit from further investigation.

Conclusions

It was the English politician Benjamin Disraeli who once noted wryly 'there are three kinds of lies: lies, damned lies and statistics'. However statistics have become increasingly important to all areas of public policy. We live in a world that constantly bombards us with official facts and figures' but it is always worth pausing to consider what such statistical evidence means. It is only by probing more deeply that statistics can begin to yield valuable insights into social behaviour.

As a result of the football financial revolution that took place during the 1990s, the game of football has become an event, no longer enjoyed in the main by the working class, but by people from all walks of life. With arguably all sections of society represented in the crowd, do they all have the same values of behaviour at a match? This can be where a club ejection policy is at the heart of a very complex issue in setting out minimum standards of spectator behaviour. But do fans know what this is? It has been suggested that the club ejection policy should be an integral part of each club spectator charter with openness and transparency being the keys to its operation in practice. It has also been argued in the research that ejection statistics say more about club policies than actual fan behaviour.

With no guidance available to assist in establishing a national code of practice relating to spectator ejections, variations in policy, procedures and recording practices makes comparisons between clubs and the national scale of spectator ejections difficult to quantify. As the research found, there is no guarantee that every ejection will find its way into the statistics or that every breach of a ground regulation will in fact lead to an ejection. Many breaches will result in a warning by stewards, which will never be recorded. Mass disobedience by fans, such as persistent standing in seated areas will not find its way into the statistical data. At present with so many variables it is difficult to judge the true value of the statistics in understanding spectator behaviour or the club management of events.

The research indicates that confidence in recorded ejection statistics will only develop with consistency in enforcement, counting, recording and harmonising club policies. If this is established it would also enable a more robust examination of stewarding performance to take place. It has been argued that only by establishing a more open and transparent system will there be any confidence in the statistics and the information they can provide. At present the lack of objective data on spectator ejections makes it difficult to place them in the context of our current understanding of spectator behaviour inside stadia.

Reasonable conclusions can however be justifiably drawn from the evidence presented in the research process. Spectator ejections are not a new phenomenon. Since the early 1990s the most significant changes have been the switch from police to steward action and from a police to club and FSOA recording system. The most significant change has been the lack of published ejection statistics since 1992, despite the FSOA establishing a database for such information in 2000. It could be argued that if the statistical information was regarded as useful public information up to 1992, is there any reason to question its public relevance at the present day?

Each year the authorities appear to place great significance on the annual football-related arrest statistics as a barometer for measuring spectator behaviour and policing activity. The media also tend to use the statistics as an indicator of improving or worsening football spectator behaviour despite the shortcomings in the way the arrest statistics are presented. Given the significance placed on these statistics, with a quarter of matches now taking place without a police presence and over half the arrests taking place outside of grounds, it may seem surprising that no significance is given to the number of ejections which occur each year, particularly with ejections exceeding arrests. Is there not a case, as identified in the research, for both the arrest and ejection statistics to be published by the Home Office and the football authorities, if only to provide a fuller picture of sanctions being taken against football fans?

The research identified the difficulties involved between recording the details of the person being ejected and the reason for the ejection. Given that the majority of safety officers record the reasons for an ejection, the problem in the present system is how this information is recorded both locally and nationally. At national level, whilst the recorded ejection figures are known, there is no system in place to analyse their meaning. In the context of understanding spectator behaviour the present system is meaningless. The research identified the importance safety officers place on good intelligence to assist them in planning each event. A system of analysis of the reasons for spectator ejections could lead to the identification of particular trends in spectator behaviour and thus assist clubs in planning their events.

Part of the research process involved identifying a distinction between stewarding activity in enforcing ground regulations and the criminal law inside stadia. The research indicated the primary role of stewards in dealing with aspects of safety, security, control and customer care through the ground regulations, but there is no information available to assist in identifying the types of offences or conduct which led to over 4,000 ejections in the 2003/04 season. Most safety officers would support a system of coding ejections based on the ground regulation number with another code to identify a criminal offence ejection. However it is argued that it will not be enough merely to provide a more detailed set of statistics. The shortcoming of this is evident in the way the arrest statistics are presented. Unless there is a detailed explanation of what the statistics mean, they could present a distorted view of real trends and patterns in spectator behaviour.

At a national level the Safety Officers favour the FSOA as the most suitable body to collate and analyse the spectator ejection data. This was not a view shared by some of the interview respondents, who favoured the introduction of an independent element into the system. Whether the likes of the Home Office, Football Licensing Authority or the University of Leicester would welcome such a role is debatable. It could be argued however that the FSOA is not a 'football authority' in that it was established to represent its members much like a trade union. Is there not therefore a case for a 'football authority' such as the Football Association or the Football League to undertake the central collation and analysis function?

Whilst the research identified that the majority of the respondents favoured publication of the ejection statistics, the safety officers did not favour general accessibility to the data. This contrasted with the interview respondents, who generally advocated transparency in the provision of the information. The safety officers concern in the main stemmed from their suspicion of the way the media would be likely to misrepresent the data, in much the same way that the arrest statistics can be misinterpreted. However with football related arrest statistics being widely published a dilemma exists. In much the same way that the media and others can misrepresent published statistics, secrecy about ejection statistics could be equally misrepresented as having something to hide.

Despite the misgivings of the safety officers about the publication of the statistics, there was general agreement by them that the lack of such published information gives a false impression of spectator behaviour inside stadia. This view was not shared by the interview respondents who argued, not about a false impression, but instead that the lack of such information resulted in an incomplete picture of spectator behaviour being presented. What is clear from the research is that the lack of published ejection statistics hides the detail of sanctions at club level against spectators whose conduct is considered unacceptable during an event.

It was a Chinese philosopher who once said that every long journey starts with the first step. In the absence of any previous research into spectator ejections at football grounds, this project could be the first step in what may be a long journey through the murky water of ejection statistics. Whilst the research project may have added to our knowledge about spectator ejections, it has also raised other questions requiring development in depth.

2.2. COMMENTARY BY STEVE FROSDICK – SPECTATOR EJECTIONS

I had the privilege of supervising Jim Chalmers undergraduate dissertation when he was a (very) mature student at the University of Portsmouth in 2005. I thought that his research was important and worthy of publication for four main reasons.

The first and most straightforward reason was simply the quality of the work, for which Chalmers was awarded a first-class mark. He has done something original and he has done it very well.

The second reason is the validity and reliability of Chalmers' work. It is very unusual for any researcher, let alone an undergraduate, to get such a high response rate (82.6%) to a questionnaire survey. This response rate and the results show the esteem in which Chalmers is held by his football safety colleagues and their confidence in his integrity in dealing with their data. It is also rare for a researcher to have such unfettered access to expert stakeholders in their field, which is what Chalmers was able to do for his follow-up telephone interviews. As readers, we can be confident Chalmers has obtained a pretty full and accurate picture of spectator ejections and what the people that matter think about the subject.

The third reason is that Chalmers research adds something new to our knowledge about the nature and extent of football hooliganism. In Robert Newton's and my discussion of the attrition rate in article 2.1, we comment that only a small proportion of incidents will make it into the official arrest statistics. Many incidents will be overlooked, some will result in a warning and others in an ejection by the stewards. Since official sources stopped collecting and publishing ejection statistics in 1992, there has simply been no data on ejections in the public domain.

We now know that, for the season 2003/04, some 4,000 people were ejected in addition to the 3,000 or so who were arrested. About 85% of ejections were for breaches of ground regulations whilst about 15% were for criminal offences which could also have resulted in an arrest by the police.

Of course the same problems of interpretation and media misrepresentation exist for ejection statistics as they do for arrests, but the figures collected by Chalmers do give us a more rounded feel for the extent of spectator misbehaviour in football grounds.

The fourth reason is that Chalmers was ahead of his time in calling for spectator ejections to form part of the data set gathered about spectator behaviour in football grounds. In January 2011, the Football Association wrote to all Premier and Football League clubs pointing out a potential gap in information and intelligence when people were ejected from stadia without the details being recorded. This was the thrust of Chalmers' conclusions six years earlier. In 2011, clubs were at last being asked to try and obtain the personal details of people being ejected and to share the information with the police.

Although statistical data could be the by-product of such data collection, the idea in 2011 is that the police might then be able to use such information as part of an application for a civil ban under section 14B of the Football Banning Order legislation. There is a whole civil liberties debate about section 14B banning orders, however it is fair to say that such action by clubs would support the UK government, police and football authorities' policy of excluding the risk fans whilst empowering the non-risk fans.

2.3. WHO ARE THE HOOLIGANS?

This paper is derived from a previously unpublished 2005 MSc dissertation, *Can a profile of a football hooligan be achieved?* The paper may be cited as Conrad, C. and Frosdick, S. (2011), 'Who are the Hooligans?' In J. Chalmers and S. Frosdick (Eds.) *More Safety and Security at Sports Grounds*, pp. 129-137. Rothersthorpe: Paragon Publishing.

Introduction

The principal researcher is a police officer who has spent a lot of time commanding public order units at 'Rovers United' football matches. At each match, officers have been briefed on details of known 'hooligans' so that they knew who to look out for. It appeared that the Football Intelligence Officer's identification of such 'hooligans' was subjectively based on the frequency and intensity of the subjects' interactions with police. A group of 160 'hooligans' was therefore known. Personal details were also available on a further 795 subjects who had been arrested at 'Rovers United' home matches. Given the privileged access to these two data sources, the initial idea for the research was to compare the two groups, aggregate the data and explore whether the aggregated profile could be used for predictive purposes.

A review of the literature on profiling quickly drew the conclusion that, even if it were possible, such predictive profiling ought not to be attempted for ethical reasons. The research therefore refocused on analysing the data sources to explore the more straightforward question, 'who are the hooligans?'

Defining a football 'hooligan' is difficult. Is this someone who regularly engages in violence at football matches and for whom the actual football is ancillary to the disorder? Is it the thug who throws darts at police horses and scaffolding clips at police officers? Are football hooligans those who have come to watch a game, are passionate about their local team and may find themselves in a crowd situation which results in fisticuffs? Or are they someone who, in a fit of rage at a refereeing decision, throws some orange peel onto the pitch? Given their behaviours and the criminal offences which they represent, all of these people are capable of being defined as football hooligans.

Previous Research

The majority of previous social science research has looked less at who the hooligans are and more at why they behave as they do. Nevertheless, various previous work has included 'profiling' data such as age, lifestyle and gender. The first was the Harrington (1968) report, sponsored by the Government, which suggested that football hooligans were mainly working class people from large cities with violent subcultures. A decade later, a study by Trivizas (1980) concluded that 80% of his sample of 652 persons charged with football offences was either manual workers or unemployed. 64% had no previous convictions and the average age was 19 years. Reviewing the previous work, Dunning, Murphy and Williams (1988) then summarised that,

> Most of the evidence on hooligan offenders suggest that they are generally in their late teens or their lower twenties, that they are mainly in manual or lower clerical occupations or, to a lesser extent, are unemployed or working in the 'grey' economy, and that they come mainly from working class backgrounds.

More recent sources have taken a different view on the question of social class. The self-confessed hooligan writers, Dougie and Eddy Brimson, suggest that 'the people who take part in football violence came, and come from all walks of life' (Brimson and Brimson, 1996 p.8) They add that they, 'have known many highly paid and highly skilled professional people who have been actively involved in both the organisation and the execution of football violence' (*Ibid.* p.9). They perhaps understandably take exception to Dunning, Murphy and Williams' comments, noting that, 'they believe us all to be illiterate morons, extreme right wing, unemployed thugs from broken homes with criminal backgrounds' (*Ibid.* p.53). Although they cite a handful of examples of fellow hooligans who are company directors and the like, the Brimson brothers work is rather more populist personal testimony than it is serious research.

In 2004, the West Yorkshire police website 'frequently asked questions' page posed the question, 'Are hooligans confined to one social class?' The answer they gave was,

No, we are aware of the identity of many football hooligans and they come from many different backgrounds. The notion that hooligans are form working class backgrounds is not true nowadays, if it ever was. The persons involved have many different occupations – labourers, unemployed, and office workers. Recent arrests in West Yorkshire have ranged from a deep-sea fisherman in Grimsby to a managing director of a company in the Home Counties.

Both these sources are anecdotal. The scarcity of other sources suggested a lack of contemporary empirical data on the gender, age, ethnicity and employment status of football 'hooligans'. This made this research project clearly worthwhile in 2005. The continued lack of such data in the public domain means the publication of the results is still useful in 2011.

Methods and Ethics

The personal characteristics of two groups of subjects were collated and analysed. The first group of 160 subjects were those who had been identified by the Football Intelligence Officer (FIO) as having come to notice either following conviction at Court or by police officers who had witnessed their involvement in disorderly or criminal behaviour at and around football matches. 40 of these subjects had been deemed to be 'Category C' or 'hard-core' hooligans because of the frequency with which they had come to notice. Although the FIO's criteria for selecting subjects were subjective, nevertheless the files held on them were comprehensive and had been built up over a long period of intense observations. These 160 subjects were termed the 'hooligan group' because they appeared to be central in organising and motivating others in pre-planned or spontaneous disorder and were recognisable amongst other fans as being a distinct group who travelled, drank and stood together at matches.

The second group of 795 other subjects were those who had actually been arrested for any offence at a 'Rovers United' home match during the 2003/04 season, whether this was drinking in view of the match, having a forged ticket, criminal damage, assaults or public disorder.

The data on the two groups was then compared to see if the subjective profiling done by the FIO matched the data on those who had been actually been arrested.

Proper authority was sought before the study was commenced. The anonymity of individuals was preserved by anonymising the data during the collection process. This does create the problem that the second group of 795 arrested persons might have included some of the 160 'hooligan group' members, but the ethical requirement for anonymity means there was no way of separating them out. The identity of the club where the research was carried out has been protected by using the pseudonym 'Rovers United'.

Findings

The 'Hooligan Group'

Table One shows the ethnicity and gender of the 'hooligan group'. The ethnicity was not broken down any further than White, Asian or Black because this was how the source data was categorised.

Table One – 'Hooligan Group' Gender and Ethnicity

Male	Female	White	Asian	Black
160	0	144	3	13

No females formed part of the 'hooligan group' studied by the FIO. During private conversations, he stated that there were in fact a few girls who followed the main hooligan group but played no significant part in their disorder activities. This supported the 1968 Harrington Report in which only one of the 497 hooligan subjects was female.

The ethnicity breakdown shows that the majority of the group (90%) were white. Black subjects formed 8% of the group and Asians a minority 2%. The location of 'Rovers United' was a deprived inner city area where 196 different languages were spoken. The diversity of the hooligan group did not match the diversity of the area in which the club was situated. This leads one to suggest that the group members came from outside the area, perhaps as a result of their families moving away from city life after the Second World War, but retaining their historical links with the club.

Table Two shows the age ranges of the 'hooligan group'.

Table Two – 'Hooligan Group' Ages

15-20	21-25	26-30	31-35	36-40	41-45	46+	Total
0	12	12	50	48	38	0	160

It is interesting to note that the 'hooligan group' was somewhat older than one would expect from the previous research, which, as we have seen, refers to the typical football hooligan as being in their late teens or early twenties. Yet this 'hooligan group' has more than three-quarters of its members aged over 30, more than half aged over 35 and about a quarter aged over 40. The 'hooligan group' at 'Rovers United' thus appeared to be ten to twenty years older than the previous studies would suggest.

Given the passage of time, can it be that the subjects who were studied in the 1980s and the members of the 'hooligan group' were in fact the same generation of people? Had the 'young hooligans' of the 1980s grown up to become the hooligans of the 1990s and 2000s? Would football hooliganism therefore eventually die out?

It is interesting to hypothesise where the 'missing' youngsters had gone. Perhaps with greater public intolerance of anti-social behaviour and the use of Anti-Social Behaviour Orders (ASBOs), there were fewer youths willing to risk being caught? Perhaps the group of youths who would have become hooligans twenty years ago had needed to find another outlet for their delinquency because of the anti-disorder stadia infrastructure of CCTV and increased stewarding? The Football Offences Act (1991) also went a long way to dissuading fans from engaging in disorder and crime at matches.

The 'Arrested Persons'

Table Three shows the 795 subjects who were arrested at 'Rovers United' home matches during the 2003/04 season, regardless of whether they were home or away fans. This provides a useful 'check and balance' to see if the FIO's subjective study of hooligans mirrored the demographics of those who were actually getting arrested.

Of course some of the 160 'hooligans' may form part of the 795 subjects, but there is no way of establishing that or indeed knowing if the same person has been arrested more than once in the season. However the large sample size should iron these issues out.

Table Three – 'Arrested Persons' Gender and Ethnicity

Male	Female	White	Asian	Black
790	5	767	15	12

As with the Rovers hooligan group, white males form the majority of the subjects. Only five women were arrested and account for less than 1% of the total group. Asian and Black arrestees compose a similar number of persons arrested (less than 2% each), whereas white subjects make up the majority of 97%.

Table Four shows the age ranges of the arrested persons.

Table Four – 'Arrested Persons' Ages

15-20	21-25	26-30	31-35	36-40	41-45	46+	Total
9	45	114	157	140	10	10	795

The clear majority of subjects arrested at 'Rovers United' home matches were aged between 26 and 40, representing 52% of the total. This is again out of line with the previous studies which described hooligans as being young men in their late teens and early twenties.

Comparing the Two Groups' Ages and Ethnicities

There are clear comparisons between the age ranges of the two groups. The only striking difference is that there was a higher percentage of those aged 26-30 in the arrested persons group (14.3%) than in the FIO's group (7.5%). This could be because the younger persons were not engaging in disorderly behaviour but were those arrested for other football-related offences such as drinking alcohol in view of the pitch.

The ethnicity data do not show anything unexpected. In line with previous studies, the vast majority of hooligans were indeed white.

Employment Classification

The 'hooligan group' data on employment classification is more accurate than the arrested persons group because the FIO has researched the hooligan's life styles. The arrested persons, however, when asked on arrest what their occupation is, may either deliberately give wrong information, perhaps to exaggerate their status, or else say nothing. In the former case, the data is recorded at face value. In the latter case, the person will usually be shown as unemployed.

The employment classification was coded by the researcher on a subjective 'best guess' basis. 'Unemployed' was where the subject self-defined as such or failed to give an occupation and was so classified by the custody officer. 'Unskilled' occupations included labourers and 'semi-skilled' included painters, lorry drivers and shop workers. 'Semi-professional' included sales persons and supervisors, whilst 'professional' included nurses, accountants, insurance brokers and stock brokers. 'Managers' referred to company management staff.

Table Five – Employment Classifications

Classification	Hooligan Group	Arrested Persons
Unemployed	24 (15%)	43 (5%)
Unskilled	58 (36%)	177 (22%)
Semi-skilled	49 (31%)	292 (37%)
Semi-professional	25 (16%)	204 (26%)
Professional	3 (2%)	74 (9%)
Management	1 (1%)	5 (1%)
Total	160	795

Given the tendency for arrested persons to exaggerate their employment status, the two data sets are broadly consistent, showing that the majority of both groups were semi-skilled at best. This is again consistent with the previous studies.

Previous Convictions

Since resource and timescale issues meant it was impracticable for the research to code the previous convictions of everyone in both groups, this part of the study was limited to the 40 'hard-core' members of the 'hooligan group'.

Table Six – Previous Convictions of 40 'Hard-Core' Hooligans

	1	2	3	4	5	6	7	8	9	10
Disorder	2	4	2	5	3	2	5	20	4	4
Assault	0	4	1	0	2	3	2	13	1	0
Drugs	2	0	0	1	0	0	0	0	0	0
Autocrime	1	0	3	0	1	2	0	5	0	0
Damage	0	0	0	1	0	0	1	2	0	0
Dishonesty	1	0	1	1	5	8	3	24	0	0
Total	6	8	7	8	11	15	11	59	5	4

	11	12	13	14	15	16	17	18	19	20
Disorder	3	1	1	3	2	2	4	3	7	6
Assault	1	2	4	3	1	2	1	4	5	1
Drugs	0	0	2	0	0	0	1	0	2	0
Autocrime	0	1	0	0	0	0	2	1	3	0
Damage	0	1	0	0	1	0	0	0	2	0
Dishonesty	1	0	0	2	1	3	0	3	4	1
Total	5	5	7	8	5	7	8	11	23	8

	21	22	23	24	25	26	27	28	29	30
Disorder	3	2	1	1	2	2	1	3	4	1
Assault	0	1	2	2	1	5	1	1	2	2
Drugs	4	2	0	0	0	0	0	0	0	0
Autocrime	1	0	1	0	1	2	0	2	0	1
Damage	3	0	2	1	1	0	1	0	2	0
Dishonesty	8	1	1	1	2	4	0	7	1	0
Total	19	6	7	5	7	13	3	13	9	4

	31	32	33	34	35	36	37	38	39	40
Disorder	2	1	11	4	2	3	1	1	12	1
Assault	1	0	4	1	0	0	0	2	5	0
Drugs	2	1	0	0	1	0	0	0	0	0
Autocrime	0	1	1	0	0	0	1	5	1	0
Damage	0	1	4	1	0	1	2	0	9	2
Dishonesty	1	1	3	0	0	1	0	1	14	1
Total	6	5	23	6	3	5	4	9	41	4

Disorder refers to public order and football-related offences. *Assault* goes from common assault to grievous bodily harm. *Drugs* includes all misuse of drugs offences. *Autocrime* includes all vehicle offences except vehicle theft, which is dishonesty. *Damage* includes all offences under the Criminal Damage Act 1971. *Dishonesty* includes all offences under the Theft Acts 1968 and 1978.

Table Six shows that every one of the 40 members of the 'hard-core' group did indeed have a history of previous convictions. On an averages basis, the group members typically had three previous convictions for disorder, two previous convictions for dishonesty and two more for assault. Although this is clearly a small sample and not at all representative of either of the main groups studied, it is perhaps unsurprising that a 'hard-core hooligan' should have convictions for these types of offences.

Conclusion

This work began during 'Rovers United' home matches when the researcher and FIO attempted to differentiate hooligans from legitimate fans. Existing profiling by the FIO was based on subjective observation. This study therefore explored the possibility of more objective profiling techniques. The results showed that the group of individuals engaged in criminality at football matches was male, white and predominantly working class. This was in line with previous studies. However the results also showed that football hooligans were some ten to twenty years older than previous studies had suggested.

If similar results were obtained through research at other clubs, there might be a national phenomenon of hooliganism either growing up or else moving out of football. It may be that the FIO-profiled 'hooligans' and those who are getting arrested now are the same people who were being arrested ten to twenty years ago. If that pattern continues, then disorder and hooliganism may 'grow out' of football, as the increasing ages of the hooligans will eventually prevent them from engaging in active disorder.

References

Brimson, D. and Brimson, E. (1996) *Everywhere We Go – Behind the Matchday Madness.* London: Headline.

Harrington, J.A. (1968) Soccer Hooliganism. Bristol: John Wright.

Dunning, E., Murphy, P. and Williams, J. (1988) *The Roots of Football Hooliganism: An Historical and Sociological Study.* London: Routledge and Kegan Paul.

Trivizas, E. (1980) 'Offences and Offenders in Football Crowd Disorder', *British Journal of Criminology*, 20(3): 281-283.

2.3. COMMENTARY BY STEVE FROSDICK – WHO ARE THE HOOLIGANS?

Chris Conrad studied for a Masters degree at the University of Portsmouth and it was my honour to be his dissertation supervisor. It was quickly obvious that Conrad had uniquely privileged access to a very rich data source. His job role meant that he was able to view original police records concerning a major English football club. He could thus collate and analyse a range of characteristics of persons being monitored by the local Football Intelligence Officer, as well as of persons actually arrested at the club's matches.

Conrad took an important academic journey to come to the conclusion that there were substantial theoretical, ethical and practical reasons for not seeking to predictively profile people as football hooligans on the basis of their fit with certain demographics. This journey was an important part of his postgraduate studies but has been edited out of the published essay. What is unique about Conrad's work and makes it worth publishing is his access to data, and, above all, his findings.

Not since 1988 has there been an empirical study of who the hooligans are as opposed to why they behave as they do. A large data set from 2003/04, albeit restricted to one club, therefore makes an important contribution to knowledge about football hooliganism.

Conrad's research confirmed the findings of previous studies in terms of the gender, ethnicity and social class of football hooligans. But what is fascinating are his findings about age. His conclusion that football hooligans were getting older is solid and empirically grounded, but confined to one club. He does however have anecdotal support from the online journalist, Duleep Allirajah, who writes for *Spiked*. On 30 May 2002, Allirajah commented,

> Hooligans just seem to get older and fatter, particular when you see the footage from the 1980s of skinny teenagers in Pringle jumpers running amok. Whereas hooliganism in the 1970s and 80s was primarily an adolescent phenomenon, today it is largely the preserve of portly forty-something *hoolidads*. I expect they'll be trashing day centres and dial-a-ride minibuses in 20 years time.

We may thus feel fairly confident that Conrad's study supports the notion that the football hooligans of the early noughties were older than those of the late twentieth century.

But to what extent might this still be the case in 2011? Fast-forwarding to 2010, evidence began to emerge of a new younger generation of football hooligans. Writing for BBC online on 8 October 2010, Rowan Bridge reported on Association of Chief Police Officer (ACPO) statistics which showed there were now 290 teenagers who were the subject of Football Banning Orders. Furthermore, 47% of reported football disorder incidents in England, Wales and Northern Ireland the previous season had involved youths. Bridge quoted Assistant Chief Constable Andy Holt, the ACPO spokesperson on football-related disorder, as saying that,

> If they're engaging in football-related disorder at an earlier age then we're going to be stuck with that sort of behaviour potentially for some while. So it is something that we are acutely aware of. People are coming through and engaging in football disorder who perhaps weren't around in the heyday of football violence 15-20 years ago. So it is a worrying trend that the younger element are starting to pick up on this sort of behaviour.

By way of supporting evidence, I have carried out match day observations with the local police at my own club (Southampton) in 2011 and seen evidence of a group of teenage risk supporters.

2.4. CONFLICT MANAGEMENT

The original citation for this article is Frosdick, S. and Joyce, G. (2005) 'Conflict Managers', *Stadium and Arena Management*, August 2005, pp. 24-26.

Steve Frosdick and Graham Joyce explain how stewards in the UK are receiving additional training on how to deal with conflict in the stadium.

Spectator behaviour often presents problems. Historically these were dealt with by the police. More recently, stewards have become the first line response – even including the ejection of fans from the stadium. This trend is spreading across Europe. New regulatory requirements in the UK mean that all football stewards now need to be trained on how to deal with conflict in the stadium. This article therefore looks at the work recently undertaken to develop a conflict management module within the UK Training Package for Stewarding at Football Grounds.

The training package was previously updated in 2003 and covered seven training modules: general responsibilities; maintaining a safe environment; response to spectators, emergency aid, basic fire safety; contingency and evacuation plans; and dealing with racism and disability discrimination.

There has been a substantial debate in the UK as to whether stewards are security staff. If so, they would fall foul of the licensing regime of the new Security Industry Authority. Notwithstanding that it was clear that the Government had never intended that stewards should be licensed, it has taken many months for common sense to prevail – but on the strict understanding that stewards will receive additional training in conflict management.

The Training Package for Stewarding at Football Grounds has therefore been further revised to include a new module on this subject. The new training module was drafted by Graham Joyce, a former personal safety trainer with Dorset Police and the current Safety Officer at Yeovil Town FC. The module was edited and incorporated within the Training Package by *S&AM* contributor Steve Frosdick.

The new training module aims to enable stewards to identify and manage conflict situations. It also aims to enable 'designated' stewards (i.e. those who have volunteered, been selected and received the practical training) to be able to undertake safety ejection procedures where appropriate. As with the seven preceding modules, the new module has been designed to assist in the safety management of the venue. Ejections are carried out for the safety of the offender or those around them. Where serious security incidents occur, the matter should always be referred to the police.

Like the rest of the training package, the new training module has been written using Microsoft PowerPoint presentation software. So, for each topic, there are slides and notes pages which include the learning objectives, the suggested training content, the assessment criteria, and the suggested assessment methods.

Delivering this training requires considerable expertise. It is essential that trainers are occupationally competent and appropriately insured, so it will be usual for clubs to commission this training from a specialist trainer.

The conflict management training covers seven main topics. The first topic is 'Stewards and the Law', which seeks to familiarise stewards with the legal aspects of the use of force. Section 3 of the Criminal Law Act 1967 provides the legal definition that 'A person may use such force as is reasonable in the circumstances in the prevention of crime, or in the effecting or assisting in the lawful arrest of offenders or suspected offenders or persons unlawfully at large.'

They key concept is the word 'reasonable'. Stewards may use force to deal with offenders, providing that the force is reasonable in the circumstances; an absolute necessity; the minimum amount necessary for the purpose; and proportionate to the seriousness of the offence. People are often not aware that powers of arrest are not always limited to police officers. Certain serious crimes have a particular legal status which means that, as well as police officers, any person, including stewards, have certain powers of arrest too.

The next topic aims to familiarise stewards with the key principles of 'Conflict Resolution'. Looking first at communication, the key point is that what you say forms only a small part – about 7% – of your message. Your vocal tone, volume, intonation, pitch and pace convey about 38% of the message, whilst your body language or non-verbal communication form about 55%.

When communicating in a potential conflict situation, stewards are encouraged to remember the mnemonic 'LEAPS':

- Listen – listen actively;
- Empathise – show understanding;
- Ask – if you need more information;
- Paraphrase – facts in your words; and
- Summarise – condense the facts.

A simple model used in training for people who deal exclusively in conflict and people management is known as 'Betari's Box' (See Figure One).

Figure One: Betari's Box

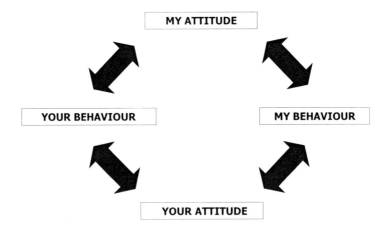

The model shows the way in which stewards and subjects can get locked into a cycle of behaviour which, if it remains unchecked, can escalate out of control. Because the role of a steward is to deal effectively with a situation, and because stewards are the very people within the stadium complex who have authority, it is their role to break the cycle of attitude and behaviour.

When stewards are confronted by an angry person, they should try to preserve their personal space. One way to do this is to break away or back off and to raise your palms. This tells the person that you do not accept their behaviour and that you do not want them to come closer. If stewards see a colleague using this posture, they may be facing a difficult situation that might require assistance.

'Initial Action and Options' looks to enable stewards to identify and deal appropriately with instances of spectator misconduct which may compromise safety. The priority question to be asked in any such situation is this – does this person need to be removed immediately? Stewards must not wade straight in to a crowd situation without careful planning and preparation. It is often not necessary to go straight into the crowd. It is sometimes appropriate to wait until the offender goes onto the concourse or even to wait until the conclusion of the match. There is plenty of video footage of poor decision-making causing stewards and/or police to go into the crowd unnecessarily and inflame a situation.

Stewards are encouraged to follow the 'L A A R' (Look and Listen, Assess the Situation, Act Appropriately and Report) action process developed for other modules. Where the appropriate action is confined to doing nothing, keeping observation or giving advice or a warning, stewards should remember to report the facts appropriately.

Where the appropriate action is to eject or even arrest the offender, then there are two possible approaches. Designated stewards may proceed to eject or arrest the offender in accordance with their training and club policy using no more force than is reasonable and necessary in the circumstances. Stewards who are not designated will inform their supervisor in order that the police or designated stewards may be deployed.

The 'Use of Force' topic gives the steward the points to consider when reasonable force is required to be used. There are four basic questions to consider. Is there a need to use force? What is the relationship between the resistance offered and the force used? Can control be established without causing injury? Is the force being applied in good faith?

Where it has been determined that the use of force is absolutely necessary in the circumstances, then the stewards need to consider whether such use of force is

- Tactically sound –will it work in that stadium area?
- Medically sound – is there potential for injury?
- Legally sound – is this a reasonable use of force, in line with training and policy?

The Steward must be able to show they had the perception that the person had the opportunity, ability and intention to do them or others harm (or were reckless about harm being caused).

Common Law then provides a defence of 'self defence' which may be relied on by stewards who use reasonable force to deal with an offender. However a steward may be committing an assault if they use force maliciously or where it is not absolutely necessary, or if they use more force than is reasonably necessary for the purpose.

Under 'Evidence', the training helps the steward understand the need for evidence to support their actions. CCTV footage provides excellent supporting evidence for descriptions of actions taken within the stadium complex. Before any action is taken, the situation should be covered by a CCTV camera with video recording in place. Original notes of the incident should be made as soon as practicable after the incident, including what was heard, what was seen, how the steward felt, what they did, and the actions of others working with them.

For the next topic, the steward needs to understand and at all times apply the maintenance of 'Personal Safety'. In order to anticipate and recognise the risk involved in a potential use of force situation, stewards need to consider what is known about the offender and their behaviour. Key questions include: is the subject compliant or aggressive? Is the subject showing any verbal resistance or gestures? Is there passive or active resistance from the subject? If the resistance is active, is this aggressive or even aggravated, e.g. involving a weapon?

Where such resistance exists, planning and preparation will be required to remove or avoid the risk. This may involve decisions about timing, numbers of personnel and the involvement of the police. The steward's presence and bearing will have a major impact on the offender's attitude and behaviour – remember the Betari's Box model. Finally under this topic, stewards whose job requires the use of personal protective equipment must always use the official equipment provided.

The last topic deals with 'Escort and Safety Ejection Techniques'. All stewards need to be aware of these, whilst designated stewards need to be able to apply them in practice.

[The basic escort hold involves holding the person's wrist with one hand and underneath the shoulder with the other]. Note that this hold is never applied by a designated steward on their own. The basic escort is always carried out by a pair of designated stewards, one each side of the subject. For this reason, designated stewards should know who they will 'buddy up' with for conflict resolution or escort and safety ejection purposes.

Where the offender shows active resistance, or the designated steward reasonably perceives the likelihood of such active resistance, then the reinforced escort is used. [This involves enclosing rather than simply holding the person's shoulder]. Again, the reinforced escort is always carried out by a minimum of two designated stewards. In many cases, a third designated steward will be needed to control the offender's head in order to prevent injury. In cases of serious or continued resistance, then it would be normal for the police to become involved.

There are a number of other advanced holds which may be taught to and used by designated stewards at some grounds.

Offenders who are to be ejected or who have been arrested may be taken in the first instance to the 'police room' or similar facility within the stadium complex. Where it exists, stewards must be aware of the location of this detention facility and the correct way of getting there. It is usually bad practice to travel around the pitch perimeter. The offender should normally be taken down the nearest vomitory or exit and escorted through the concourses or even around the outside of the ground.

The new training module is now being rolled out at football clubs across the UK in preparation for the 2005/06 season. The UK football authorities are once again setting the standard for stewards training. The new module represents a further enhancement in the professionalisation of stewarding and we have been privileged to be part of that process.

2.4. COMMENTARY BY JIM CHALMERS – CONFLICT MANAGEMENT

The article written by Frosdick and Joyce explains the introduction in 2005 of a conflict management module into the joint football authorities' stewards training package. This was a further addition to the original stewards training package which is dealt with in Part V of *Safety and Security at Sports Grounds*. The article fully explains the background and content of the conflict management training and requires no further comment from me in this regard. In this commentary I will bring the topic up to date by referring to the managing conflict module in the brand new stewards training package, *On the Ball*, introduced by the English and Welsh football authorities in October 2010.

There are many factors that contribute to the pleasant and safe experience that fans should enjoy at our football grounds. One of these factors is how stewards react to and manage conflict situations. It is therefore very important to train stewards how to recognise and respond to any conflict they are likely to face in their role.

What I felt was missing in the article was for conflict to be defined, since this should provide the starting point for any training. This has been resolved in the new *On the Ball* module with conflict defined as,

> A disagreement through which the parties involved perceive a threat to their needs, interests or concerns.

Emerging from this simple definition, *On the Ball* highlights several important points.

> *Disagreement.* Generally we are aware there is some level of difference in the positions of the two or more parties involved in a conflict. Conflict tends to be accompanied by significant levels of misunderstanding and the true disagreement may be different from the perceived disagreement. If we can understand the true areas of disagreement, this will help us solve the right problems and manage the needs of the parties.

Parties involved. We often get confused over who is involved in conflict. Sometimes people are surprised to learn they are a party to a conflict while at other times we are shocked to learn we are not included in a disagreement. On many occasions family, friends and colleagues readily 'take sides' based upon current perceptions of the issues, past issues and relationships, roles within the organisation and other factors. The parties concerned can become an elusive element to define.

Perceived threat. People respond to the perceived rather than the true threat facing them and behaviours, feelings and ongoing responses become modified by that evolving sense of threat they confront. If we can work to understand the true threat and develop solutions that address it we are acting constructively to manage conflict.

Since the article was written, Graham Joyce has remained very involved in personal safety training and is still very much an expert in this area of managing conflict. His initiative in developing the original module is indicative of the multiple skills base which exists within the Football Safety Officers' Association and it is to his credit that the training was developed within the football industry rather than from any external source.

The conflict management module from 2005 was universally accepted across all the football leagues in England and Wales and I have used it at my own club, Kidderminster Harriers FC, ever since it was introduced. The success of the module lies in the way Joyce and Frosdick combined theory with practice. As a trainer and assessor myself, I found the best training medium to be simulated conflict scenarios in a classroom setting. The stewards would role play conflict situations to examine how they and their colleagues would respond to the situation. They found this to be interesting, rewarding and stimulating. These sessions also provided me with an insight into the character and temperament of my stewards and their ability to manage the stress of conflict. The training also provided some surprises, with some whom I thought might be weak and indecisive in conflict proving to be positive and assertive and vice versa. I learned more about my stewards' strengths and weaknesses in this module than in any of their other training.

During the training the stewards found the input on 'Betari's Box' – how to break the cycle of behaviour which could lead to conflict – the most rewarding. It helped stewards understand the difference between talking themselves out of trouble and talking themselves into it. They also said that for the first time they came to understand how simple communication and body language techniques could help resolve conflict, not only in their role as stewards, but in their everyday lives at work, home and play. One steward explained how they were constantly in conflict with their manager at work and how this was affecting them mentally and physically. After the training session they took a look at how they spoke to and expressed by body language their attitude towards the manager. They realised that the conflict was not the manager's fault but their own! The steward was able to adjust their style at work and this resolved the stress and anxiety they had suffered for some years. In another case a steward had for years been involved in a dispute with a neighbour over a boundary fence. After the training, they changed their approach to the neighbour which resulted in the problem being amicably resolved.

The success of the conflict management training can be judged from the review which I carry out with each steward at the end of their training and assessment programme. In the review I ask every steward to rate the top three training modules for both 'interest' and 'usefulness'. In the 2009/10 season training programme the overall top three modules for 'interest' were conflict management, emergency aid and the general responsibilities of a steward. The top three for 'usefulness' were emergency aid, conflict management and basic fire safety awareness.

In discussing the responses with my stewards it was clear that the training modules which scored highly in both categories were those which they felt would have an impact on their everyday lives. Conflict exists in society and knowing and understanding how to manage this better is beneficial. Over the years, stewards have also explained how they have used their emergency aid and basic fire safety awareness training in responding to real life situations. In one case a steward was able to revive a man who had collapsed in the work place and had stopped breathing. In another case a steward was able to deal with a chip pan fire in a neighbour's house as result of the fire safety awareness training.

So is conflict management training necessary and has it proved of value in stewards training and practice? In my opinion the answer to both questions is a resounding 'Yes'. Conflict exists in every walk of life. In the football environment, conflict exists between the teams and between both sets of supporters and it will generally be the steward who finds themselves in the middle. How many times do you see on television fights involving players or supporters where the stewards are the first line of response and have to try to restore normality? However it is not just acts of violence or disorder which can bring a steward into a conflict situation. Even minor incidents can quickly escalate out of control if a steward does not respond in a calm, disciplined and rational way. I tell my stewards in their conflict management training that it is they who have had the benefit of conflict management training, not the supporters, so if anyone is going to break the cycle of conflict then it must be the stewards.

Examples of minor incidents which occur at my club and which can escalate unless managed properly include complaints from fans about the quality of the food and drink being sold, running out of match day programmes, someone sitting in the wrong seat, complaints about refereeing decisions, grievances about the chairman and board of directors, the incompetence of the manager, people smoking in a non smoking area, bringing drink into the viewing area against ground regulations, persistently standing in a seated area, a car parked in the wrong place on the club car park, the noise emanating from a fan with a large drum on the terrace and so on and so on. Every safety officer will tell you the same story which is that you can please some of the people some of the time but not all of the people all of the time. Whatever the complaint or grievance, it is the way the steward manages that potential conflict situation which will mean a peaceful resolution or escalation into an ejection scenario.

To emphasise the necessity and value of the managing conflict training, the module in *On the Ball* is a standalone module in its own right. The module is based on the concepts of managing conflict developed by Joyce and Frosdick but the recommended training style differs considerably. The new module is divided into two training sessions and has a recommended training time of three and a half hours. Session one deals with the theory of managing conflict whilst session two deals with the practical response to a conflict scenario.

The main differences between the former and the new modules is that the *On the Ball* resource is,

> ... an interactive, engaging and informative platform; placing the focus on learning by experience as opposed to learning by teaching. The programme centres on delegate centred exercises that allows stewards to learn with and from each other in a way that will complement the practical nature of the stewarding role. In this respect there is a far greater emphasis in the new module on group activity, role playing interaction and debating responses to conflict situations. There is far less emphasis on Powerpoint usage and far greater emphasis on video scenarios to provide the opportunity to discuss and debate spectator and steward reactions. There are seven training videos in Module 5 and all of them provide excellent visual representations of conflict both from a spectator and steward perspective. They provide the ideal opportunity for stewards to debate the difference between good and bad managing conflict experiences.

The new videos speak volumes in helping stewards understand the difference between good and bad managing conflict responses. The new module relies more on the trainer encouraging discussion on managing conflict than the traditional sit down and be talked at by the trainer. On a selfish note therefore the new module represents more my style of managing conflict training and the videos provide me with something which has been lacking in my training tool kit.

The new module has advanced the use of technology in the steward training environment and I believe this will make the training more interesting, more stimulating and more exciting for both the trainer and the stewards. I certainly look forward to using the new training tool. However as the new programme is gradually rolled out across the country it will be interesting to gauge the responses of different safety officers to the suggested new style of training.

The importance of managing conflict training can be judged from the possible repercussions for stewards and their clubs if allegations of improper use of force are made in a conflict situation. In a small piece of non academic, non scientific research which I conducted with my FSOA colleagues in January 2011 I posed the questions:

- Please advise me of details of any steward prosecuted for any alleged use of force whilst carrying out stewarding duties at a club.

- Please advise me of details of any steward or club having civil action taken against them for damages as a result of any alleged use of force whilst carrying out stewarding duties at a club.

- Please advise me of any complaints you have received about any alleged use of force by stewards whilst carrying out stewarding duties at a club.

Anonymity was guaranteed in any responses I received. The research was carried out through the forum section of the FSOA website with negative responses not required. 85 of my colleagues logged onto this topic and the responses I received included the following cases.

In a local derby fixture between Manchester United and Manchester City at Old Trafford in September 2009, a City supporter who was being escorted out of the ground by two United stewards alleged that they shoved him down some steps fracturing his left heel and right shin. He reported this to the police and both stewards were charged with assault. At a Crown Court hearing in November 2010 the jury returned a 'not guilty' verdict for both men. This case was reported in the press.

At another club during a fracas inside the stadium it was alleged that a steward retaliated against the supporters involved. The steward and a number of fans were arrested and charged but the charges were later dismissed.

There was another case where a steward from a visiting club alleged that excessive force was used by stewards during the course of an ejection. This matter is being pursued through the civil courts but is being strongly defended by the stewards involved and their club.

My research therefore found no evidence of any steward being successfully prosecuted either through the criminal or civil courts for alleged misuse of force during the course of their duties.

I appreciate that my colleagues may well have been reluctant to share with me details of any unnecessary use of force by their stewards in the course of their duties but over the years as President of the FSOA I must admit that this has never been an issue of concern raised at any national or regional meeting or by the police or the sports regulatory bodies. I am fairly confident that were this to be something which was happening on any regular basis I would have heard about it through these various bodies, particularly the police. So in the absence of any evidence to the contrary it may be reasonably concluded that stewards by and large carry out their duties having due regard to their training in managing conflict.

In the 2009/10 season there was a total spectator attendance in excess of 39 million at regulated football matches in England and Wales. At every fixture the potential for conflict will always exist given that there will always be two sets of opposing fans in a contained and closed arena. It is estimated that there are over 14,000 stewards employed at football clubs in England and Wales and it is they who will provide the first line of response to any conflict situation. During the 2009/10 season 47% of all matches were classed as 'police free', indicating the confidence the sports ground regulatory bodies have in the ability of the club safety management personnel to safely manage their events, including managing conflict.

This is certainly the case at my club when we have had only one 'policed' fixture in five seasons. The Safety Advisory Group are totally confident in our ability to manage our own affairs. That includes being able to manage conflict and indicates at a national level the success story of managing conflict training in England and Wales.

PART III – CASE STUDIES

Introduction

This part of the book contains six UK and European case studies of different aspects of safety and security at sports grounds. The cases cover responses to violence in France, safe standing in Germany, non-league football in England, business continuity after floods and storm damage in football and horse racing, and preparations for the London 2012 Olympic Games.

3.1. Stade Marcel Picot and Parc des Princes

This *Stadium and Arena Management* article from 2007 covers two French football grounds in Nancy and Paris. Both had experienced problems with violence; Nancy with the visit of the Feyenoord of Rotterdam and Paris with the murder of a Paris Saint Germain fan. Frosdick reports on a safety and security assignment he carried out in Nancy and on a study visit he organised for the City of Paris. The article concludes with an assessment of the impact of these interventions.

The commentary looks beyond this French work to other UK 'exports' of safety and security expertise around the world, including Chalmers' own work in Guatemala following the Mateo Flores stadium disaster.

3.2. 'Safe' Standing in Dortmund

This *Stadium and Arena Management* article from 2007 looks at developments in the debate about standing up to watch football matches. One part of the debate concerns what to do about fans who persistently stand in all-seated areas. The other part is about whether safe standing areas might be re-introduced to the top two divisions of football in England and Wales. As part of his research, Frosdick visited Borussia Dortmund's 25,000 capacity Südtribune in Germany, the largest standing terrace in Europe. Whilst he had reservations about some aspects of the design and management of this terrace, Frosdick could not deny the fantastic atmosphere generated by the crowd's expression of collective identity.

The accompanying commentary notes that persistent standing has become more and more pervasive and outlines the efforts made to manage this issue. Chalmers notes how safety officers have gradually come to the view that persistent standing is more of a customer service issue than it is a safety one. In order to avoid creating public order problems, safety officers have to accept the inevitable – that persistent standing is here to stay – and manage around it as best they can.

The commentary also brings the debate on safe standing up to date by referring to Don Foster's 2011 Private Members Bill and its passage to a second reading in the UK Parliament. Speaking as an expert individual rather than in his role of President of the Football Safety Officers' Association, Chalmers' clear view is that he fully supports the call for safe standing to be allowed to return to all levels of UK football. He is one of the first safety officers to publicly express this view, which is not currently supported by the UK football authorities.

3.3. Smaller Scale at Stevenage Borough

This 2008 article from *Stadium and Arena Management* shows how non-league football safety officers face the same array of safety and security issues as the colleagues in the higher leagues – but on a smaller scale.

Being a non-league safety officer himself, Chalmers commentary empathises with the article. His commentary highlights the financial difficulties facing non-league clubs and the implications these can have for safety standards. On the plus side, smaller scale allows stronger relationships to develop, provides the satisfaction of delivering safety despite sparse resources, and gives aspiring safety officers a career stepping stone.

3.4. Flooding at Hillsborough Stadium

In this *Stadium and Arena Management* article from 2008, Frosdick interviews Alan Roberts about the seven key business continuity lessons to be learned from the June 2007 floods at the Hillsborough Stadium, Sheffield. A Herculean effort from all sides ensured that the club was able to fulfil its fixture commitments for the new season.

3.5. Storm Damage at Cheltenham Racecourse

In a further *Stadium and Arena Management* article from 2008, Frosdick talks with Cheltenham Managing Director, Edward Gillespie, about his venue's extraordinary business continuity recovery from overnight storm damage and the loss of the a full day's racing.

Chalmers commentary deals with both the business continuity articles together. Integrated contingency planning and the exercising of such plans are two of Chalmers' key areas of expertise. He therefore uses the commentary to outline the key principles behind these concepts.

3.6. London 2012

This *Stadium and Arena Management* article from 2009 looks at progress with the safety and security preparations for the London 2012 Olympic Games. Frosdick discusses the five 'S's of strategy, stakeholders, staffing, students and society, highlighting the novel 'Bridging the Gap' initiative to bring further education college students into the London 2012 and legacy workforce.

Cross reference is made to Jim Chalmers detailed update on London 2012 in his commentary on article 5.2. in Part V of this book.

3.1. STADE MARCEL PICOT AND PARC DES PRINCES

The original citation for this article is Frosdick, S. (2007) 'French Safety Focus', *Stadium and Arena Management*, October 2007, p. 20-23.

Steve Frosdick reports on problems and the search for solutions in French football over the last two seasons.

Safety and security problems have been associated with football, both whenever it has been played throughout history and wherever it has been played across the world. France has been no exception to this principle. The most serious French incident was in Bastia, Corsica in 1992, when 17 people were killed by the collapse of a temporary stand. More recently, in April 2000, there were serious problems for English fans from Arsenal at their UEFA Cup semi-final at the Stade Felix-Bollaert in Lens. Supporters complained of being crushed in overcrowded sections of the ground and of being beaten by riot police batons.

The season 2006/07 saw at least four further serious incidents. On 28 November 2006, following the murder of a Paris Saint Germain (PSG) fan after a UEFA Cup match, the authorities and the club together ordered the closure of the lower tier of the Boulogne stand at the Parc des Princes. Two days later, Feyenoord of Holland visited Nancy-Lorraine (ASNL), also in the UEFA Cup. The Feyenoord supporters smashed the plexiglass segregation barrier in the Stade Marcel Picot and attacked the security forces. Play was interrupted for twenty minutes and the match completed in a surreal atmosphere after the Nancy fans had been evacuated from the stadium. Back at Lens in February 2007, the Stade Felix-Bollaert was being used by Lille for a UEFA Champions League match. The Manchester United fans made similar complaints to those of Arsenal two years previously. One fan was quoted as saying, "I couldn't believe the state of the ground. We were fenced in like cattle only treated worse." The police, he said, had been barbaric. Lille were later fined by UEFA for the safety and security breaches. Finally, in March 2007, a match between St Etienne and Lyon was suspended for twenty minutes when fans threw flares at each other and tear gas ended up on the pitch.

The repetition of similar problems in Lens might raise concerns that the French authorities are not learning lessons from previous incidents. The good news, however, is that this charge cannot be levelled at Nancy or at Paris. During 2007, I have been fortunate enough to work with both cities. The purpose of this article is therefore to show two examples of the positives in recent safety and security progress in French football.

Nicolas Holveck is Chief Executive at ASNL. Following a visit to a UK and European stadium managers meeting organised by *S&AM* publisher Alan Levett at Arsenal's Emirates stadium, Nicolas invited me to visit Nancy with John de Quidt, Chief Executive of the Football Licensing Authority. The purpose of the visit in late January 2007 was twofold. First we were to hold a seminar for representatives from the club, the police and the local authorities. Second, I was to carry out a safety and security audit before, during and after the ASNL match against St Etienne.

Our host for the visit was the ASNL Director of Security, Louis Begey. We had not been sure if our visit would be welcome but Louis and his assistant were both very friendly and open. Notwithstanding his long police career and several years in post at ASNL, he was still keen to learn and to act on any recommendations arising from the audit.

At the evening seminar, John de Quidt highlighted the developments in UK safety policy and practice since the 1989 Hillsborough disaster. His thesis was that everybody needed to work together in an integrated and coherent safety management system. The UK's key achievements had been:

- an improved atmosphere which had attracted new kinds of spectators;
- substantial improvements in stadium structures and facilities;
- clarity about who was responsible for what;
- new safety measures such as CCTV and stewarding systems;
- maintaining a balance between the needs of safety and security; and
- new legislation and stadium regulations.

I then spoke about the differences between safety and security (see *S&AM* August 2006), the need to balance both safety and security with other aspects of risk management, such as the commercial business, the fans demands for atmosphere and enjoyment and the locality needs for minimal disruption.

The following day, I carried out a visual inspection of the Stade Marcel Picot. There were a few maintenance issues discovered which were repaired very shortly after the audit. The ground has two distinctive features. First, it was at that time the only stadium in France with turnstiles at all the entrances. Second, it was constructed with a substantial moat between the stands and the pitch. The moat serves as the internal concourse containing the toilet and catering facilities. It also acts as an effective segregation barrier – eliminating any need for fences – and also as the entry and exit system. Because the moat has the capacity to take double the stadium capacity, the ground empties very quickly at the end of the match, or indeed in any emergency.

In the evening, I observed the operational performance of the safety management system. The game was being broadcast live by Canal Plus and so the club had invested in a pitch cover and hot air blowers to counter the freezing conditions – there was heavy snow all around. The pitch was fine but the challenge for the ground staff and stewards was clearing the gangways and staircases of snow and ice before the ground was opened. This was a serious safety concern because of the risks of slips, trips and falls in a crowd situation, and was a good example of the importance of clarifying who was responsible for what. During the match, I had been asked to pay particular attention to the behaviour of the ASNL supporters in one particular block and to make observations about the policing and stewarding. Following the audit, I prepared an 8,000 words report – with photographs – and made 16 recommendations for possible improvement. These covered both physical and management aspects of the stadium. The recommendations were discussed with and accepted by the club.

A few weeks after the murder in Paris, Pascal Cherki (Deputy Mayor responsible for sports) contacted Lionel Dreksler (President of ESMA – the European Stadium Managers Association). He asked him to use his contacts to set up a study trip to London for a delegation from the

City of Paris. Lionel and I then decided to organise a seminar involving the UK's leading experts on aspects of safety and security. We would also visit a Premier League match. Thus on 30 March 2007, Pascal Cherki and Lionel Dreksler arrived in London with a delegation comprising representatives of all the main political parties in Paris, policy staff, and Philippe Boindrieux, Chief Executive of Paris St Germain.

We had been invited to hold the seminar at the offices of the UK Football Policing Unit, headed by Bryan Drew, who is also a UEFA Security Officer. The cast of speakers began with Bryan and David Bohannan, the senior civil servant responsible for government policy on football disorder. They spoke about the preventative measures adopted in the UK since the nadir of Euro 2000. 946 English fans had been either arrested or deported at those Championships and this had been the catalyst for a new football disorder strategy. Key outcomes had been the development of partnerships in recognition of the fact that no one agency could deal with all the safety and security issues. There had also been greater clarity about who was legally responsible for what – the government and police for football disorder and the football authorities and clubs for crowd safety and management in the stadium.

The cornerstone of the UK security strategy had been stronger football banning orders to prohibit violent fans from attending matches. These had been supported by work to influence the expectations and tactics of host cities abroad, to encourage ordinary fans to self-police and so to isolate the minority of troublemakers. The aim was to promote mass inclusion by excluding high risk fans and positively influencing those fans who might be drawn into bad behaviour. The results had been positive with 43% of matches being completely police-free, arrests down and falling, and no incidents or arrests at 68% of matches.

John de Quidt and I gave broadly the same presentations we had given at the ASNL seminar a few weeks previously. The other speaker was John Beattie, Stadium Manager at Arsenal's Emirates stadium and Chairman of the UK Football Safety Officers' Association. He spoke about the practicalities of crowd safety management, including the UK system of stewarding, stewards training and stewarding qualifications.

The following day the delegation was welcomed to the Boleyn Ground for the match between West Ham United and Middlesbrough. John Ball, the Stadium Manager, gave us a tour of the Control Room and explained the match day safety operation. We then observed the senior staff briefing and wandered around the ground. The delegation particularly noted the low key arrangements for supervising the arrival of the visiting supporters, which contrasted with the much harsher reception found in France. At the end of the visit, the feedback was that the delegation had found the visit very useful and were returning to Paris with various ideas in their minds.

Now that the months have passed and we are into the new season, I wanted to find out if the seminar and audit at Nancy and the conference for the Parisians had made any difference to their policy and practice.

At Nancy, Louis Begey was able to confirm that the club had implemented those recommendations arising from the audit which were solely within their control. For example, the issue of keys to exit gate staff had been improved. The stewards' were smarter and were all now wearing black trousers. Briefings to senior stewards had been tightened up – the briefings were now scripted and available in writing. Canal Plus was being required to cover up their cable runs where these presented a trip hazard. The Control Room was being fitted with new CCTV monitors and the design of the room changed so that it would accommodate 15 persons rather than nine. Additionally, Louis Begey had been asked by the League to write new guidance on Control Rooms to be implemented at all clubs. All good stuff.

Some of the recommendations, such as the installation of emergency telephones and an additional turnstile for the visiting supporters, would require agreement beyond the club and expenditure by the municipality. These recommendations had not yet been implemented, however Nicholas Holveck reported that discussions were continuing and that the club was being listened to sympathetically.

At PSG, Philippe Boindrieux told me that the club had installed a new access control system which made forced entry almost impossible. The ticketing software had been changed to allow a much better quality interface with the access control system. The club was also continuing to make improvements in the identification of spectators. As well as checking the personal details of all ticket purchasers, the club had added photographs to membership cards. These photos were taken at the stadium and had been uploaded into the customer database.

Work at the political level had resulted in CCTV outside the stadium being reinforced. As well as their traditional role in maintaining law and order, the police were making more efforts to be proactive and to identify undesirable individuals. There were also moves towards extending from three to nine months the duration of the stadium ban for violence or other unacceptable behaviour.

I was very pleased to hear of the progress made in both Nancy and in Paris. For Lens, French contacts have reported that work is being undertaken to remedy some of the physical problems with the stadium. I have no doubt that safety and security problems will continue in France – as of course they will in every country. The encouraging thing is that there is good evidence from last season of French professionals working positively to make progress with their local situations.

3.1. COMMENTARY BY JIM CHALMERS – STADE MARCEL PICOT AND PARC DES PRINCES

In the article published in 2007, Frosdick outlines some of the problems experienced in French football and how UK experiences may have provided part of the solution. This entailed a visit by him and John de Quidt, then Chief Executive of the Football Licensing Authority (FLA) to the Stade Marcel Picot in Nancy, the home of AS Nancy Lorraine (ASNL), and a visit to the UK by a delegation from Paris involved with the Parc Des Princes , the home of Paris Saint-Germain (PSG).

To set the article in context, I would have welcomed a pen picture of both stadiums, and so have provided my own. Nancy is located in the north east of France. Although the original stadium was built in 1926 it was completely rebuilt in 2003, providing a modern facility with a current capacity of 20,087. Work is continuing to increase the Stadium capacity to 35,000 with a retractable roof. The Parc Des Princes in Paris was built in 1972 and has a current capacity of 48,712. It was originally the national stadium but was replaced by the Stade De France for the French World Cup in 1998. Interestingly, the stadium is owned by the city of Paris.

In his introduction, Frosdick summarises some of the problems experienced in French football, including the Bastia Stadium collapse in 1992 which resulted in 17 deaths. The summary of violence and disorder (including the death of a PSG fan in Paris) only highlights the fact that no country is immune from crowd related problems associated with football. The article is not, however, another dialogue about 'football hooliganism', but instead explains how the UK experiences in dealing with safety and security at matches is being shared internationally, hopefully to the benefit of other nations.

The visit by Frosdick and de Quidt to Nancy and the visit to the UK by the Paris delegation are only a small part of the contribution made by UK experts in explaining to representatives from other countries how the football experience has changed in the UK since the 1989 Hillsborough stadium disaster. It is encouraging that over the years since the disaster, other countries have learned and benefitted from the changes made in our stadia and how they are managed.

As a member of the FLA Inspectorate during the early 90s, I was fortunate enough to be invited (with my colleagues) to speak in Europe on issues relating to stadium design, safety systems, safety management and stewarding. One of those visits included addressing the Council of Europe in Strasbourg. Our then Chief Executive, John de Quidt, regularly travelled far wider than me. As Chair and later Vice Chair of the Standing Committee of the European Convention on Spectator Violence and Misbehaviour, de Quidt was instrumental in promoting across Europe the UK best practice and procedures in spectator safety management and stewarding.

The visit by the Paris delegation in 2007 reminded me of my visit to Paris in the mid 90s (along with de Quidt and a fellow inspector) to speak to a high powered delegation of government officials and senior police officers on the changes made by the UK in the way grounds were being managed and stewarded. They listened with interest to what we had to say, but as we were leaving, a senior police officer said to me that, whilst it was interesting, there was no way that the control and management of crowds at football matches would ever be transferred from the police to civilians. I would like to think, therefore, that our visit sowed the seeds of change for the FIFA World Cup of 1998, when the UK concept of stewarding was very evident at all the matches in France.

It is always difficult to judge whether talking to representatives from other countries about our experiences in the UK makes any difference in attitude and practice towards safety and security. This was brought home to me at a very personal level when Jim Froggatt (a fellow member of the FLA Inspectorate) and I were invited by the government of Guatemala to assist them in determining the cause of a football related disaster at the Mateo Flores stadium in Guatemala City in October 1996. 82 fans were trampled to death inside the stadium at a World Cup qualifying fixture. When we visited Guatemala there was no safety at sports grounds legislation, no means of regulating the stadium and no safety guidance such as our *Guide to Safety at Sports Grounds* (the Green Guide). Without the relevant legislation, regulation and guidance to advise upon and enforce safety, then spectator safety is always likely to be in jeopardy.

As an example, without the establishment of the FLA in 1991, and given the previous legal framework and authority to monitor and enforce safety at UK football grounds, then change would never have occurred in the aftermath of the Hillsborough disaster. Even after 96 deaths there were still Club Chairmen saying that Hillsborough was a one off and would never occur again. This was very much the attitude which prevailed following other UK disasters – they were always one offs and there was no need to change.

Part of our brief in Guatemala was to make recommendations on how such a disaster could be prevented in the future. Froggatt and I made a total of 20 recommendations relating to legislation, regulation, stadium design, safety systems, safety management and policing. At the time, it was probably the Guatemalan equivalent of the Taylor report into the 1989 Hillsborough stadium disaster. To the present day, neither Froggatt nor I know if any of our recommendations were implemented by either the Guatemalan government or the country's football authorities. We both would have welcomed the opportunity to return to the country to carry out an independent audit to see if our visit had made any difference in either the stadium design or its methods of operation.

This contrasts with Frosdick's experiences, where he was able to follow up on Nancy and Paris to see whether they had made any progress. Not everything which was recommended was in place, but there was strong evidence at both stadiums that much of the advice given had been acted upon. In this regard it was welcoming to see that his intervention had made a difference in changing attitudes to safety and security. However, I do not think that the article can be seen as suggesting that all French grounds may be as progressive as the Stade Marcel Picot and the Parc Des Princes. France has its share of old and decaying stadia with lower standards of safety and security.

It would therefore have been interesting to know whether in France there was an equivalent body to the FLA keeping safety at sports grounds under review, and with authority to enforce safety if ground management and municipal authorities do not. Northern Ireland has only recently introduced their equivalent of the FLA indicating they have learned something from the other UK experiences.

So whilst over the years UK representatives have travelled extensively around the world to speak on issues relating to safety, security and policing at sports grounds, I suspect the majority may have left wondering if their visit did make any difference. Having personally hosted international visitors to the UK, I often wondered if their visit had changed attitudes and beliefs, and whether that would be translated into practice on their return to their respective country. I would like to think that sharing UK best practice and procedures in safety at sports grounds has made a difference, and perhaps where this has been most noticeable is how over the years in many countries the police have been replaced by stewards inside the stadium.

If you viewed overseas football matches on television in the mid 1990s, they remind me of what our stadia were like in the 60s, 70s and 80s, with police stood shoulder to shoulder around the pitch perimeter. In many instances the police were in paramilitary uniform. There was never a steward to be seen. Contrast that with the present day, when at overseas matches you rarely see the police on the pitch perimeter, the officers having been replaced by stewards.

In October 1990, during my time as the Police Commander at Aston Villa, the club played Banik Ostrava in the Czech Republic during the UEFA European Cup. I was in charge of a small contingent of West Midlands police officers which accompanied the Villa fans. Despite my reassurance to the local police that the Villa fans would not cause any problems, I was appalled at the level of security in place for the game. It comprised military detachments with armoured vehicles and police paramilitary groups. It looked as if the security forces were prepared to repel an invasion by an armed force. Stewards were not a known commodity in the Czech Republic at the time. The small group of Villa fans were extremely well behaved but I had grave fears for their safety if anyone had spoken out of turn, since the military and paramilitary forces at the ground were just waiting for the opportunity to step in and crack a few skulls. On the return leg, the police commander from Ostrava was amazed at the small number of police officers in the ground, and even more amazed to see a safety officer and stewards in charge of the event, with the police only there in support. However I had my doubts whether, on his return to the Bazaly stadium, anything would have changed in his attitude towards crowd management by anyone other than the military and police.

Without sounding arrogant, it was and arguably still is the UK which leads the way in professional safety management and stewarding. I would like to think that one of our most significant contributions to other countries has been in changing attitudes towards the way spectators are managed and controlled at sporting events, with the emphasis changed from policing to stewarding.

I remain confident in the years ahead that UK experts will continue to preach our sports grounds safety and security gospel overseas, and representatives from abroad will continue to visit the UK and learn from our experiences. I believe that we will continue to offer a great deal of practical knowledge, skill and expertise within the sports grounds market place, with regards to safety legislation, safety regulation, stadium design, safety systems, safety management and policing, with models of best practice and procedure which overseas governments, authorities, clubs and other agencies can use to improve their stadium safety standards. This is not arrogance, but experience has shown that we do lead the world in stadium and spectator safety and the way our crowds are policed. It is therefore only right that we should share with others how this has been achieved and the effect on the overall stadium experience from the spectator perspective.

The difficulty will always be in judging to what extent the UK models have benefited other countries. In individual cases (such as in Nancy and Paris and the consequent follow up) the UK experience has made a tangible difference. To what extent that difference can be judged in the wider international context is far more difficult to say.

3.2. 'SAFE' STANDING

The original citation for this article is Frosdick, S. (2007) 'Safe Standing?', *Stadium and Arena Management*, December 2007, p. 10-13.

Steve Frosdick investigates recent developments in the debate about fans who want to watch football standing up.

Over the last fifteen years, spectators have had to get used to all-seated stadia. But a sizeable minority have never liked sitting – and frequently ignore the regulations. This poses problems for the authorities. Short of draconian measures, it is impossible to make a large crowd sit down. There has thus been an ongoing debate about 'safe standing'.

There are two aspects to the debate. First is whether the authorities should 'tolerate' persistent standing in seated areas. You can stand up on entry, at times of excitement, at half-time and on egress. So what, supporters ask, is the problem with standing during open play? The fans' case is set out in detail on the 'Stand Up Sit Down' website at *http://www.standupsitdown.co.uk*. I've previously written about persistent standing (see *S&AM* June 2003) and won't cover the same ground here. Suffice it to say that fans stand up week after week, often with the tacit approval of the safety authorities, who have to develop plans to manage the standing safely.

The second issue is whether standing terraces might return to grounds. Properly designed and managed, standing is not inherently dangerous and there are English lower division grounds with 'safe standing' approved by the authorities.

There are many reasons why clubs cannot convert most seated stands into terraces. The fans understand and accept this. But a recent campaign by the Football Supporters Federation (FSF) has proposed a 21st century 'safe standing' solution to re-ignite the debate. The FSF report can be downloaded from *http://www.fsf.org.uk/media/pdfs/safe-standing-report-web.pdf*.

Dr Malcolm Clarke (FSF Chair) was invited to present the report to the UK Football Safety Officer's Association (FSOA) Autumn conference on 16 October 2007. Clarke began by emphasising what the fans were <u>not</u> asking for. Safety was paramount, thus they were not asking for a return to massive Kops. Nor should anyone be obliged to stand. The FSF estimated that about 10-20% of capacity would meet the demand. Clarke was not in favour of permitting standing in seated areas – the choice to stand would strengthen the case for expecting other people to sit down. Finally, the FSF did not want to compel clubs to introduce standing. This was a commercial and policy decision to be debated between clubs, regulators and fans at the local level. For example, the opportunity might arise if a club was considering filling-in the corners of the stadium.

The FSF case is that the current regulatory prohibition is illogical, not in line with the government's view of risk and regulation and prevents choice. It is absurd to say it is safe for fans to stand when the club is in a lower division but not safe to stand on the same terrace in the third season after the club has been promoted. It is illogical that standing is allowed at other sports grounds or at other events in a football ground, e.g. pop concerts. Nothing is 100% safe anyway. The (then) Prime Minister Tony Blair had stated that the balance between risk and regulation had gone awry because of unintended consequences. The FSF argument was that the all-seating introduced after the Hillsborough disaster had had unintended consequences – particularly the loss of atmosphere – and so needed reviewing in the light of changes and circumstances.

Clarke's presentation drew a mixed response from safety officers. Some acknowledged the persuasiveness of the arguments, but there were doubts whether the football industry would support bringing back terraces. Speaking on Sky Sports News, FSOA Chair John Beattie of Arsenal FC commented that, 'Clubs have spent a fortune making the facilities better for fans, making them all-seater. It's not a simple matter of pulling the seats out and being able to stand. It would result in the clubs having to spend more millions of pounds to revert to something that everyone seems to think is a backwards step, apart from the supporters'.

The FSF campaign won strong support from members of the UK parliament and a debate was held on 24 October 2007. Summarising the views in favour, Roger Godsiff said, 'Football supporters do not want to watch football in unsafe grounds; they do not want to see a return to the mass terraces of old; they do not want to stop people sitting if they want to; and they do not want to force clubs to have safe standing areas, if the clubs do not want them. What I and other football supporters want is to be allowed the choice of safe standing; I want clubs to have the option, if they choose, and if there is a demand from the fans, to put in a safe standing area.'

Unfortunately for the FSF, both opposition spokesmen lined up with the government to oppose any changes. Liberal Democrat Don Foster concluded that, 'nothing I have heard in this debate, or read in the (FSF) report, persuades me that there is a strong enough case to call for a change.' Conservative Hugh Robertson promised that a future Conservative government would reconsider the matter with all the evidence to hand. If the authorities remained opposed, however, he concluded, 'It would be an extraordinarily brave and, many would say, foolish Minister who, with the Hillsborough issue sitting on their shoulder, overturned the current situation'.

Labour Minister for Sport Gerry Sutcliffe reviewed the history of the policy debate at length. He noted his huge responsibility to ensure spectator safety and concluded, 'I have considered the matter carefully, and I have not heard anything to make me change my mind'. The only encouragement for the FSF was that the Minister also commented that he was, 'not shutting the door' to future discussion.

The FSF case relies partly on the German Bundesliga. Remember that Germany successfully staged the 2006 World Cup in grounds with all seated stands which had been temporarily converted from standing. But the shadow of Hillsborough is a major factor in explaining the different UK and German perceptions of the 'safe standing' risk. UK politicians and regulators simply cannot chance another Hillsborough, however negligible the risk. Germany is also a highly regulated country, but has an unblemished stadium safety record. The German authorities also emphasise the social importance of allowing young football fans to express their collective identity and generate atmosphere. Without the dread of a disaster, Germany has thus retained standing in all bar one of its major football grounds.

To find out more, I visited Signal Iduana Park, home of Borussia Dortmund's 25,000 capacity Südtribune, the largest standing terrace in Europe. Borussia's Head of Administration, Dr Christian Hockenjos, explains why the club constructed the Südtribune. There was tradition – Germany had always had standing places and the UEFA and FIFA requirements were only recent. There was value for the fans who pay only twelve euros a ticket. Most important, however, was the question of atmosphere.

Crushing through overcrowding is the greatest risk to be managed on standing terraces. There are three key issues here: access control, crowd behaviour and structural design. Hockenjos explained that the Südtribune is divided into eleven self-contained blocks each with a capacity between 1,500 and 2,500. Each block has its own entrances and has radial and lateral fences to prevent people changing blocks. Following problems with crowd migration towards the central blocks, which had become overcrowded, the radial and lateral fences had been heightened to stop people climbing. Access control by stewards should ensure only ticket holders for that block were admitted. The crowd was monitored by CCTV and there were stewards at each gate in the pitch perimeter fence.

Hockenjos invited me to put the club's three-stage access control system to the test. The gates opened a full two and a half hours before kick-off. Compared with the UK, I was surprised at how many fans arrived so early to get a good position and begin their noisy and colourful rituals. Stewards searched fans at the approaches to the turnstiles and any prohibited articles were binned. Tickets were checked by a barcode reader at the turnstile – I used my 'print at home' ticket purchased via the Internet. Finally, tickets were checked again by a steward at the entrance to the block.

It was this third check where I found the system had some problems. For League matches, the Südtribune is all season ticket holders. I visited a Cup match for which about 7,000 of the places had been sold by 'print at home' tickets, which the Südtribune stewards are not used to. Even though Borussia Dortmund instructs its stewards to check every ticket, I was able to access most of the blocks by showing my Block 13 'print at home' ticket. Stewards checked I had a ticket but only two stewards also checked my block number. Hockenjos recognises the problem with 'print at home tickets' and extra controls will be introduced for the next Cup match. This was an unusual situation, but the risk is that, if lots of fans access the favoured blocks behind the goal with the wrong tickets, then overcrowding could result. That this has not happened is because the Germans tend to be more compliant than the English; and because the crowd densities in the lower tier blocks were fairly low. Even when my Block 13 (the most popular) was full, fans could still just about get in and out to buy beer or visit the toilet.

Hockenjos echoed the German authorities' view that the standing crowd's behaviour was self-policing. The Borussia fans thought of the Südtribune as their 'living room' and so intervention by stewards or police was rarely needed. Some illness and injury was normal in an 80,000 crowd, but there was no greater rate of injuries in standing than in seating. Nor was there any greater rate of arrests or ejections. Tellingly, there was no problem with persistent standing in any of the seated areas.

The design of the upper and lower tiers is very different. The upper tier features continuous crush barriers with 4,500 tip-up seats. 9,000 standing places are sold in this tier and the fans distribute themselves at will. Even so, the crowd density is very low. There are also radial stairways which are kept clear during the match.

The lower tier by contrast has staggered crush barriers, no radial gangways at all and only a single lateral gangway towards the front. I was not comfortable with the design when the stadium was empty because I could not see how people would move when it was full. A further issue was a gap in the radial fence between Blocks 14 and 15 which allowed uncontrolled crowd migration. However I saw that these design issues were mitigated during the match because the low crowd density permitted some radial and lateral movement even when the blocks were at full capacity.

The fold down seats mean no changes are needed to the upper tier for all-seated e.g. UEFA matches. In the lower tier, temporary seating reduces the capacity of the whole Südtribune from 25,000 to 11,500. Hockenjos explained that the club charges the same 12 euros as for standing and that the fans all stand up anyway – especially towards the centre – making a complete nonsense of the all-seating rules.

The front of the lower tier had a high pitch perimeter fence. The key issue with such fences is emergency egress. Although the Südtribune is designed to be evacuated in eight minutes without using the pitch, nevertheless additional exit gates onto the pitch are also provided. There is electronic advertising all around the pitch perimeter but this moves if the exit gates are opened. The fans had been allowed to tie banners along the fence and gates, but these banners had been cut into sections so as not to cause any obstruction to the exit gates.

Whilst I had reservations about some aspects of the Südtribune's design and management, I cannot deny the benefits for atmosphere. Here in Dortmund, happy fans were guzzling beer, smoking, chanting, singing, waving flags and generally having a lovely time – active participants in the spectacle. I loved it – and had paid less than £10. The following Saturday I sat miserably in my seat at an English ground, banned from smoking (although I don't); banned from drinking beer; passively consuming another mediocre performance in a largely silent crowd. I had wasted my afternoon – and paid £28 for the privilege.

These contrasts help explain the FSF's persistence. Clarke told me that, 'The campaign continues. We welcome the Minister's statement that the door is not closed and will continue the dialogue. We remain confident that logic and an evidence-based approach to risk analysis will win the argument'.

3.2. COMMENTARY BY JIM CHALMERS – 'SAFE' STANDING

The article published by Frosdick in 2007 continues the debate on the provision of safe standing in the Premier League and Championship League of English football. In the article he reflects on a submission to government by the Football Supporters Federation (FSF) in June of that year, in which they call for the return of standing terraces at clubs in our top two football divisions. He then comments on his experiences during a visit he made to a football stadium in Germany to examine how seating and standing can operate in practice in the same viewing area.

In his introduction to the article, attention is drawn to the issue of football fans who persistently stand in seated areas in our top two football Divisions. Frosdick goes on to suggest how this cannot be divorced from the debate on the provision of standing terraces at stadia in these leagues. Putting it very simply, if the fans did not persistently stand then there would be no debate on the return of standing terraces in all seated stadia. The two issues are therefore inexorably linked.

Frosdick and I debate the history of these issues at length in Part VI of *Safety and Security at Sports Grounds*. There is therefore no point going over this background again since this is already well documented. It is more important to reflect on the position as it stands in 2011 and the implications for the future.

In 2005 I stated that the debate on both issues would rumble on and indeed it has to the present day. There are rarely safety advisory group meetings, local and national FSOA meetings and conferences, Core City Group meetings and football regulatory body meetings, which do not discuss the issue of persistent standing. I think it likely therefore that the debate on both issues will continue into the future, unless some form of compromise can be found between government and the hopes and aspirations of a sizeable section of football fans who want to see a return of some standing terraces in all seated football stadia.

In his article Frosdick refers to his previous articles on the topic of persistent standing and that he did not intend to go over old ground. Neither do I, but it has to be recognised that the phenomenon of persistent standing has not diminished with the passage of time. If anything, I would suggest that the situation has continued to worsen as time has gone on. One only has to look at any televised game in the Premier or Championship Leagues to see how the majority of home and away fans, particularly at the goal ends, stand throughout the game. The experience from visiting games in these divisions will only confirm that it is now the norm at many grounds for fans to stand throughout the game. They will then generally only sit down during the half time break.

In *Standing in Seated Areas at Football Grounds*, published in 2002 by the Football Licensing Authority (FLA) in conjunction with the football authorities, the FSOA, the Association of Chief Police Officers and Local Authority Groups, the causes and methods of tackling persistent standing are debated at length. The document can be found on the FLA website at http://www.flaweb.org.uk. In the conclusion to the report the contributing bodies said,

> Tackling standing in seated areas will require a concerted approach by all the relevant bodies acting together over a prolonged period. Wherever possible, the ground management and the football authorities should be given the opportunity to address the issue through education, persuasion and positive ground management before the local authorities or FLA take action to reduce capacities. Should such action be necessary, the Local Authorities should receive the full public support of the Clubs collectively and of the football authorities.

Members of the FSOA will tell you how education, persuasion, positive ground management and, in some cases, reduction in capacities has not persuaded standing fans that they should sit down. If anything it has encouraged more to join in the practice. The simple fact is that if several thousand fans want to exercise what they see as their right to stand at football grounds, then no amount of education, persuasion or authoritarian actions are going to prevent this from happening. You can see the results at almost every Premier or Championship League match.

Although the FLA document was published in 2002 we should not lose sight the fact that the phenomenon has been going on almost from the first introduction of all seated stadia in England and Wales. The simple fact is that no one has found a solution to the problem. I believe it is now time to admit that we have lost the battle in persuading fans to sit down at football matches. In other words, it is 'people power' which has prevailed. In many cases ground management have given up trying to enforce all seating. Even the football regulatory bodies have accepted the inevitable, that in the overall scheme of things, persistent standing is not a priority. At a time of cut backs in staff and budgets at both local and central government levels, there are far more pressing issues to occupy the mind than persistent standing.

Over the years since the phenomenon became so prevalent, calls for the curbing of the practice have stemmed from a perceived risk that persistent standing is unsafe. In 2009 Crowd Dynamics (a consultancy specialising in safety and crowd behaviour) were commissioned by the Premier League to conduct a study into the safety issues surrounding fans standing in seated areas at football grounds. In their report, one of the discussion points was on what constitutes persistent standing. As I said in *Safety and Security at Sports Grounds*, the only organisation which has sought to define persistent standing is the FSOA and this still remains the position. One would have thought by now that there would at least have been a commonly agreed definition of what is meant by 'persistent standing'. If we cannot even agree what it is it seems unlikely that a cure will ever be found.

In their report, Crowd Dynamics conclude that standing in seated areas alone carries a negligible statistical likelihood of triggering a spontaneous progressive crowd collapse. They highlighted that safety issues in seated areas are not solely related to persistent standing, since the level of risk will be greater at moments of excitement, especially when fans suddenly leap to their feet, rush forward or jump up and down. Crowd Dynamics also highlight that a progressive crowd collapse is not possible if the crowd is all seated but stands at moments of excitement. The standing crowd however, may jump in excitement and this carries a higher likelihood of a progressive crowd collapse. This is a simple fact already well known to the safety officers who have to manage the problem.

The Crowd Dynamics report goes on to say that the rake of the deck – steeper being more dangerous – and whether the crowd is dynamic or stable – dynamic being riskier – will significantly affect the likelihood of a progressive crowd collapse. The impact of such a collapse can be serious and as such, standing in seated areas must be regarded as a significant risk.

So in certain circumstances, persistent standing is said to pose a significant risk, whilst in other cases it presents a lower or negligible risk. It all depends who carries out the risk assessment and what their perception of the risk is. This is usually the safety officer exercising a professional judgement on the basis of their knowledge of their ground and experience of their crowd.

In the report, Crowd Dynamics suggest that, where persistent standing is anticipated, a considered approach to the problem should include the measures set out below. The italics indicate where to my personal knowledge clubs or venues have tried some or all of these recommendations:

Design

- *Consideration of avoiding areas where steep rake applies;*
- *Assessment of front barriers heights;*
- *Application of 'S' factors to maintain 'fire breaks' (empty rows of seats particularly in front of the upper tiers);*
- *Application of 'S' factors to maintain empty seats adjacent to radial gangways (standing spectators require more space than seated);*
- Introduction of strategically placed barriers in seated areas;
- Revision of seat and spacing dimensions.

Information

- *Use of positive communication to encourage sitting (sit down and enjoy the show);*
- Development of neuro linguistic programming options in support of a communication strategy;
- *Consistency of message;*
- *Good rapport between safety officials and spectators;*
- *Accurate, timely and relevant intelligence.*

Management

- *Crowd safety risk assessment;*
- *Management policies on risk assessment with clear ownership of the persistent standing risk, monitoring of areas where persistent standing is anticipated, focus on vulnerable areas/spectators in particular;*
- *Education of safety personnel regarding risks from progressive crowd collapse;*
- *Education of spectators.*

The fact that so much is in italics indicates that there is little new in the Crowd Dynamics report, since many of the recommendations were debated and included in the 2002 FLA publication. The majority of the measures have already been tried in some form or another, or in combination with other club initiatives such as mass ejections. However no one single measure or combination of measures has had any significant impact on the problem.

My view is that the Crowd Dynamics report does very little to progress our knowledge or understanding of the problem or how to tackle it. Their new recommendations are to install barriers into the seated areas and to revise seat and spacing dimensions. When I come onto discussing the return of standing terraces to all seated grounds, one of the main stumbling blocks is the cost of conversion. Changing existing seated areas with revised seat and spacing dimensions or the installation of barriers is unlikely ever to happen, due to the substantial costs involved. Even if such measures were introduced, I do not believe they would encourage the fans to sit down – if anything, I believe they would only encourage them to stand and lean on the barriers.

It has long been argued that a consequence of persistent standing is an increased risk of spectators being injured. However, during my twelve years as an FLA Inspector I saw no conclusive evidence to support that contention. To a degree, my view is supported by the FLA annual analysis of the reported injuries to spectators at football grounds in England and Wales. The statistics can be found on the FLA website. In the 2008/09 season, the FLA examined in greater detail whether there had been any obvious link between standing and injury rates in the top four English leagues. They looked at three different scenarios:

- Grounds that still retain standing accommodation;
- Grounds where home supporters have been reported as standing in large numbers in seated areas;
- Matches where visiting supporters have been reported as standing in large numbers in seated areas;

The FLA concluded that they had been unable to establish any clear link between the type of accommodation and the number of reported injuries; and that they had been unable to establish any pattern between supporters standing in seated areas and the distribution of reported injuries in different areas of the grounds in the top two divisions. In reaching these conclusions the FLA said it could only proceed on the basis of reported injuries, despite some evidence of under reporting. The FLA had observed a number of cases where spectators have been injured whilst standing in seated areas but had not sought treatment. These injuries had thus not been reported.

From this analysis it appears unlikely that a spectator faces any greater risk of injury from persistent standing in seated areas than they do from any other risk associated with crowd movement in confined spaces, such as entering or leaving the seated viewing areas. This is not in any way to condone the practice of persistent standing, but it may give an understanding why in terms of management and resolution of the problem, it is not regarded by safety officers in the top two divisions as posing a significant threat to safety. At many grounds this is reflected in the risk assessments.

Safety officers accept the phenomenon has to be managed and many feel that the situation is being well controlled, so that the risks around persistent standing are reduced to a level which is as low as. reasonably practicable. Despite their professional risk assessment judgments, suitably documented, safety officers will tell you that the certifying authority and the FLA keep badgering them to do something about it, although those bodies themselves do not have any answers. This is where my colleagues get so frustrated. They feel they have done all they can to control and manage the problem, but because they have not found the solution, they are constantly being criticised.

It is about time the regulators acknowledged that there is no answer. Instead of constantly threatening sanctions, they should accept the safety officers' professional risk assessment judgments on the issue.

It will be interesting to see what happens with the new and less directive style of safety certification preferred by the FLA (See my later commentary on sections 6.1 – 6.2). This requires the ground management (i.e. the safety officer) to use risk assessments to identify the conditions which it considers reasonably necessary to secure the safety of spectators. These conditions are recorded in an operations manual and incorporated into the safety certificate. So if a safety officer assesses that persistent standing at their ground is not a significant safety risk, I wonder how the authorities will react. As the FLA 2010 *Guidance on Safety Certification* confirms, ground management has the sole responsibility for safety at their venue. So will the certifying authority or FLA step in and disagree with any such risk assessments? Surely not. If the safety officer is acting responsibly and reasonably, then the regulators should leave matters to those who know their ground and the fans best, namely the safety officers.

Persistent standing is now an everyday occurrence which is no more unusual than fans celebrating a goal or moving in and out of the viewing areas. Over the years, the recommendations on how to tackle the problem have, at best, contained it but have certainly not solved it. Thankfully there is no evidence to suggest that persistent standing has led to any substantial increase in spectator injuries. Nor do I believe there is any substantial evidence that persistent standing spoils the enjoyment of those who would prefer to sit. Although I know that some safety officers do receive letters of complaint from time to time, I am not aware of any notable conflicts between fans in areas affected by persistent standing. If anything, I think there is a unifying effect in such areas as the groups come together with the common purpose of standing. The only time conflict arises is when clubs take some action against such standing. This is why so many safety officers, in an effort to prevent conflict, are prepared to accept the inevitable – that persistent standing is now a fact of life. I believe that, unless some new and radical solution can be found, then persistent standing is here to stay. This leads me into the debate on the other issue linked to persistent standing – the return of safe standing in the top two divisions in England and Wales.

In his article, Frosdick summarises the case made by the Football Supporters Federation (FSF) in their submission to government in June 2007, *The case for Safe Standing at Major Football Stadia in England and Wales – a 21st Century Solution*. When the 51 page document was published, I considered it to be a well researched, well presented and well argued case for the return of small standing terraces in the Premier and Championship Leagues. The FSF submission was not based on emotion or nostalgia for a return of the dark old days of standing terraces, but instead made a valid argument for fans to have a choice of either standing or sitting to enjoy their football, if their club wished to give them that choice. At the time of the submission Cardiff City was in the process of constructing their new stadium and was prepared to incorporate safe standing terraces into the development. However, current regulations prevented this from happening. This would have been the ideal opportunity to test the feasibility of providing some standing terraces in an all seated stadium, but sadly that opportunity was not taken by government.

I was present at the FSOA Conference when Dr Malcolm Clarke, Chair of the FSF, presented their case. Like the report, he gave a clear, articulate and very persuasive presentation. Of course not everyone agreed with the case, but there were many delegates who were privately very supportive of the argument for the return of safe standing. This is not surprising since, again in private, many of my colleagues have said that they would much rather manage and control safe standing terraces than have to contend with the present scenario of persistent standing. However, most safety officers are reluctant to speak out openly in favour of a return of safe standing for fear of upsetting their employers, the football authorities and the sports regulatory bodies. As commented upon in the article, for a safety officer to speak out in favour of the FSF argument, they would ultimately be placed in a head to head disagreement with the Chair of the FSOA. So whilst publicly the FSOA will argue against the return of safe standing, this is not a view held by many of its members.

Over the years there have also been parliamentary pressures from various Members of Parliament who support the FSF case. The most recent parliamentary debate was in a Private Members Bill proposed by Don Foster MP. His motion on 'Safe Standing (Football Stadia)' is reported in Hansard columns 188-190 of 7 December 2010. The Bill will be presented for a second reading on 17 June 2011. Private Members Bills generally have little chance of becoming law unless the government of the day supports them. The Minister for Sport has agreed to consult relevant bodies but at the time of writing it is not clear what stance the government will eventually take. I do however honestly believe that it will only be a matter of time before a government will be prepared to take the bull by the horns and give clubs and fans the opportunity to safely stand in the top two divisions.

The Hillsborough Stadium disaster occurred over thirty years ago and, whilst the memories of that day are still very vivid in my mind, so much has changed in the quality of design and management of our stadia. Would it therefore be such a retrograde step to allow safe standing facilities in the Premier and Championship Leagues? Is it right to say to the fans in our top two divisions that they will be forever deprived of the opportunity to enjoy their game of football in a standing environment, if that is what they and their club wish? I do not believe the safety card can be played every time this issue comes up for debate. As an example that safe standing can be implemented in the upper divisions, consider this scenario. A club promoted from League One into the Championship League, and who might be promoted the following season into the Premier League, is allowed three seasons in which to take their standing terraces out of use and provide only all seated accommodation. If they can be allowed to operate safe standing for three seasons or more, what is suddenly risky in season four? It makes no sense at all to say that despite the fact that a club has operated safe standing for many years whilst in the lower leagues of football, they cannot continue to operate those safe standing facilities once promoted into the higher leagues.

The provision of safe standing in our top two divisions is therefore perfectly feasible for those who wish to go down this path. For many it would be cost prohibitive, but if a club wished to provide such a facility for the fans it would not (in my opinion) be unsafe for them to do so. I would therefore fully support the FSF and the recent Private Members Bill to allow the return of safe standing in our top two divisions. The design and control measures already exist for the provision of safe standing. All that is necessary to give the fans what they want is a bold step and a leap of faith by government responding positively to the call for a return of safe standing.

Frosdick paints another vivid picture of his experiences at the Signal Iduna Park Stadium in Germany, the home of Borussia Dortmund's 25,000 capacity Südtribune - the largest standing terrace in Europe. Whilst his experiences are of interest, there is no possibility of such a large standing area ever being introduced into any UK stadium. Part of the stand is seated but capable of being easily converted into a standing terrace. This of course is only one such example of the dual usage of stands in providing either standing or seated accommodation by simple conversion. From the description of the stand, this would not meet the UK safe standing criteria with regard to barriers and radial gangway configurations. It is therefore important to recognise that, in the call for a return to safe standing, it is UK standards of safety which must be met, not another country's.

There is no call for the reintroduction of such large standing terraces in the UK by either the FSF or the parliamentarians, who envisage small standing terraces of between 2,500-3,000 capacity. This is the norm in the lower league football grounds. Whether any club wants to install a pure standing terrace or a hybrid design to include seating will be a matter for each to consider, and decide upon the best option to meet their particular circumstances. What is perfectly clear is that the design and engineering solutions do exist, and so there is no reason why safe standing cannot exist in our top two divisions if there is a will to allow this at government level.

Using Hillsborough as the reason not to return to standing terraces in is unreasonable. I would suggest that it is very unlikely that a disaster of this nature could occur again in the UK. The type of scrutiny exercised by the FLA and certifying authorities means that the criticisms made by Lord Justice Taylor are unlikely to be repeated. In Chapter 19 of his final report, Taylor described the performance of the certifying authority as inefficient and dilatory. Their failure to revise or amend the safety certificate over the three years preceding the disaster, despite important changes in the layout of the ground in 1981 and 1985, was a serious breach of duty. There were, as a result, no fixed capacities of the pens in Leppings Lane. Taylor concluded that a number of breaches of the Green Guide standards had been permitted, e.g. the spacing of crush barriers, the width of perimeter gates and the gradient of the central tunnel. These types of failures are extremely unlikely in the UK in 2011.

I believe the time is right to look forward and not keep looking over our shoulders at the spectre of Hillsborough. We cannot change the past, but I believe we have learned from the history of Hillsborough. The results can be seen in both the physical sense (with the modern stadia we have in the UK) but equally important in the very professional way in which safety is managed on a match day.

When government relaxed the all seated requirements for clubs in our lower football leagues, they accepted that safe standing was possible in those leagues. The safe standing criteria have been maintained through the FLA licensing remit. The government now needs to accept that there is nothing which would prevent the reintroduction of safe standing terraces in our top two divisions. The mechanism for monitoring their operation already exists. The standing terraces in our lower leagues have never been deemed 'unsafe'. Nor do they in any way contribute to football related antisocial behaviour.

The conclusion of Frosdick's article compares his experience at the football match in Germany with his experience of a match in the UK. The German experience won hands down. For those who want it, safe standing is more fun.

I have to agree with Dr Clarke, Chair of the FSF when he says, 'We remain confident that logic and an evidence based approach to risk analysis will win the argument'. I hope that optimism for the future gets its just reward, and in doing so helps resolve the persistent standing phenomenon.

3.3. SMALLER SCALE AT STEVENAGE BOROUGH

The original citation for this article is Frosdick, S. (2008) 'Smaller Scale', *Stadium and Arena Management*, April 2008, p. 31-32.

Steve Frosdick visits a non-league football ground and finds the usual safety and security issues – but on a smaller scale.

Running a stadium or arena always poses operational challenges for managers – irrespective of the size of the venue. Having previously reported on larger European venues, I thought it would be interesting to make a case study of a smaller sports ground. Thus one foggy Wednesday evening in February I found myself stuck in horrible traffic on my way to Stevenage Borough's Broadhall Stadium for their Conference (English fifth division) clash with Forest Green Rovers.

It was a good job I was two hours early as the usual car park opposite the ground had a huge circus tent plonked in the middle of it – meaning that there would be parking problems for the fans. Coupled with the evening kick-off, the fog, the cold and the traffic chaos, it was no surprise that a crowd of only 1,500 was expected – about 800 down on the average gate.

The Broadhall Stadium is neat and compact. Unusually for the UK, the ground is owned by the municipality and leased by club. The 7,107 capacity venue has two modern seated stands. The 2,002 capacity home stand down one side incorporates corporate hospitality facilities and the 1,402 seats behind one goal are for the away supporters – tonight all 55 of them! There are then two covered standing terraces, one holding 3,008 noisy fans down the full length of the pitch and the other providing 695 spaces behind the other goal.

Safety Officer Sean Comerford has a Fire Service background and is also a recently retired senior referee. He knows his safety and he knows his football. His Deputy Safety Officer is Steve Fanthorpe. Both work part-time for the club, mainly on matchdays. Yet both are full members of the Football Safety Officers' Association (FSOA) and both have completed the FSOA Certificate in Event and Matchday Safety Management – voluntarily and in their own time. As a founder member of the FSOA myself, I was delighted to see the professional approach to their own development adopted by these two dedicated individuals.

This commitment to good quality safety is also evident in the stewarding operation at Stevenage. The safety certificate specifies 24 stewards and one additional steward for every 250 spectators. With a crowd of 3,000, they would thus need 32 stewards. To ensure this number are available, there are 46 stewards on the books. 34 had signed in for this match, which was fine.

The stewards are provided with smart reflective jackets and their supervisors carry radios. Stewards normally work in the same positions for every match, thus they become familiar with their own stand and the regulars in the crowd around them.

Some of the stewards also work at Watford Football Club and already hold one of the acceptable Level 2 qualifications – the Certificate in Event and Matchday Stewarding. To bring the remaining stewards up to standard, Sean Comerford has entered into a partnership with North Hertfordshire College to train and assess the stewards for a Level 2 National Vocational Qualification in Spectator Safety. For the first 19 stewards, the six learning sessions have already been delivered and the workplace assessment is in hand.

The four car park stewards had been briefed before their earlier deployment. The fog and bad traffic meant that many of the stewards were delayed getting from their day jobs to the ground. However by 6.10 pm all the supervisors bar one and twelve of the stewards were present for Sean Comerford's briefing. The briefing was later cascaded by the supervisors to the stewards in their stands.

Thus in their ratio to the expected crowd, their appearance, briefing, training and assessment, the stewards were what one might have expected to find at a Premier League club – but on a smaller scale.

The current control room forms part of the commercial manager's office and is equipped with base stations for the emergency telephone system and the supervisor's radios. There is also a turnstile counting computer, which showed that the final attendance was 1,628. Stevenage Borough are doing well and may get promoted to the

Football League next season. To be fully compliant with the ground requirements, plans are in hand to install CCTV inside the ground and to build a dedicated control room.

The fog meant that the referee's pre-match inspection was critical. Would he call the game off before the gates were opened to admit spectators? Would he decide to play but later have to abandon the match? Opening the gates was delayed as long as possible. After two inspections and careful discussions, the referee decided to play and the fans began to enter through the turnstiles.

Sean Comerford now faced the same issue any Safety Officer would have to address in these circumstances. There was clearly a risk that the match might be abandoned before half-time – in which case the fans would have to be given a voucher for the replay. Accordingly, Sean activated the relevant contingency plan. Vouchers were printed on the club's ticket stock and distributed to the supervisors so that they would be readily available for the fans if required. I was impressed at this quiet efficiency, which was of course invisible to the spectators.

It had been expected that visibility would improve as the floodlights burned the fog away. But unfortunately things got worse. Although the referee could see, the fans in the end stands could not even see the half-way line at times. This led to some amusing cheering of supposed goals (there were none) and mock appeals for penalties and bookings from the fans who could not see.

For the second half, a small group from the East terrace migrated onto the North terrace One of them had previously been ejected for vile verbal abuse towards a steward. This type of bad behaviour is not uncommon at grounds of all sizes. As one would expect, the group were closely monitored by a steward and supervisor. Whilst there was plenty of witty banter, the abuse was not repeated and the group provided some amusement for the otherwise bored crowd.

Two local police officers attended the match but had neither told Sean that they were coming nor even that they had entered the ground. This was impolite and represented a microcosm of the issues at some larger grounds where the relationship between the stewards and police is sometimes tense.

Interestingly, the biggest safety problem is outside the ground, where the fans have to cross a busy dual carriageway before and after the game. Steve Fanthorpe has asked the local authority to install barriers on the central reservation but they have so far declined to do so. In a previous article on safety and security in France (see *S&AM* October 2007), I reported how Premier League club AS Nancy-Lorraine had found difficulties persuading their municipality to pay for recommended ground improvements.

There were thus various aspects of safety and security at Stevenage which represented on a smaller scale the types of issues one might find at any size of ground. But it would be a mistake to assume that these similarities imply that a small-scale venue team could be asked to run a large-scale venue. Away from Stevenage, both Sean Comerford and Steve Fanthorpe are also employed as supervisors – not as Safety Officers – at the new Wembley Stadium. Yet the senior managers of at least one major venue have been guilty of making this mistake. Their Safety Officer having left, they assumed that any qualified Safety Officer could be asked to run an event, rather than appreciating how essential it is for the Safety Officer to have experience in a similar sized venue. The spans of command, complex inter-relationships with other agencies, volume of incidents in parallel and the sheer numbers of people all combine to make the larger scale venue an altogether different proposition.

3.3. COMMENTARY BY JIM CHALMERS – SMALLER SCALE AT STEVENAGE

Frosdick has written about sports grounds around the world. In this book alone you will find his experiences from visiting major stadia in France, Germany, Spain, Portugal and America as well as the UK. But I am glad that he also found the time and interest to visit Stevenage on a cold and foggy evening in February 2007 to experience what life is like for the safety officer at the grass roots level of football.

When the article was published I had an immediate empathy with everything he wrote about and the people he referred to. Having been the deputy safety officer at Kidderminster Harriers (my club) since 2003, I have shared many seasons with Stevenage in the Football Conference. I know the club, the safety officer and deputy safety officer well. They were always very professional in their approach. They were also members and staunch supporters of the Football Safety Officers Association (FSOA) and it was my privilege to share many conferences with them. They could always be relied upon to contribute sensibly to any debate, giving the smaller club perspective.

Stevenage and my club also shared some memorable occasions. We played them in the final of the FA Trophy Competition in 2007. Sadly we lost 3-2. The fixture will however go down in history as the first competitive Cup Final to be held at the new Wembley Stadium. In the 2009/10 season we also played them at home in the game which secured their promotion into the Football League. So Frosdick's references to their expectations if promoted have become a reality.

Over the years many clubs, including my own, have been relegated from the Football League into the Conference League. However there is no lessening of safety standards when clubs are relegated and the authorities expect proper standards from all Conference clubs. That comes across very clearly in the article.

All Conference League clubs occupy either designated grounds (under the Safety of Sports Grounds Act 1975) or else have regulated stands (under the Fire Safety and Safety of Places of Sports Act 1987). In either case the club will have a safety certificate issued by the local certifying authority and setting out the terms and conditions they must comply with. My Club with a capacity of 6,444 occupies a designated ground and this means we have the same safety certification requirements as Manchester United and Arsenal. As Frosdick rightly says in the article it is only the scale of the ground and its capacity which will vary, not the safety and security demands placed on the club and managed by their safety officer. This must be right since, whether a spectator walks through the turnstiles at Stevenage or at Manchester United, they should have the same right to expect to be and to feel safe in the ground.

Similarly, the *Guide to Safety at Sports Grounds* does not have a sliding scale of safety and security expectations. Old Trafford in Manchester and Stevenage's Broadhall Way stadium are both sports grounds. So you will find just about the same terms and conditions in the safety certificates issued to both Clubs. The safety officers and their deputies will be expected to have a Level Four spectator safety qualification on the relevant qualification framework. Steward supervisors will be expected to hold a Level Three qualification and stewards a Level Two. Whilst Stevenage has 46 stewards to train and assess, Manchester United will have some 1,300. However both will use the same training materials and the standards of training do not vary. So it matters not whether a club is in the Premier League or the Conference, the safety documentation and safety qualifications remain the same. It is only the scale which is different.

Frosdick's match day experience at Broadhall Way showed that the safe management of the event was no different from any other fixture in any other division. The pre match stadium checks and the stewards briefing were what you would expect to find at any club. In the likes of the Premier League, the safety officer is able to delegate many of the pre-event functions which I suggest that the safety officer at Stevenage had to carry out himself. However the bonus is that in the lower leagues the safety officer will know the stewarding team personally and understand and their individual strengths and weaknesses. Another benefit for small clubs is that the turnover of stewards is normally very low. This is because most of the stewards are local people who support their local team and this is their way of being part of the local football community.

The main disadvantage is the lack of finance at the grass roots of football. I speak from personal experience when my club came close to going out of existence in 2010 due to financial problems. Most clubs in the lower leagues of football are struggling find the money even to pay the players and staff their wages. So it is a real struggle to find the money to pay the match day stewards, to ensure that they are properly equipped and that there are sufficient radios to enable communications between the match day safety staff. It is also a constant struggle to find money to maintain the structural integrity of the stadium and to ensure that safety systems such as CCTV, public address, turnstile counting, emergency lighting and fire fighting equipment continue to operate and function effectively.

I know of some clubs where lack of funding has meant that the ground and safety systems have been allowed to deteriorate. I fear therefore that it will not be too long before there will be a serious incident at a lower league ground when the main contributory cause will be the lack of proper maintenance. Reasonable structural maintenance and safety management costs money and is very often the first area where senior management look if they have to cut costs. The commercial department can show the chairman it has brought in so many thousands of pounds whereas all the safety officer has to offer the balance book is that there have been no injuries or deaths as a result of any stadium structural or management defect.
However with regards to safety it is not a question of saying 'Can we afford it?' It is more a case of saying 'Can we afford not to do it?' when the possible consequences can be death or serious injury to a spectator or employee with the resulting criminal or civil litigation or both. A responsible club chairman and board of directors must therefore ensure they do all they can to finance the reasonable safety of their stadium and the way it is safely managed on the day of the event. Every paying customer who comes through the turnstiles should expect this as a minimum standard for their care and well being. To do otherwise is in my opinion criminally negligent and morally indefensible.

I know of one Safety Officer who paid the price by losing his job when he spoke about serious safety failures at his club. Instead of supporting him the chairman resented his honesty and sacked him. I recall a chairman at my club saying to me that due to the lack of funds I would have to cut the stewarding staff by half. My stewarding plan supported by the safety certificate required the club to provide 37 stewards for a capacity gate. I told the chairman that I would have no problem halving the steward numbers, however he would have the problem of deciding which two of our four stands he was going to close! Four sides of the ground continue in use to the present day.

Despite the problems there are undoubted benefits in being involved in safety management in the likes of the Conference and, after eight years involvement in safety management at my club, I certainly would not swap this for a similar role in a higher division. Everything is up close and personal whatever you do and whoever you do it with at a smaller scale Club. At my own club, with the exception of the manager and the players, there are only six full time members of staff. So the safety officer only has to walk along a small corridor to meet and talk to the key personnel involved in running the club. There is also a very close relationship with the chairman and board of directors. Everyone works very closely together as a tight knit team. Since the links are so close, the risk of a communications breakdown is considerably less than you will find in a larger club.

Another advantage in working at a smaller scale club is that the stewards and the fans are generally all local people and get to know each other well. Some of our visiting teams only bringing a small number of supporters and these have got to know the stewards who work the visitors areas. It can be like an annual re-union when the fans, the supervisor and the stewards start chatting to each other about what has gone on since their last visit to our ground. Another benefit in a small club is that you can quickly identify any of the home fans who may decide it is a good idea to engage in some form of anti-social behaviour. Thankfully extreme anti-social behaviours such as acts of violence or serious disorder are extremely rare at Conference games. They do happen from time to time but the clubs with which this is likely to occur are very well known and action can be taken to plan for their visits. Anti-social behaviour by my own club's fans is a rare occurrence, but if it does happen then we have adopted an early intervention approach.

Following an initiative by our local West Mercia Police Football Intelligence Officer, Police Constable Sian Stockton, my club and the

Police introduced a scheme known as acceptable behaviour agreements. In effect an acceptable behaviour agreement is the equivalent to a 'yellow card' served on any of our fans whose conduct we consider is likely to damage the good name and reputation of the club whether at home or away and whether at the ground or in the town. The supporter has to give an undertaking to be of good behaviour and if they do not sign the agreement then they are banned from attending our games. The scheme has proved very effective in identifying potential trouble makers at a very early stage. By taking positive action at this stage we can prevent their conduct escalating into the more serious anti-social behaviour which can harm the good name of the club.

The success of the scheme relies heavily on the involvement and cooperation of the police since it will normally be the police who become aware of any anti-social behaviour away from the ground either at home or away. In such cases we rely on the information provided by the police to secure the acceptable behaviour agreement and it is always the police who serve the document on the offender to reinforce the seriousness of their actions. At a small club it is so much easier to identify any potential 'football hooligan'. Nipping their conduct in the bud can only benefit the fan, crowd safety, the club, the police and the wider community. That has certainly been our experience.

Smaller clubs can also provide an excellent opportunity to those who want to serve their safety management apprenticeship before moving up the ladder to a club in a higher Division. Using my club as an example, Peter Smith joined the club in 2003 as the safety officer after serving as a senior steward at a larger Club. However he had no previous experience as either an assistant or deputy safety officer. So he was quickly thrown into the deep end and he would either sink or swim. One of the first things he did was to attend and successfully pass the FSOA six days event and match day safety management course. He went on from this to achieve a Level Four qualification in spectator safety management. As the safety officer he completely revolutionised the club approach to safety management with the introduction of a very professional audit trail. For the first time in the history of the club he introduced a stewards training programme and under his leadership all stewards and their supervisors attained the relevant Level Two and Three qualification. Following his success at my club he was appointed the safety officer at the new Ricoh Arena, the home of Coventry City. After similar success at that club he was appointed the stadium manager/safety officer at Birmingham City, a major Premier League club. I am sure Peter would agree that his time at my club gave him the training, qualifications and experience which provided a solid base on which to build his safety management career as he moved to higher division clubs.

This is where I disagree with Frosdick when he says it would be a mistake to assume that a small scale venue team could be asked to run a large scale venue. I consider Peter Smith proved otherwise in moving from a smaller scale club with a capacity of nearly 6,500 to a much larger stadium and club with a capacity of over 25,000. I know from personal experience that he had no problems in making the transition and proving himself as a first class safety officer in the larger venue. There are other examples where safety officers from smaller venues have taken charge of larger venues and have been successful in the venture. It is also a fact that at many clubs, including the Premier League, the safety officer has been recruited directly into the post from another career background, but with the appropriate training has proved themselves to be very competent and professional in the role. There are therefore probably more cases and evidence to support the contrary view to that expressed by Frosdick in the article.

Dave Preece, the current safety officer at my club, started as a steward and has worked his way through the stewarding ranks to hold his current post. Like Peter Smith, he successfully completed the FSOA course and subsequently obtained his Level Four qualification. Dave had no previous safety management experience but has demonstrated his competency by hard work, training, qualifications and experience. Whether Dave will move on in the future to a larger Club is speculation but I have no doubt that, if he does choose to do so, he will have no problem in adjusting to the demands of a larger venue with larger capacities. In my opinion it is all about confidence and ability and both he and Peter Smith have these qualities in abundance. They are perfect examples of where smaller scale venues can provide all the training and experience necessary for a professional career in spectator safety management.

The financial drawbacks of working at a smaller club are offset by the satisfaction of planning and executing successful safety management operations on a shoe string. There is also a sense of pride and achievement that, despite the paucity of resources and less than ideal control room and safety systems, safety officers can still achieve the three main objectives that all fans arrive and enter the ground safely, all fans enjoy the game in safety, and all fans leave the ground safely.

Whatever the size of the stadium or the attendance figure, if these objectives are achieved for every match day operation then the safety officer and their team can reflect on a job well done. Whilst the smaller scale clubs may never get the recognition for their achievements, nevertheless at grass roots level these objectives are being achieved week in and week out throughout the football season. It can also be very rewarding to achieve the same high standards of stewards training and qualifications as those clubs in the upper echelons of football. I also know from personal experience how some safety systems and procedures which have been developed by some smaller scale clubs have been adopted by clubs in the higher divisions. With all due modesty, I would have earned a small fortune if I had sold on the copies of the medical plan, stewarding plan, contingency plans and operations manual which I developed at my club, instead of giving them away to my safety officer colleagues. The main thing in safety management is that no one person or no one club has the monopoly of knowledge. The largest clubs in the country can learn from the smaller scale venues and vice versa.

Frosdick's article brought home very forcefully that up and down the country there are people at smaller clubs who are capable of operating just as professional a safety management operation as their colleagues in the Premier League. So the next time you are listening to the football results and you hear Stevenage or Kidderminster Harriers mentioned, just remember that behind the scenes at these smaller scale clubs is just as capable and dedicated a group of men and women as you will find at the likes of Manchester United or Arsenal. The main difference with the smaller scale clubs is that you won't see these men and women on televised games nor will they ever get the publicity or recognition they deserve. Frosdick's article went a small way towards addressing that imbalance.

3.4. FLOODING AT HILLSBOROUGH STADIUM

The original citation for this article is Frosdick, S. (2008) 'In Deep Water', *Stadium and Arena Management*, February 2008, p. 34-36.

Steve Frosdick looks at the business continuity lessons to be learned from the June 2007 floods at the Hillsborough Stadium, Sheffield.

Fires, explosions, storms, structural collapses, systems failures and floods – these are the kinds of disasters which can take a facility completely out of use. Apart from the risks to life and limb, the damage to property and the sheer havoc from such events, the consequential loss of revenue streams can quickly bring the commercial business to its knees. Planning for business continuity is thus a key challenge for facility managers.

The business continuity cycle covers normality, mitigation, readiness, continuity during response and recovery and the subsequent return to normality. The floods which devastated the City of Sheffield in June 2007 also left the Hillsborough Stadium in deep water. I spoke with Sheffield Wednesday FC's Operations Manager, Alan Roberts, to see what lessons other stadium managers might learn from his experience.

There are a whole host of perils for which managers carry out risk assessments and put appropriate mitigation measures in place. Fire prevention, physical security, planned maintenance and testing are examples. But a flood at Hillsborough was simply not on the radar. Yes, the River Don did flow in a deep cutting past the back of the main stand, but the river was some eight metres below the boundary wall and nobody could have imagined the water level rising by such a huge amount. There had never been a flood in that part of Sheffield.

As Alan Roberts explains, 'This was a once in a thousand years scenario'. So spending money on flood defences would have been a disproportionate response to the very low risk. Preparing a specific contingency plan for a flood was not appropriate either.

That said, Roberts had already been thinking about business continuity. Over the preceding months, he and his counterpart at

Sheffield United had begun exploratory talks with a view to reciprocal ground sharing in the event of a disaster. The discussions had thrown up lots of difficult management issues. How do you relocate season ticket holders and corporate box holders from one stadium to another when the designs and capacities are different? How do you manage ticketing? How do you deal with supporter animosity arising from historical rivalry between the two clubs? The intention had been to prepare a document for the two Boards of Directors, but these were early days and nothing was in place at the time of the flood.

Not being ready to ground share is not an immediate disaster. Clubs can always fulfil their fixtures by playing at a borrowed ground. Most stadiums can stage a match at fairly short notice – cup replays for example. The host venue has its own staff, can sell tickets and ensure the attendance of the emergency services. So had the flood happened during the season, an alternative venue could have been quickly negotiated. The issue, of course, is the long-term commercial damage from lost revenue streams.

As it was, Roberts and Head Groundsman Steve Kiddy were faced with a nightmare following a week of prolonged heavy rain. After the River Don burst its banks, the stadium was under three metres of water, with fish floating on the surface. There was nowhere for the water to subside as the whole area was flooded. Houses, businesses and people's lives were devastated – this was a disaster for the whole community. There was nothing to do except wait for the surrounding flood levels to subside.

Before the flood, the pitch had been in perfect condition for the first game due on August 4th. 'My initial reaction when I saw the flooded arena was total shock', Steve Kiddy recalls. In addition to the severe damage to ground floor structures, bars and changing rooms, the pitch was left a stagnant mess. All the end-of-season renovation work had been washed away. 'Because of the silt level on top of the grass we were left no option but to returf.'

Carl Pass, managing director of Premier Pitches and a Sheffield resident himself, had carried out the renovation work of fraise mowing and reseeding weeks before the flood. 'I've never seen anything like it in my life. Our main problem was the silt that covered everything. We used protective gear at first because of the infection risk from raw sewage. Silt had been capping the drains preventing water loss so our first job was to clear them. The drains were fine and the fibresand pitch was still intact. Once the water had fully drained, the silt was removed and we spent three days preparing the ground for the new turf.'

The first rolls were precision cut at 3.00 am in 1.2 metre wide rolls incorporating plastic wrap during the harvesting process to ensure the grass surface remained in pristine condition. The turf was laid just four hours later. Over three days, twenty articulated lorries delivered 8,400 square metres of turf to the stadium. There were three weeks until the first match.

Whilst the new turf meant the club would be able to play its games, the damage to the rest of the ground was a commercial disaster. 'Everybody was concentrating on the pitch,' explains Roberts, 'But it was the close season when selling season tickets and corporate hospitality for the coming year is at its busiest. We had no power at all for the first four days, then several days of three hours on and three hours off. As well as the dressing rooms, we lost both the club shop – with its entire stock – and our ticket office accommodation. None of the turnstiles were working either.' This was not the sort of event for which you could dust off a pre-planned response. Sometimes, as Roberts puts it, 'You just have to roll your sleeves up and get stuck in'.

Once the waters began receding, the whole ground was left stinking, filthy and wet. The fire brigade, who had been helping local residents for the first few days, were then able to come in and pump out the rest of the water – which took them three days. Thereafter, cleaning contractors were brought in to jet spray the flood damaged structures, which then had to be tested for contamination. Only once the ground was clear of the filth and power had been restored could the recovery work begin.

Staff relocated from the ground floor had to squeeze into other offices on the upper levels. 'The conditions were appalling', says Roberts. 'But the staff were wonderful, working hours and doing things way beyond the call of duty. Some people stayed at the ground on the night when the flooding started and so were already on site. Others had to wait until the water subsided a little. We had people with rubber gloves retrieving soaking wet season ticket applications and trying to decipher them. Some people didn't go home for several days, even though their own houses were flooded'. Roberts also commends the understanding and patience shown by supporters and sponsors, who had sent payments for season tickets or booked corporate hospitality packages.

Whilst Steve Kiddy busied himself with the pitch refurbishment, the vital commercial continuity and recovery was led by Chief Executive Kaven Walker, supported by the Catering Manager. The various pre-booked weddings and parties were able to go ahead using kitchen and banqueting facilities on the upper floors. Alan Roberts still had his usual pre-season preparations to make to ensure operational and matchday continuity. So who would lead the stadium refurbishments? The decision was quickly taken to find specialist project managers to lead the recovery operation. Bond Bryan was appointed and immediately deployed three senior full-time staff.

There was a huge amount of expensive recovery work to do. For example, one main kitchen had to be gutted and completely re-equipped. Repairing the turnstiles cost £26,000. Six months on, only the dressing rooms have been reinstated on the ground floor. The ground is still a building site and local residents are still dealing with their own flood damage.

The Hillsborough flood makes a useful case study. With the benefit of hindsight, Alan Roberts thinks there are seven key lessons to be shared with other facility managers.

- You can't plan for everything – some risks are not reasonably foreseeable and so mitigating them is not appropriate.
- The unexpected happens – so ideally you should have reciprocal ground sharing arrangements already in place.
- What happens off the pitch is at least as important as the pitch itself.

- Specialist support – you need to know which experts you will call on before you need to use them. You also need to bring them in immediately to ensure the quickest possible response to the disaster.

- Contractors and equipment – suddenly everybody will be competing for the available resources. As with your experts, you need to know who your suppliers will be before you need to call them in.

- Longer term damage to the stadium fabric after it has dried out – six months on, the turnstile doors are rotting and some of the concrete terracing is crumbling.

3.5. STORM DAMAGE AT CHELTENHAM RACECOURSE

The original citation for this article is Frosdick, S. (2008) 'Calm in a Crisis', *Stadium and Arena Management*, June 2008, p. 10-12.

The 2008 Cheltenham Festival staged an extraordinary recovery from storm damage and the complete loss of the second day's racing. To find out how they did it, Steve Frosdick talked with Edward Gillespie.

The Cheltenham Festival in March each year has been described as the horseracing equivalent of the World Cup. Over four days, it attracts some 230,000 spectators – 5,000 making an annual pilgrimage from Ireland. Around the country, over £500 million is wagered on the 25 races, including the *totesport* Cheltenham Gold Cup – the highlight of the Jump racing season. This is a mammoth event.

The storms forecast for the 2008 Festival posed a severe test for Cheltenham's emergency planning. Despite having to cope with serious wind damage to the hospitality village and the complete cancellation of the second day's (Wednesday's) racing, Cheltenham managed to stage a near miraculous recovery for Thursday and Friday. The story of how Cheltenham kept going makes an excellent case study of very fast-time business continuity.

The business continuity process is shown in the figure below.

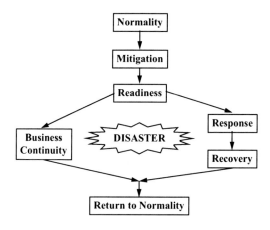

Business continuity involves assessing and mitigating risks, contingency planning, responding to crises, continuing to operate through an incident and managing the return to normality. Cheltenham Managing Director Edward Gillespie and I talked through the steps in the process to find out how they managed the storm crisis and so quickly returned to normal.

Mitigation

The 2001 cancellation of the entire Festival because of the foot and mouth crisis had reinforced the importance of proper insurance cover. But risk mitigation involves far more than this. Cheltenham had raced in November 2007 when the winds were at the 56 kph (35 mph) maximum for safe racing. They had been monitoring the weather forecasts and already knew that even higher winds were likely. This awareness meant they could liaise with the Irish trainers and get their 80-odd horses over early before the ferries got cancelled. Over the weekend before the Festival, a break in the winds allowed Cheltenham to remove the vulnerable roof of a large temporary grandstand. They also closed the hospitality village site overnight and relocated away from the temporary structures any staff etc. who were sleeping in tents or caravans.

Readiness

The run up to the Festival had seen a series of structured emergency planning meetings involving all the emergency services and staffing agencies. The planning culminated in a table-top exercise held the week before the Festival, when high winds were (deliberately) one of the scenarios exercised. There was thus a general state of readiness and people had exercised around the most likely risk.

Monday Crisis and Response

When Gillespie arrived on site at 0600 on the Monday morning, he found that the strong winds overnight had demolished a 700-person marquee in the hospitality village and damaged surrounding structures. Work immediately began to clear the mess, which was completed by 1430. Staff were also deployed to relocate or reschedule the 700 persons for each day. People who could not be moved into the spare hospitality capacity or who could not attend on an alternative day were offered a full refund. Customers reacted with a mixture of shock, disappointment and yet understanding and were grateful for Cheltenham's efforts to re-accommodate them.

Like most venues, Cheltenham has a crisis co-ordinating group, known locally as the 'Emergency Directorate', which can be convened if needed. At Cheltenham, the key players are well known to each other and the lines of communication are very short. The Monday night forecast was for further winds and Cheltenham now knew that 67 kph (42 mph) was the safe limit for the temporary structures. Thus when the Emergency Directorate first met at 1600 on the Monday, Cheltenham was already well into response mode.

Tuesday Mini-Crisis and Response

In the event, the winds on Tuesday were lower than expected and the full day's racing was held without incident. However there were strong gusts after the end of racing and it became necessary to calmly evacuate a particular temporary structure. Because the situation was not an obvious emergency (such as a fire), this proved to be difficult – the punters were very much enjoying their food and drink! It took Gillespie, his colleague and four police officers 20 minutes to clear the tent.

The gusts and weather forecast meant that it was decided to close the hospitality site at 2000. This was a massive inconvenience for the caterers and cleaners. They were now unable to clear away and reset for the next day and would have to reorganise their work when the site re-opened.

The Emergency Directorate met at 2030. It was noted that the forecast was for winds up to 80 kph (50 mph). Although it was hoped that the winds would be less than forecast, Gillespie was now notifying the British Horseracing Authority that Wednesday's racing might need to be rescheduled.

Wednesday – Main Crisis, Continuity and Response

Gillespie was in by 0500 on the Wednesday morning and would clearly have to operate on two fronts. On the one hand, it was possible the winds might abate and the day's racing go ahead as normal. On the other, it was probable that the whole day would be cancelled. By 0530, it had been decided how to reschedule three day's racing into two and by 0600 Gillespie was sure in his own mind that racing would be off. Although parallel preparations necessarily continued, by 0630 people were also getting ready for a cancellation. At 0710 another marquee was destroyed – people clearly heard it 'pop'.

The Emergency Directorate met at 0800. For insurance reasons, any cancellation had to be not 'just in case' but on the clear advice of the structural engineers, supported by the emergency services, that it would not be safe to admit the public and to race. Accordingly, at 0810, the formal decision was taken to cancel the day's racing. The parallel continuity preparations could now be laid aside.

Because Cheltenham's communications manager had had a head start on writing the media briefing and because many media agencies were already on site, Gillespie was able to appear on television and radio from 0830 to make the announcement. The website was constantly updated and there was a formal press conference at 12.30. The central messages were public safety, refunds and what was going to happen on Thursday and Friday. The delivery was calm and assured. It was clear that the Cheltenham team was on top of events. Many people heard the news before they left home and travel companies were informed so that others were able to abandon their journeys.

Meanwhile the Racing Director was working with the British Horseracing Authority to talk to sponsors and trainers and secure their agreement to the revised race schedules. Races were now on different days and even on different courses (Cheltenham has two which are used alternately). Fortunately, the sponsors and trainers were all very supportive and keen to race.

At the same time, the various staffing agencies were in contact with their personnel to reorganise work schedules and deployments.

'When I walked back into the office at 12 noon,' Gillespie told me, 'the scene was one of enormous calm. Everybody was just getting on with their jobs, for example arranging additional stabling for the horses'.

By 1300, the race programme for Thursday and Friday had been fixed. Racing would start earlier at 1230, the race orders had been completely changed and the card had been extended by four races on Thursday and two on Friday. The news media were informed so that they could update their racing pages and the Tote now had to decide which races would be the jackpot etc.

'By now', said Gillespie, 'we had moved from response to recovery mode'.

Recovery and Return to Normality

Over the next three hours, Cheltenham gradually returned to normal. 'People found it remarkable that Thursday's race card came out looking like it had always been like that. But actually, each day's card is finished by 1600 and printed overnight, so before 1600 we were back in the normal zone', explained Gillespie.

The Emergency Directorate met at 1600 to confirm the plans for Thursday. At 1630, the hospitality site was re-opened. The caterers and cleaners could now get in to do what they could not do 24 hours earlier and so get ready for the next day.

Gillespie was again on site by 0500 on Thursday. The wind had calmed, everything was fine and the whole site was able to open as normal. The rearranged final two days of the Festival were then Cheltenham's usual triumph, enjoyed by over 50,000 racing fans each day.

Lessons Learned

Gillespie felt that there were four lessons learned that could be of wider benefit to *S&AM* readers.

- It is very difficult to evacuate a hospitality tent – once the customers are in full swing, they will not want to leave.

- To keep the public informed and to maintain goodwill, it is essential to get the media messages right. The words to be used on the website and in briefings need to be carefully crafted. Media broadcasts need to be monitored and any misinformation quickly corrected.

- To support an insurance claim for business interruption, it is important to get the decision-making process right. The decision to abandon must be informed by the clear and certain advice of the emergency services and structural engineers.

- The successful management of the crisis and the rapid recovery proved the value of multi-agency planning, the table-top exercise and the 'Emergency Directorate'.

3.4. AND 3.5. COMMENTARY BY JIM CHALMERS – FLOODING AT HILLSBOROUGH STADIUM AND STORM DAMAGE AT CHELTENHAM RACECOURSE.

Frosdick's articles on the flooding of Hillsborough Stadium in Sheffield in 2007 and the storm damage at Cheltenham Racecourse in 2008 illustrate only too clearly the raw power of nature at its worst. However both incidents, whilst serious in their own right, pale into insignificance compared to natural disasters such as the 2011 earthquakes in New Zealand and Japan. Nevertheless, both articles demonstrate the importance of contingency planning and business continuity management, these being the underlying themes in both scenarios.

Business continuity management can be described as a holistic process that identifies potential impacts which could threaten the organisation and provides a framework for building resilience and the capability of an effective response to those threats. In so doing it safeguards the interests of the key stakeholders and the reputation of the organisation.

I agree with Alan Roberts, the then operations manager at Hillsborough Stadium, that the flooding of the stadium was a once in a thousand years scenario. But what is not a once in a thousand years scenario is the possibility of a sports grounds business being unable to continue to operate due to some calamity such as adverse weather conditions. There can be numerous other causes which can affect business continuity such as fire, structural failure (as occurred at Cheltenham), terrorist incidents, explosions, serious crime or even industrial action. The list could go on but these are just examples of serious incidents which could affect spectator safety or disrupt the normal operations of the sports ground. Incidents such as at Hillsborough and at Cheltenham occurred suddenly and unexpectedly and it is up to ground management to decide how best to prepare for such contingencies. To use the age old expression, 'Failing to plan is planning to fail'. In that context it is interesting to compare the management responses at Hillsborough and at Cheltenham. Judging from the articles, the management at the racecourse seemed better prepared in their responses.

When the articles were originally published the content struck a chord very close to my heart. During my police career I was the chief superintendent in charge of the uniform operations department in West Midlands Police. One of my responsibilities was planning and exercising for major incident responses in the force area. This included contingency planning to deal with crashed aircraft, serious civil unrest, acts of terrorism, the spread of life-threatening diseases, nuclear explosions, industrial actions which threatened the life of the community. There was even a plan to deal with a satellite breaking up in space with parts falling to earth. So contingency planning, including restoring normality as soon as possible, was part of my everyday life for many years.

On my retirement from the police in 1991 and joining the Football Licensing Authority (FLA) Inspectorate, I took my knowledge and interest in contingency planning with me. I wrote the first FLA guidance on contingency planning in 1994 and updated this in 2002. In 2001 I also wrote the FLA guidance on exercise planning since in my experience the exercising of any contingency plans should be regarded as an integral part of the contingency planning process. It was Sophocles who said in 5 BC, 'One must learn by doing the thing. For though you think you know it, you have no certainty until you try'.

I would suggest that sentiment is equally valid in the present day. Those who may have to implement contingency plans need to be exercised in their operation so as to assess their response procedures and the effectiveness of the plan. This was obviously recognised by management at the racecourse as described in the article. However despite all that has been written about contingency planning including advice over the years from the FLA and in the *Guide to Safety at Sports Grounds*, I know of sports grounds where no plans exist, where plans are many years out of date and even where plans exist but have never been exercised. So there are still sports grounds woefully ill equipped to respond to any incident likely to affect spectator safety or disrupt their normal ground operations.

I agree with Frosdick's description of the business continuity management process and how this should form part of integrated contingency planning. Whilst within the safety organisation the development of contingency plans has gone a long way towards satisfying the business continuity plan, it is still necessary to take the widest view of the organisation to ensure that all eventualities have been considered. The ground management should involve and include their own resources, the emergency services, certifying authorities and other local agencies such as the emergency planning department, in harmonising responses to ensure a speedy return to normality. This concept appears to have been recognised at the racecourse with their 'emergency directorate'. At most football grounds they do not have an 'emergency directorate', instead using the club safety advisory group as the forum to serve the same purpose.

In my opinion therefore the basis for business continuity planning relies heavily on contingency planning in the widest context - harmonised with external agencies. To illustrate this, at most of the larger sports grounds you will generally come across three types of contingency plans:

- There is the emergency plan or major incident plan owned and managed by the local authority;
- There is then an emergency services plan relating to a specific location such as a sports ground;
- There is then the contingency plan prepared by the sports ground or venue management. It is in this plan that I would expect to find the business continuity plan.

Whatever the type of plan, the underlying aim of the planning process should be to develop flexible arrangements which will enable the sports grounds management and any related agency to deal with a crisis situation.

For example at Kidderminster Harriers (my club), since it is a small stadium, we only have a club plan and not an emergency services plan, since their initial responses to any incident at the ground are included in the club plan. The latter section of our contingency plan includes our business continuity plan. Thankfully up to now we have never had to implement this but have always included this aspect of our planning in the exercises held at the club to test and validate our plans and those who have to implement them.

In my opinion integrated contingency planning embraces a number of phased concepts. Firstly there is the prevention phase when measures are introduced in advance of an emergency situation to prevent it occurring or to reduce its severity. This could include in fire prevention the installation of a sprinkler system or to combat terrorism the building of physical barriers to prevent a vehicle being driven into a building by a potential suicide bomber.

There is then the preparedness phase when an essential part of the planning process is the assessment of hazard and risk. This planning phase also needs to be underpinned by training and exercises.

There is then the response phase by the ground management, the emergency services and the certifying authority as appropriate. The basic objectives of this phase are to save life, prevent the escalation of the emergency incident, relieve suffering, protect property and (where a crime is suspected) to enable any criminal or forensic examination to take place. Ground management very often underestimate the effect of a serious criminal incident on a venue. In the case of a suspicious fire, criminal damage or terrorist incident, all or part of the venue could be closed for months whilst the police conduct their investigations. This is when the next phase has to be planned for.

This is the recovery or continuity phase which encompasses those activities necessary to provide a rapid return to normality both for those affected by the crisis situation and those providing any support services. For example, in the case of a fire at a sports ground, how quickly could the venue re-open for business as normal?

Since both articles relate to sports grounds incidents and their business continuity planning, I intend to ignore for the purposes of this commentary any further reference to local authority or emergency services plans. I will instead concentrate on the requirements for good contingency and business continuity planning at a sports ground. Such planning is another piece of the jigsaw in the ground management's overall responsibility for spectator safety. It should be approached in the context of safety in the round and integrated with other elements such as the spectator safety policy, the safety procedures, safety personnel, safety equipment and training.

Experience has shown how emergencies can arise at a sports ground with little or no warning. Relatively minor incidents can quickly escalate into a major incident unless tackled in a controlled and systematic way. The 1985 Bradford fire was the perfect example – what was believed to have started with a discarded cigarette was within a couple minutes a raging inferno.

It is therefore the responsibility of ground management to assess the risk of any incident occurring at their ground which could prejudice spectator safety or disrupt the ground operations and which cannot be dealt with under normal circumstances. As a result of this risk assessment process ground management should prepare their contingency plans to determine their specific response actions or the mobilisation of specialist resources such as the emergency services. They should also consider their business continuity response.

Safety certificate holders will be required within the safety certificate to produce contingency plans, review and test them and keep them up to date. This should be done in conjunction with the emergency services and the certifying authority. Should the ground management fail to discharge these legal responsibilities then the certifying authority should reduce the ground capacity. It is worth remembering that risk has become a tool of our legal system. When anything goes wrong, the first question regularly posed is 'Who can we blame and how much can we claim?' Failures in contingency planning may thus expose the venue to both civil and criminal liabilities.

Effective contingency plans should lay down a structured and graduated response with clear guidance or instructions on the action to be taken in particular circumstances. These should include the actions by ground safety personnel and in particular those of the safety officer and stewards in an emergency situation. This is essential in the early stages of any incident where without properly defined and structured contingency plans there will at best be confusion and at worst disaster. This is why it is essential that ground management have a clearly defined command and control structure identified within their spectator safety policy.

Good contingency planning starts with a competent person, such as the ground safety officer, conducting a safety audit and producing the risk assessments. This follows the same principles as health and safety risk assessments, namely:

- Identify the hazards to which spectators and others at the ground may be exposed;

- Determine the level of risk;

- Assess whether the existing safety management procedures are adequate to eliminate the hazard and, where this is not possible, reduce the risk to an acceptable level by preventative or protective measures;

- Continually assess and review the adequacy of these procedures.

It is very likely that the safety advisory group will be consulted by ground management in this risk assessment phase to make sure nothing important has been missed.

All venues can be susceptible to hazards as the articles testify. Many will recall the chaos that occurred in Liverpool when the Grand National horse race was called off due to a bomb threat and the racecourse had to be evacuated. Sadly in this day and age the threat of terrorist activity is never very far away. I do not think that any sporting venue is immune from this hazard and the consequences of a suicide bomber activating a bomb in a crowded stadium will be devastating, not only for the casualties and their families but also for the organisation as it tries to recover the use its premises for business as normal. Recognising the terrorist threat is only the start of the planning process. It is not enough to wait for the hazard to occur and then start planning the response. By then it is already too late. It is working the threat through to a business continuity solution which is the sign of good planning.

In the racecourse article, Frosdick refers to the table top exercise staged at the venue just prior to the racing event. No commentary on contingency planning would be complete without making some reference to such exercises.

Exercises should be regarded as an integral part of the contingency planning process. An exercise is not a one-off event but part of an ongoing process of testing, analysing, reviewing and planning again. Testing of plans is more than just a paper review. It requires some form of exercise during which those responsible for implementing the contingency plans can practice or rehearse how to respond to a particular emergency situation.

Experience over many years has shown that exercises are the only practical, efficient and proven method by which ground management, the ground safety personnel, the certifying authority and the emergency services can test and validate their contingency planning arrangements. It is a statement of fact that an untested plan is no plan at all. The FLA 2009 publication *Sports Grounds and Stadia Guide No. 4 – Safety Management* recommends that:

- Management should hold a minimum of one live exercise every year;
- Such an exercise should ideally be preceded by one or more seminars, table top or control centre exercises;
- The exercise programme should endeavour over a maximum period of five years to cover the full range of the sports grounds contingency plans.

The FLA publication explains the different types of exercises as follows:

- Seminar – based on a classroom environment and also known as an orientation, workshop or discussion exercise.
- Tabletop – likewise classroom based, also known as a floor plan exercise.
- Control centre – in military circles sometimes known as training without troops, in a sports ground this type of exercise could be based around the actual central control point or ground control room.
- Live – also known as an on-location, site, practical, operational or field exercise.

Live exercises are logistically difficult to organise and it is very difficult to be realistic without disrupting the event. But there is no reason why ground management should not arrange a seminar, table top or control centre exercise around any scenario which would take their venue out of use for whatever period. The exercise should involve anyone likely to be involved in the business continuity solution. This would include the senior ground management, insurers, assessors, preferred contractors, the certifying authority and anyone else likely to be involved in restoring the premises to normality.

In this commentary I have only been able to provide a snapshot of the principles of contingency, business continuity and exercise planning. These are dynamic processes with the plans regarded as living documents that must be kept constantly under review in the light of experience and changing circumstances. Unless there is this constant evaluation process, how can senior ground management ever be confident that their plans and those who will have to implement them will rise to the occasion in an emergency situation such as occurred at Hillsborough Stadium and Cheltenham Racecourse? Such situations should impel senior ground management to make sure business continuity is part of their contingency planning portfolio. To do nothing with regards to business continuity is in my opinion not an option.

3.6. LONDON 2012

The original citation for this article is Frosdick, S. (2009) 'Three Years Out', *Stadium and Arena Management*, February 2009, p. 38-39.

With the Beijing Olympic Games safely behind us, Steve Frosdick reports on progress with the safety and security preparations for London 2012.

Meeting the International Olympic Committee's security requirements forms a significant chunk of spending for an Olympic Games. The scope is vast, covering asset and people protection, food hygiene, disease prevention and information security. For London 2012, the *Independent on Sunday* (28 September 2008) quoted a senior official as stating that the security costs could reach £1.5 billion, nearly three times the original estimate, largely because of the increased terrorist threat. With three years still to go, the initial preparations are now well in hand.

As a framework for what is very much an early and partial discussion, I've taken the idea of the five Olympic rings and the headings shown in Figure One.

Figure One – Olympics Safety and Security Rings

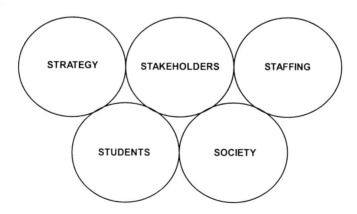

Strategy

The UK government has expressed a clear commitment to delivering a consistent and co-ordinated approach to safety and security in the 35 Olympic venues across the country. Because of the terrorist threat – a reality at the Munich and Atlanta Games – the Olympics are seen as a high profile target. Anti-terror security rather than general safety has thus understandably been the early priority. The strategic approach seems to have been top down, conceiving the Games as a global event threatened by international terrorism, and the early security strategy has focused on this high level.

Dissenting voices have argued for a bottom up approach, considering the threats to individual venues and infrastructure and then scaling up to the overview. Wembley manages to host 80,000 people for three days in a row for the end of season football play-offs with parallel concerts going on in the adjacent Wembley Arena. The Olympics might be seen as something conceptually similar, albeit with more venues, a larger audience and over a longer timeframe.

2008 has seen changes in the identities of some of the most senior security players, and this may have been a reflection of the political debate about security strategy, which remains unresolved.

But what about safety in the venues and the transport infrastructure? Andrew Amery is the Head of Security for the London Organising Committee of the Olympic Games (LOCOG). He explained that safety presently sits within the venues functional area. Key early priorities have been ensuring alignment with the various regulations and official guidance such as the *Green Guide to Safety at Sports Grounds*. Thus whilst the safety and security functions are currently correctly separated, Amery feels that, 'this will need to change when we move to operational planning'. Amery's view is that 'operational crowd management would benefit from being in the same planning area as security'. This will be developed at the appropriate time as LOCOG migrates from operations into event delivery.

Mindful of the Grozny stadium bomb, which was placed during the construction of the building, safety and security are being built into the designs of the venues and the Olympic Park. A host of technology will be deployed, however, as Amery explains, '2012 is not the time to be test-bedding new kit'. Accordingly, there is a technological lock-down so that only technologies which have reached a particular level of maturity will be permitted.

Consistency across the venues is an important feature of the strategy. As Amery explains, disproportionately target-hardening the eight venues in the Olympic Park could simply displace the risk elsewhere in the country.

Stakeholders

Strategy is being developed within what Amery describes as 'a complex international stakeholder map'. To name but a few, this map involves governing bodies, regulatory organisations, commercial sponsors, suppliers and individual athletes. All will have varying safety and security needs, all of which will have to be met. In the UK alone, the organisational complexity is extraordinary, with a legion of different organisations involved in a plethora of steering groups, working parties and the like. Amery recognises the complexities and challenges in this area and is working closely with the Olympic Security Directorate, which is responsible for co-ordinating and implementing the strategy in partnership with the stakeholders.

David Evans is the London 2012 Project Director for the British Security Industry Association (BSIA), which is acting as the lead voice for the private security industry. Debriefs from previous Games around the world have noted a lack of co-ordination or integration between the industry and the police, who along with the venues form the three key stakeholders at the operational level. London 2012 provides an opportunity to break new ground by creating the mechanism for a public/private partnership to deliver safety and security on the ground.

Andrew Amery considers that this partnership could comprise four tiers. The lowest tier would involve trained volunteers who would act as ushers, giving help and directions to spectators on the approaches to the venues and around the Olympic Park. The second tier would be safety stewards of the type one finds in stadia and arenas, monitoring crowd ingress and egress, supervising the viewing areas and on hand to deal with any emergency evacuation.

The third tier would be those stewards requiring Security Industry Authority (SIA) licences to carry out security duties; searching, intervention and ejecting people from the venues. Finally, the fourth tier would be the public police, who would patrol to provide reassurance but also take responsibility for counter-terrorism, crime and major incidents.

Staffing

The Games will require about 100,000 temporary staff to work in catering, cleaning, merchandising and other spectator services as well as in safety and security. Whilst many of these people will be volunteers, there will be challenges in sourcing the workforce. In parallel with the Olympics, all the usual summer and weekly events will still be taking place, all of which will require their usual staff. This will be a highly competitive market where premium payments may be offered to avoid staff being tempted away.

Evans points out the common problem that venues and the police make their plans in isolation from the private security industry, assuming that it can supply whatever they decide they need. 'Which it either can't,' says Evans, 'or sometimes won't', particularly if there is other more lucrative work elsewhere.

For 2012, says Evans, 'the London candidate file reports that the industry needs to supply 6,500 safety and security staff; and that this is within its capabilities given the appropriate notice.' Subsequent work by the venue profiling team now estimates that the peak requirement will be on day seven of the Games, when 8,000 safety and security staff will be required.

Evans explains the various factors affecting capacity. The industry runs under establishment and people routinely work long hours. Many stewarding staff are on the books of more than one company, so there is double-counting. It will be the summer holidays and some staff will want to watch the events as spectators. Most importantly, the key lesson from the Commonwealth Games in Manchester was that companies should not neglect their long-term customers and so make sure that all their existing contracts were fully resourced.

According to Evans, the stark truth is that the industry can probably supply about one in eight of the staff required, i.e. 1,000 of the 8,000. As Evans puts it, 'There is a huge gap between the requirement and the industry's current capacity to supply.'

One option might be to use the Wimbledon Tennis model. Here the military are deployed as ushers, and about 600 university students are trained as stewards and security staff, who are SIA licensed. But this model, says Evans, 'is less 'plannable' for the volume required, as planning normally takes place in the year before the Championships. It also leaves less legacy than the concept of using Further Education students for 2012.'

Students

The notion of 'Bridging the Gap: the Further Education Concept' was presented on 3 July 2008 following discussions between the BSIA, SIA, London Development Agency, Skills for Security and the Association of London Colleges.

Further Education Colleges in London and the Home Counties have thousands of students aged 16 to 19, many from the more deprived boroughs in the East of London where the main venues will be housed. The idea is to target those who will be 18 or 19 in four years time and offer them the opportunity to obtain an additional vocational qualification in stewarding and security; the chance to work during the Games; and the legacy of long-term career opportunities in the security or uniformed industries. 'Bridging the Gap' will be particularly relevant for students on public services and sports courses. Colleges in the host Boroughs will take the lead and staff tutors could be deployed as supervisors.

Society

'Bridging the Gap' envisages a legacy of social benefits. As well as a network of colleges with a common approach to enrichment and additional qualifications for learners, there will be new employees entering the security supply chain and reduced unemployment in the host Boroughs. 'Bridging the Gap' could provide a model for future events such as Glasgow 2014.

Evans is excited about how the 'Bridging the Gap' legacy could be enhanced by organising a Jobs Fair after the Games, offering students the opportunity to investigate careers in the uniformed services (military and police) and in the private security industry. Of wider social significance, Amery can see the potential for 'Bridging the Gap' to prevent the young men and women of east London being drawn into extremism or gang related culture by providing them with a gateway to a responsible career in the police or security industry – model citizens with higher expectations for the future.

3.6. UPDATE ON LONDON 2012

Jim Chalmers has included a detailed update on the safety and security preparations for London 2012 in his commentary on article 5.2. in Part V of this book. The information has not been repeated here.

PART IV – MYSTERY SPECTATOR VISITS

Introduction

Part IV comprises seven articles by Steve Frosdick and a composite commentary by Jim Chalmers. The articles cover 'mystery spectator visits' between 2006 and 2010 to venues in the UK, Europe and the United States. The commentary notes the variety of venues and match day experiences and suggests that these demonstrate that UK lessons-learned are being applied internationally.

4.1. World Cup Weekend

In the first article, published in *Stadium and Arena Management* in 2006, Steve Frosdick and Andrew Rawlings give a father and son perspective on facility safety and the fan experience at the World Cup in Germany.

4.2. Emirates Experience

Also in 2006, Steve Frosdick and Andrew Rawlings told *Stadium and Arena Management* about the fan experience at Arsenal's new Emirates Stadium.

4.3. Live at Wembley

Moving on to 2007, *Stadium and Arena Management* carried Steve Frosdick and Rachel Rawlings' report on the first sell-out concert at the new Wembley Stadium.

4.4. Wembley Progress

In 2009, Steve Frosdick returned to Wembley Stadium with his two sons for an end of season play-off match between Millwall and Scunthorpe United football clubs.

4.5. Estádio da Luz

In the next *Stadium and Arena Management* article from 2009, Frosdick and his son go to Portugal to look at how UK-style stewarding and 'friendly but firm' policing have become embedded.

4.6. Nou Camp Night

This *Stadium and Arena Management* article from 2010 carries a report on the logistical complexities behind organising a night out *at Barcelona's Camp Nou stadium.*

4.7. O-Rena Orlando

The final *Stadium and Arena Management* article from 2010 reports on a visit to the City of Orlando's Amway Arena for a Friday night Arena Football game.

4.1 - 4.7. Commentaries

Chalmers comments individually on each of the 'mystery spectator' reports. He concludes that, in terms of safety management, there is little the UK can learn from Frosdick's visits overseas – rather that the visits go some way to evidencing the export of UK expertise, particularly in Europe.

4.1. WORLD CUP WEEKEND

The original citation for this article is Frosdick, S. and Rawlings, A. (2006) 'World Cup Weekend', *Stadium and Arena Management*, August 2006, pp. 8-9.

Steve Frosdick and Andrew Rawlings give a father and son fan perspective on facility safety and the fan experience at the World Cup in Germany.

We were among the fortunate few to succeed in the FIFA ticket allocation process – Angola v Portugal in Cologne on Sunday 11 June. So we planned a weekend taking in the Fan Fest in Frankfurt for the England v Paraguay match on the Saturday.

We could write about many things. But we're not going to talk about the (generally good but occasionally embarrassing) behaviour of our fellow countrymen in our hotel, in the bars or on the trains. We're not going to report on the security successes arising from the 'friendly but firm policing' tactics in the host cities. We will forgive FIFA the excessive commercialism – we're still laughing about the official phrasebook with such gems as, 'Acceptieren Sie Mastercard?' – and inadequate ticket allocation to fans rather than sponsors. But we do want to comment on the safety and fan issues we experienced on our trip.

Saturday morning saw us on the train. All around Frankfurt station was heaving and we were advised to get straight down to the Fan Fest by the River Main. This was an excellent concept, allowing ticketless fans to experience the atmosphere whilst watching a giant screen – in Frankfurt's case set up in the middle of the river! There were plenty of portable toilets and food and drink concessions on the site.

The Fan Fest was almost full but we got in and found seats in a temporary stand. Shortly afterwards, the authorities closed the entrances because the safe capacity had been reached. The site was full but by no means overcrowded. This was good crowd management. Inside the site, the stewards kept the stairways clear but left the good humoured fans to get on with it. I had no concerns letting Andrew (aged 12) make his own way round the site.

The primary safety measure was the access control. At the barrier, we had to dump all bottles. It was roasting hot and people were complaining they would need water, but the stewards were very firm – only open plastic beakers were permitted, but most people didn't have these. We could see fans stuffing bottles down their trousers, but the stewards inside the barrier carefully searched everybody and confiscated them.

The sun was oppressive and it was over 30 degrees. Many fans drank nothing but beer and must have got sunburn, however the loudspeakers kept encouraging us to drink water and the Fire Brigade were brought in to spray their hoses on the crowds. People were queuing for over an hour to buy drinks so we ended up using a discarded plastic cup and drinking the water from the taps in the portable toilets. Overall, safety had taken precedence over welfare. Fair enough, since the overarching safety requirement was to minimise missiles.

England did not play well but it was great to just 'be there' with thousands of other England fans. We also enjoyed the Fan Fest for other matches and fan groups back in Cologne's Heumarkt. This was again well managed with the same access control arrangements and good temporary facilities. Since it was a much smaller venue and not often full, the queues for food and beverage were fine.

The advice was to arrive early, so on Sunday we got to the stadium three hours before kick-off. Again the primary safety measure was access control, supported by high profile stewarding. The police presence at the ground was unobtrusive. Fans had been warned that tickets would be checked against passports but we saw no evidence that this happened. There were barriers at the entrance to the stadium grounds where we were searched by stewards and our tickets were checked. Again, no bottles were permitted and it seemed clear the rules were consistent at the different venues.

We were then able to buy programmes, merchandise, food and beverage in the stadium grounds – but all at inflated prices. It seemed a rip off to prevent us bringing drinks in on safety grounds and then sell us bottled water decanted into beakers for €3.50 – three times the shop price. And we had to pay a €1.50 deposit on each beaker!

Entry to the stadium was through a low turnstile where our tickets were checked in a data reader. Tickets were then checked at three further points as we made our way up the stairs and vomitories to our seats.

We were right next to a block of 2,000 Angolan supporters and they were loud. It was great that the organisers had taken a far more permissive attitude towards the fans, who were allowed to bring drums, instruments, flags and banners into the ground. Fans were allowed to drink beer in their seats, in contrast to the total ban on alcohol at UEFA matches. And apart from the blocks of fans with team series tickets, there was no segregation at all. This all contributed to a noisy, good humoured and exciting atmosphere.

Having strictly controlled the access, we were interested to see how active the stewards would be inside the stadium. The Angolan fans were all stood up and it was difficult for late comers to find their seats. So they stood or sat in the gangways, which creates a safety risk associated with emergency access or evacuation. We were impressed that the stewards did not ignore this behaviour, but one by one escorted the fans to their correct places and cleared the gangways. The stewards were friendly but firm – the ideal approach. A similar situation arose in the adjacent stand around half time. Again, we could see the stewards were active in dealing with it.

Inevitably at such a big tournament, there will have been reports of safety and customer care things that did not go so well elsewhere. But ours was a very positive experience. We always felt safe, the Fan Fest concept worked well and the facilities we experienced were generally good. To have been at a World Cup match together was brilliant – and the sausages weren't bad either!

4.2. EMIRATES EXPERIENCE

The original citation for this article is Frosdick, S. and Rawlings, A. (2006) 'Emirates Experience', *Stadium and Arena Management*, December 2006, p. 35.

Following on from their 'World Cup Weekend', Steve Frosdick and Andrew Rawlings report on the fan experience at Arsenal's new Emirates Stadium.

Having toured the 60,000 seater Emirates Stadium at the October meeting of the UKSMA (*S&AM* October 2006), Steve Frosdick was keen to sample the matchday experience. 12 year-old Andrew volunteered to test the pies and hot dogs! So the scene was set to check out the access control, concourse facilities and the stadium bowl for Arsenal versus Hamburg in the UEFA Champions League.

The stadium approaches were well controlled with filter cordons of police officers, whilst club stewards patrolled the external podium and entrances. These were clearly marked and we easily found our way to our turnstiles, which were full height to prevent unauthorised entry. There were no turnstile staff and access was by inserting a 'smart' ticket into a reader. We couldn't work out which end to insert but a steward was quickly on hand to help us. Once inside we took the stairs to the upper tier. The clear signage meant we quickly found our block. There were stewards at the exit from the vomitory. They didn't check our tickets but they helped us find our seats when we asked them. We noticed that, as it got busier, the stewards became more active in ticket checking and directing people to their places. Throughout the match, the stewards worked hard keeping the vomitory and gangways clear. Overall, we thought the access control was very good – thorough without being obtrusive.

The catering outlets were bright and clean with plenty of staff – a promising start. The food was nicely presented but the prices over the top – we paid £9 each for a hot dog, pie and soft drink. We thought each item was at least £1 overpriced. Sauces, forks, etc. were available at separate 'Sauce Stations'. We sampled the fare only minutes after the stadium opened but the bottles of mustard and ketchup had been put out nearly empty and with the lids all messy.

Not impressive. The food itself was only ok although the branded soft drinks were good. At half time the queues at the outlets were long and did not clear until ten minutes after the start of the second half. Overall then, we were disappointed and thought the concourse catering was poor value.

The concourses themselves were spacious with great views through the glass walls over the surrounding area. The concourses were clean, with plenty of rubbish bins. There were lots of toilets and we noticed that cleaning staff were on hand throughout the match. Even after the game, the toilets were still in good order, so a definite thumb up here.

Emirates is a distinctive and beautiful four-tiered stadium. Even in the upper tier, the design of the continuous bowl optimises viewing – the corners sweep down so there are no seats too far away from the pitch. The excellent view is enhanced by the seat comfort – every single seat in the bowl is upholstered, generously sized and with plenty of leg room. This was the most comfortable 'ordinary' stadium seat we've ever sat in. The public address system was loud and clear and the two jumbo screens superb – great for seeing the goals over again. The striking roof design amplified the crowd noise within the bowl. The Hamburg fans were in good voice after an early goal and, as Arsenal gradually fought back, so the atmosphere continued to build, reaching a crescendo towards the end of the second half. When Arsenal took the lead we all went mad!

In summary, we had a great night out. Arsenal's new home is a fantastic football ground and we loved it. Who's to say where we'll turn up next?

4.3. LIVE AT WEMBLEY

The original citation for this article is Frosdick, S. and Rawlings, R. (2007) 'Live at Wembley', *Stadium and Arena Management*, August 2007, p. 36-37.

Continuing the S&AM series of 'mystery spectator' visits, Steve Frosdick and Rachel Rawlings report on the first sell-out concert at the new Wembley Stadium.

Following George Michael, UK trio Muse were scheduled to play the second live concert at the new Wembley, which was finally completed in time for the *Stadia and Arena 2007* event. The June 16th date was announced in December 2006 and we booked four tickets online within the first 30 minutes of their release. Muse are a huge draw and the gig quickly sold out – an additional date was added later.

Seven months later, three excited teenage girls and their driver set out for Wembley. The iconic arch means you can see the stadium from a long way off, the route was well sign posted and we had a smooth journey in. Parking is limited, so the authorities are encouraging fans to travel by train. The station has been rebuilt and the walk down Olympic Way, the stadium rising majestically in front of you, is as evocative as ever. We paid £20 for the car park – Central London prices – but we arrived early and had no problems.

The access information on the ticket and the signage around the stadium were clear, so we found our entrance easily. Our bags were checked efficiently and there was no silliness about not bringing plastic drinks bottles or snacks in. Rachel had a metal aerosol in her handbag which the steward found but sensibly decided did not pose a threat to public safety.

We were in Level Five – the upper tier – which is a long way up. But there are no more stairs to climb at the new Wembley and we ascended under the close supervision of the 'escalator stewards'. Our tickets were carefully checked at the vomitory to our block and the stewards pointed us towards our seats, midway up the tier. We were opposite the centre line yet we were fairly side-on to the stage. A good third of the seats in the bowl were unusable, but of course there were lots of people on the pitch, which had a protective covering.

There were three support acts and the show lasted over six hours, however the seats remained very comfortable throughout. The leg-room was exceptional and the sightlines great. Just one problem – in a 90,000 seater stadium the upper tier is so far away from the stage, the performers look like ants. On the plus side, the overview of the mosh pits and the whole crowd was really spectacular. We certainly felt part of something big.

Throughout the show, there were engineers patrolling the gangways to monitor the sound quality. And here lies Wembley's first big problem. The roof design enhances the atmosphere and minimises sound pollution at sports events by holding the sound inside the bowl. But for concerts, this means the sound bounces around. This was worse the higher you went. In the upper tier, we were getting the sound through the public address system rather than the speaker stacks. The sound was blurred and there was a visible time lag between the performers playing a note and us hearing them. I spoke with one of the engineers during one of the support acts and he used the word 'atrocious'. Things did improve for Muse but the overall sound was disappointing.

The second gripe was with the food and beverage. Yes, there were a huge number of outlets all around the concourse and these were all fully staffed and well equipped. Yes, you could see that a lot of thought had gone into the design of the food offering – scotch beef burgers in a classy bun with tasty cheese and relish served in stylish boxes with greaseproof paper overprinted with details of Wembley legends. Doubtless this was all intended to justify the premium pricing – £7.50 for a burger, chips and soft drink.

But the delivery was sadly lacking. Till staff were standing around and some queues built up because the full-cook staff couldn't get stuff out quickly enough. What did come out wasn't evenly distributed – for example one concession had five lots of chicken but no burgers or fish whilst the next door one – supplied from the same kitchen – had burgers but nothing else.

All four of us used different concessions and three of us had branded soft drinks served warm and flat – apparently there were problems with the dispensers. And some of the food wasn't properly cooked – the man in front of me sent two lots of fish back because the middles were still raw. Two out of three of our burgers were tepid and the fries soggy. Only one was fresh and hot. Bizarrely, you could not buy chips on their own, so vegetarian Sophie was limited to one choice – a snack size pizza baguette for £4.

Wembley clearly know they've got teething problems with the catering because there were monitoring staff from an outside company auditing the service delivery.

We're not alone in voicing these criticisms, although other fans were full of praise. Rachel surfed a few Internet forums after the event and the comments below are typical of what the fans were saying.

- 'I felt too far away. There wasn't any atmosphere back there. Mr Bellamy was 1.5 cm tall when I could spot him. Since I watched everything on the screens anyway, I really felt that I'd have been better off watching it on telly at home. Still, that Wembley is dead smart these days.'
- 'Lots of moshing, crowd surfing and shoving. Was good. Muse rule!'
- 'The visuals were outstanding, as one would expect from Muse, with some fantastic backdrops for several songs.'
- 'Perfect gig, perfect venue.'
- 'I was standing and the view of the stage was bad, even quite near the front. Should the stage be higher? Maybe.'
- 'The acoustics in the stadium were appalling, what a waste of money.'
- 'Despite vastly increased facilities, queues were formidable for both toilets and refreshments, while during the interval thirsty concert-goers at drinks outlets were informed that the stadium had run out of beer.'
- 'Wembley was a great venue and the acoustics were great.'
- 'It's the sound that's the problem.'

- 'Even though I was at the back seating, for which Matt Bellamy was the size of an ant (a red one!), it was still a superb atmosphere.'
- 'And you can't buy a portion of chips without it being part of a meal.'
- 'It was as if [they] were shouting into the walls of a cave and the only echoes that could be heard sounded like school playground noise with drilling going on in the street outside.'

The new stadium boasts over two thousand more toilets than the old. These remained in fairly good order and there were housekeeping staff cleaning and replenishing throughout the show.

The most notable feature of the stadium management was the exceptionally high staffing levels. There were safety stewards and response team staff everywhere – on escalators, on stairways, in the concourses, in the vomitories and distributed throughout the bowl. Supervisors and managers were also very evident. In all my event experience I have never seen so many staff on duty. We felt very safe.

The crowd behaviour seemed good. Of course everyone stood all the way through the Muse set, but the mood was very happy and the gangways were kept clear. Almost everyone observed the 'no smoking' rule – and we weren't sure what the few disobedient ones were smoking anyway!

Egress after the show was straightforward with ample capacity on the stairs. We were fortunate in being parked near the end of a row and had no trouble getting out of the car park and away.

All in all, of course we had a good day out. There are operational teething problems, but the new Wembley has been worth the wait. Like the old stadium, however, there are question marks against its suitability as a music rather than sporting venue.

4.4. WEMBLEY PROGRESS

The original citation for this article is Frosdick, S. (2009) 'Wembley Progress', *Stadium and Arena Management*, August 2009, pp. 22-23.

'Mystery fan' Steve Frosdick returns to Wembley Stadium with his two sons for an end of season soccer match.

Having previously visited Wembley with my daughter for the second live concert held at the stadium (see *S&AM* August 2007), I was keen to make a return trip to the 90,000 seater venue. Millwall's qualification for a play-off final against Scunthorpe provided the opportunity. Millwall fans have a poor reputation with the authorities, so I like to spend time with them to experience safety and security close up.

Wembley is a 'public transport venue' and so many fans arrive by train from Central London. As with most Wembley matches, the South Africa public house in Baker Street is a lively meeting point. We used the toilets there and found the atmosphere carnivalesque rather than frightening.

For financial reasons to do with cross-charging, the Metropolitan Police and British Transport Police now restrict themselves to their own 'footprints'. This means lost continuity in observing risky fan groups moving on and off the railway system. Our journey supervised by the Transport Police was very noisy, with many fans illegally drinking alcohol, but we never felt uneasy. There was even a lone Scunthorpe fan in our carriage. He was barracked good humouredly but without menace.

Joining the crowds down Wembley Way, jurisdiction passed back to the Metropolitan Police until we reached the turnstiles, where the Wembley stewards took over. We were politely and efficiently searched on entry, but I was surprised when the stewards asked Andy his age – he is 15 – and then said that they were not allowed to search him. Searches of youngsters should be done with sensitivity, but no search seemed a security error. Young people are quite capable of carrying prohibited articles for themselves or their elders, which is why airports don't decline to search them. As it was, we saw and heard several air horns in the stadium. Wembley don't allow these – but if you don't search you can't stop them.

The concourses have fantastic facilities and plenty of space. The catering delivery had much improved from my previous visit. The quality of product, service and staff was much more consistent and queuing was vastly reduced. Our seats were on level one behind the goal. The sightlines and legroom were exemplary, although the viewing distances are inevitably longer in a large venue.

One unique feature of Wembley's safety and security is the horizontal pitch perimeter fence. This preserves viewing quality for the front rows but still prevents access to the playing area. More venues should consider using this system.

Millwall had sold 45,000 tickets, more than any other play-off team since the new Wembley opened. Scunthorpe had only about 12,000 fans in one quarter of the ground and were vastly outnumbered.

Reflecting something of their geographic and cultural heritage in a rough part of South London, the Millwall fans were very loud, some had drunk too much and some were menacing and aggressive, although not to each other or to us. We noticed a small group behind us wearing surgical masks – echoing the 1970s hooligans known as 'The Treatment', who attacked opponents with scalpels. At the segregation lines, there was sometimes vicious abuse of Scunthorpe fans and one middle aged man (on the club level) climbed across several rows and a segregation net to confront them. His girlfriend was spitting and screaming at the stewards who intervened.

Stewards afterwards commented that Millwall were the worst behaved of the six play-off teams this year. The fact that fewer Millwall were arrested than Burnley or Gillingham, two of the other teams, may have reflected different tactics towards a more difficult crowd. But the vast majority of this 'bad behaviour' was anti-authority – the flouting of regulations rather than hooliganism or violence. For example, we noticed large numbers of fans smoking in the toilets in contravention of the ban.

At our end, the fans stood up throughout the game. Facing such mass non-compliance with the all-seating requirements, the two stewards in our gangway understandably made no attempt to sit people down. Whether persistent standing is a genuine safety concern or not (see *S&AM* June 2003 and December 2007), there are compelling safety reasons for keeping the gangways clear to allow free passage and for emergency access. Yet the fans in our area stood blocking the gangways throughout the game. A Wembley Quality Assurance person came through and pointed this out to the two stewards, who simply shrugged. One of the stewards later said to a fan opposite me, 'could you try and keep across?' The fan, who was much taller than the steward, looked down at him with sneering disdain and just ignored him. Elsewhere, another steward asked a man to sit down and was told, 'You're not big enough'.

These are good examples of the challenge of balancing safety with security. There were clear safety reasons to keep the gangways clear. But there were compelling security reasons not to. It would have needed a large force of stewards and police to enforce compliance and no doubt have led to some unpleasant public disorder.

Of course the management challenge also involves balancing safety and security with commercial considerations. Given that the stadium was only two thirds full, one might have thought that it would have been easy to enforce the segregation by leaving large empty blocks between the two sets of fans. But doing this would have ruined the television spectacle. The opposing fans occupy the two ends and so the gaps would have been opposite the television cameras, giving the appearance of an empty stadium. In fact the segregation line opposite the cameras was densely populated with opposing fans either side of the netting, whilst other parts of the stadium were left empty.

Notwithstanding these hostilities towards the authorities and opposing fans, as members of the vociferous Millwall crowd we felt safe and secure throughout the match. Any anti-social behaviour was directed outwards rather than among us. We had a wonderful day out in the sunshine, tarnished only by the fact that Millwall lost a thrilling match by three goals to two.

4.5. ESTÁDIO DA LUZ

The original citation for this article is Frosdick, S. (2009) 'Lightness of Being', *Stadium and Arena Management*. April 2009, p. 14-15.

Continuing the S&AM series of stadium safety and security visits, Steve Frosdick travels to Lisbon's Estádio da Luz.

In the last edition of *S&AM*, I looked at safety and security for the London 2012 Olympics – three years out. I now want to look at stewarding in Portugal – five years on from the European Football Championships when the Portuguese adopted both UK-style stewarding and the 'friendly but firm' policing style.

I had met Eduardo Rodrigues from Prosegur when we worked together on the Superleague Formula motor racing series at Estoril a few weeks earlier. There had been a high standard of stewarding at the circuit and I was delighted when Rodrigues invited me to observe a UEFA Cup match at the Estádio da Luz.

Sport Lisboa e Benfica's home has a 65,000 capacity set out over four levels – public, club, VIP boxes and again public – a classic contemporary configuration. The design ensures superb sightlines and viewing distance for all spectators.

Reflecting best European practice, the control complex was multi-agency, accommodating the Prosegur match commander and CCTV operators, the Portuguese Security Police (PSP), the Fire Brigade (who also provide paramedic services in Portugal), lift engineers, local authority Civil Protection staff, public address, video screen, entry counting and other life safety systems and personnel.

There are normally about 500 stewards and 500 police deployed for a full house. However very few fans were expected for this fixture because Benfica could not qualify – unless they won by eight goals! Of course the deployment is more contingent on the design of the stadium and approaches than the crowd size. So although level four of one stand would be closed, there were still 300 stewards and 150 police on duty for the crowd of 6,000 which turned up.

The away zone for 1,500 fans is on level one with the option to also use levels two, three and four for a larger contingent. The segregation was pleasingly subtle, with simple low-level Plexiglas screens supported by cordons of stewards to separate the home and away areas, and large numbers of stewards sat on folding stools all around the pitch perimeter. There was no high fencing to be seen anywhere.

Portuguese legal requirements are more stringent than the UK. Not only do all football stewards have to be licensed security guards, but they also have to be licensed sports stewards and so wear two badges. At Luz, the stewards are responsible for the external concourses, stadium bowl and pitch perimeter. The stewards are the first response to any situations in these areas. The stewards were particularly smart, wearing full Prosegur uniforms and yellow tabards. Full sleeve waterproof jackets are provided for poor weather. Supervisors wear orange and white.

Prosegur have developed what they call the 'Volcano' filter cordon. This comprises a diagonal line of barrier triangles, which help reduce crowd pressure for the fans in the queue. Stewards staff the entrance gaps, which admit one person at a time. There are then bins or bags within each of the barrier triangles to allow for easy disposal of prohibited items. The 'Volcano' is used for two purposes, the first of which is ticket checking all fans on the approaches to the stadium. Risk assessment principles then determine its use for extra ticket checks and searching at the 'security zones'. These are the away zone and the two home areas occupied by two large groups of so-called 'heavy fans' – the 'No Name Boys' and the 'Red Devils'. The 'Volcano' was a novel cordon which I have not seen anywhere else.

Tickets having already been checked on the approaches and again at the security zones, access control is then through automatic turnstiles which read the microchip incorporated in each ticket.

The 'No Name Boys' enter through gates 10 and 11 at one end of the stadium. Although they have no official status, they issue their own membership cards and the ticket office will only sell tickets for these gates to people who can produce a 'No Name Boys' card. The 'Red Devils' use gate 25 at the opposite end, adjacent to the away fans.

The 'No Name Boys' and 'Red Devils' do not like each other but do not wish to fight, and so they do not infiltrate each other's areas.

Police cover the traffic, stadium approaches, external concourses and the security zones. At the entrance gates, the security zones were observed by groups of PSP football spotters – officers familiar with the groups of 'heavy fans'. Inside the bowl, the police remain out of sight unless they need to be deployed. If necessary, they will show their presence but will only deploy if the stewards cannot cope with the situation. This all represents the 'friendly but firm' approach which the PSP used so successfully during Euro 2004, and I was delighted to see it consolidated into practice five years on.

Fire brigade staff are deployed adjacent to the security zones so as to deal immediately with any pyrotechnics in the 'heavy' fan areas.

But there are always safety and security surprises for even the best run modern stadium operation. This match was no exception. Benfica TV, which had launched one week earlier, had a very long cable trailing along the ground and across entrances throughout the corridors of the VIP box level. This tripping hazard was picked up by Prosegur staff and will be fed back into the planning for the next match to ensure the risk is removed.

All in all, I have to congratulate both Benfica and Prosegur for clearly sustaining the safety and security improvements from Euro 2004. This was an impressive stadium safety and security operation with several best practice features evident:

- The Multi agency control room;
- High profile stewarding;
- Low key segregation;
- The 'Volcano' cordon for ticket checks and searching;
- Risk assessment based checking and searching for different fan groups;
- High-tech ticketing and turnstiles;
- Police football spotters; and
- The 'friendly but firm' policing style.

4.6. NOU CAMP NIGHT

The original citation for this article is Frosdick, S. and Rawlings, A. (2010) 'Nou Camp Night', *Stadium and Arena Management*, April 2010, pp. 30-31.

'Mystery fans' Steve Frosdick and Andrew Rawlings tackle the logistics behind a night out at Barcelona's Camp Nou stadium.

The Camp Nou (new field) stadium – often also referred to as the Nou Camp – has been home to FC Barcelona since it was built in 1957. At its peak for the 1982 World Cup, the stadium accommodated almost 122,000 fans. Since becoming all-seated, the capacity has reduced to 98,787. This is still one of the biggest stadium capacities in the world and certainly the largest in Europe.

Camp Nou's sheer size, coupled with the star footballing talent on display, makes it a 'must see' for stadium fans. It is also one of Barcelona's most popular tourist sights. But organising a visit is not without its problems.

The trouble is that kick off dates and times are determined by Spanish television and are set only ten days in advance. Matches can kick off at 1800, 2000 or 2200 on Saturday and 1700, 1900 or 2100 on Sundays. So visitors have to buy their tickets and make their travel arrangements not knowing when the game will be. You have to fly out on Saturday morning and back on the Monday, staying at least two nights. From February 2010, there may also be a Monday night game, which will make things even more difficult.

We bought our print-at-home tickets from the club website about five weeks before the game. Oddly, the website does not offer all the available seats and gives the impression the venue is almost sold out. We thought we had found one of the only pairs of seats left. But on the night the crowd was 'only' 75,000. There were empty seats around us and people nearby had turned up and bought their tickets at the ground. It seemed like we had lost the opportunity to buy the cheapest flights and stayed the extra night unnecessarily – mind you we did have the consolation of a visit to the Port Aventura theme park!

Setting the date and time so late causes other problems too. Small towns and cities cannot organise any other events on weekends when their team is at home in case the public services and temporary staff get double-booked. In Barcelona, the police, fire and ambulance staff do not know when they will be needed. Stewards and hospitality staff do not know when they will be working and caterers don't know when they'll have to cook. All this uncertainty is of course the price to be paid for television revenues.

Our kick-off was at 2100 on the Sunday night. Several metro lines run near the stadium and our journey was uneventful, although we noticed many of our fellow-travellers were English or American rather than Spanish. We joined the throng waiting for the gates to open and were struck by the number of (presumably illegal) merchandise stalls blocking the footway and pushing the crowd out into the roadway. There were local police monitoring the traffic but not the pedestrians. We also noticed touts selling tickets at one euro less than face value.

The gates opened at 1930 sharp and our tickets were checked by the access control stewards in their orange jackets. The external concourses are enormous and there was plenty of circulation room. The stadium entry doors were well signed. We presented our tickets to the barcode reader at the turnstile, supervised by another access control steward. Inside, there were wide ramps leading all the way up the five tiers. Signage was very clear and we easily found our tier, vomitory, row and seats. There were plenty of toilets and catering outlets. No alcohol is served but we enjoyed sampling the different hot dogs on offer.

Our stand on tier four had been recently refurbished. Previously crumbling nosings and terracing had been re-profiled. This meant there was a slight change in level from the new to the old concrete in the vomitory, which created a tripping hazard. There were new plastic tip up seats of good quality. The steep rake of the tier meant that there were barriers in front of all the seat rows and handrails down all the gangways. Because of the overlap and rake of the tiers, we were much closer to the pitch than we had expected and the viewing standards were excellent. There is no pitch perimeter fence to block people's view, although there are nets behind the goals to prevent missile throwing.

Thus the physical environment and access control were generally fine. There was good evidence of other security work too. The riot police were supervising turnstiles 87 and 88, which are used by Barca's 'heavy' fans. There were police and security stewards monitoring the couple of hundred away fans in segregated blocks on tier five. We also saw security stewards from a private company patrolling some of the other spectator areas.

The safety stewarding was not to the same standard. Stewards always appear more professional when they are smartly dressed, but the Camp Nou stewards wore shabby yellow tabards and jeans. Stewards should be deployed in each vomitory to monitor the crowd and initiate any emergency evacuation. But there were not enough stewards on duty and our nearest steward was covering at least one other vomitory. We could see that other vomitories around the ground had no steward in them either – the stewards were more in evidence on the sides than in the ends or corners. There was a group of young American men standing in our row. They were blocking people's view but there was no steward to intervene. In the end, an elderly man – clearly a seasoned Barca fan – told them in no uncertain terms to sit down.

We were surprised at the lack of atmosphere. Football fans generally chant loudly for the first fifteen minutes of the game, but there was none of this. Perhaps there were more tourists than genuine fans in the stadium? The crowd only became animated when Barca were attacking or scored one of the six goals by which they beat Zaragoza. But it was certainly excellent to experience a Nou Camp night – we loved it.

4.7. O-RENA ORLANDO

The original citation for this article is Frosdick, S. (2010) 'O-Rena Farewell', *Stadium and Arena Management*, October 2010, p. 42.

Mystery fan Steve Frosdick says goodbye to Florida's Amway Arena

The August edition of *S&AM* featured the brand new Amway Center, the City of Orlando's state-of-the-art facility for indoor sports and events. Amway Center will replace the current Amway Arena – known as the 'O-Rena' – when it opens in October 2010.

Whilst holidaying recently in Orlando, I wanted to visit the Amway Arena before it was too late. The 'O-Rena' is only 21 years old but the decision to replace it demonstrates the exponential progress in facility design and management.

IAAM colleague Allen Johnson, who operates both venues, kindly arranged tickets for the Friday night football game between the Orlando Predators and the Alabama Vipers. Arena football is gridiron, but on a quarter size indoor field, with smaller teams, faster action and higher scoring. Fortunately, the Predators won to keep their play-off hopes alive.

In terms of entertainment, we had a fantastic night out. Our seats were superbly located and my family loved the whole show, which was part sports event, part spectacle and part TV show. The advertising breaks were filled with different activities such as a big truck driving round the field with cheerleaders throwing t-shirts into the crowd – all great fun. It was also fascinating to see the television producer giving the referee a countdown to when he could restart the game. This was more obvious than in European field sports because the stop-start nature of American football allows for many more breaks.

From a professional viewpoint, I was struck by the smart appearance, service ethos, safety awareness and proportionality of the ushers. The bag searchers were relaxed – I guess because of the family audience – but I did notice that several people behind us were drinking spirits from small glass bottles they had brought in their pockets. Of course you can't prevent this without patting everyone down, which would not have been appropriate for the audience. The ticket checking using scanners was very efficient and the checker gave a smiling welcome. The ushers in the bowl were friendly, helpful and wearing 'evening dress' – more like a theatre than a stadium. The usher where we were sat was smart, calm, polite but nevertheless fastidious in keeping the aisle clear throughout the event. The police were present in small numbers to cover outside the venue but safety and security in the concourse and bowl were the venue's responsibility, just as they are in Western Europe.

The variety and quality of the food and beverage offerings was very marked. The concourse had numerous and varied concessions selling a wide choice of fare and I added to my collection of 'son eating hot dog' photos – as seen in previous editions of *S&AM!* There were also lots of sellers in the bowl, taking money handed up the rows and passing the drinks and snacks back down. The wide product selection and bowl service levels were notably different from UK arenas, where the choice can be more limited and mobile sellers are a rarity. Another big difference from UK soccer was the ability to drink alcohol in the seating bowl. The beer seemed to loosen people up as the game progressed and the atmosphere became more and more thrilling, particularly towards the end of the fourth quarter. Yet the family nature of the occasion meant there was not a hint of unpleasantness, even when we were booing the visiting team.

I had noticed the 'no camera' signs at the entrances and so was initially hesitant to use my iPhone to take pictures – particularly as I was a guest. But it soon became obvious that everyone else was snapping away, so I happily joined in! As a recent discussion on the IAAM forum noted, venue managers seek to prevent commercial photography rather than fan souvenirs.

This was my family's first experience of an American arena event, but we sure hope it won't be our last!

4.1. – 4.7. COMMENTARY BY JIM CHALMERS – MYSTERY SPECTATOR VISITS

In this series of seven articles, dating between 2006 and 2010, Frosdick is accompanied on occasions by his young sons and daughter on visits to sports and music events in Germany, England, Portugal, Spain and America. At each venue visited he gives a very graphic account of their experiences from a 'mystery spectator' perspective. What makes the articles all the more interesting is that each venue and event is being viewed through the eyes of an ex-senior police officer, an expert in theories of risk and risk management, a leading academic in the areas of spectator safety management and stewarding and a safety manager in his own right, with the unique experience of managing safety and security in Superleague Formula motor racing (see Chapter 1.3).

4.1. World Cup Weekend

Frosdick gives a very personal account of his experiences in attending the Fan Fest in Frankfurt and the Angola v Portugal game in Cologne. Having visited both cities myself in a professional capacity, I was able to put his experiences into context.

It seems clear from his article that the arrangements in Frankfurt were organised with the usual German efficiency. It was encouraging to note his very favourable impression of how the event was stewarded. Although the majority of English fans at the venue would not have made such objective judgments, Frosdick is able to reason the distinction between spectator safety and spectator welfare. It is always difficult to strike the correct balance between safety and security, but on this occasion I would say the German attitude towards bottle confiscation got the balance right.

Turning now to his Cologne experience, the message which rings out loud and clear is the very pro-active stewarding and management of the fans. It is interesting that despite being in an all-seated stadium the Angolan fans stood throughout the game. So persistent standing in seated areas at football events is not just an English disease! However in controlling this area, the stewards adopted the ideal 'friendly but firm' approach in what appeared to be a high profile stewarding and low profile policing environment – always the ideal crowd management scenario.

Whilst this was just one snap shot of a father and son experience, it is nevertheless an important part of World Cup history, since the mystery spectator's background makes it unique. Frosdick's World Cup weekend was a very positive experience of both the spectacle and the way the events were organised and stewarded.

4.2. Emirates Experience

This was another father and son 'mystery spectator' visit, this time to the Emirates stadium in London, the home of Arsenal FC, on the occasion of their home game against Hamburg in December 2006.

During his visit Frosdick looked at key areas of the stadium operation; spectator comfort, amenity and safety, all of which can be summarised as customer care issues. His description of the stadium access control systems seemed to identify the ideal scenario, whereby a spectator can access their seat from outside the stadium, through the concourses and into the viewing bowl without having to ask for directions. This would indicate very high standards of signage.

Once inside the stadium, the catering outlets were modern, bright and clean. However, the actual catering experience did not match the surroundings. Sadly, issues such as this can make or break the enjoyment of any visit. Arsenal is not alone in its disappointing catering arrangements. This is where 'mystery spectator' comments are of such value. In my opinion, 'mystery spectators' should be used far more extensively to assist venues in assessing their quality of service provisions.

In contrast, the concourse design and toilets were highly praised, with staff constantly on hand to deal with cleaning and waste management. During my time with the Football Licensing Authority (FLA), I can recall using images of the spectator toilet facilities at the Emirates stadium in my talks on stadium design and operation. The standards were evidently high, and so I used the images as an example of the standards other clubs should set for their customers. Many other new developments of the time were bare or painted breeze block with the minimum of customer amenities. Arsenal's provision does them great credit and shows they value the concept of customer care and service. Unfortunately, not every major club in England can make such a claim.

Arsenal's attitude towards good design can also be judged by Frosdick's comments on the spectator seating provisions. Sadly, at many clubs where there is new build, work is done to minimum standards due to costs. It is clear that Arsenal looked towards the maximum standards in seating dimensions and fan comfort.

Overall Frosdick was very impressed with the stadium, describing it as 'fantastic'. Having known Frosdick for many years, I know just how critical he can be in his analysis; I have rarely known him speak in such glowing terms about a stadium. With the exception of the catering, which let the club down on this occasion, it does appear that, from Frosdick's perspective, the club and the designers have got it right. Having visited the stadium myself, I must say I agree. I would describe the Emirates stadium as a jewel in the crown of stadium design and operation, which others would do well to emulate.

4.3. Live at Wembley

This article comments on the experience of Frosdick, his teenage daughter and her two friends, and their attendance of the first sell-out concert held at Wembley stadium in June 2007. Being a senior citizen, my experience of pop concerts is very limited and goes back to the time when I also had teenage daughters in the 1980s, so I looked forward to learning about the modern day pop concert experience.

On arrival at the stadium, their access to their viewing level was straightforward, which is always an indicator of good stadium design, ticketing, signage and stewarding. It should be said, however, that this was to be expected; the stadium was designed with the intention of serving as a multi-purpose venue, capable of holding concerts. Proof of this can be seen in the seating provisions, which were designed to accommodate spectators for far longer periods than the average football match. From this perspective, the stadium accommodation seemed to meet Frosdick's expectations.

I was very surprised to read his comments about the poor sound quality within the venue. I would have thought that this would be one of the major factors which would contribute to the enjoyment of the event. Hopefully lessons were learned by the venue management and the sound engineers for the future concerts staged at Wembley.

Having visited the old Wembley on a few occasions, I am well aware that one of the main complaints was the cost and quality of the catering – or more, the lack of quality. Judging from Frosdick's experience it would appear nothing had changed, which was unacceptable of our national stadium. However, it is perhaps interesting to add that when Aston Villa FC played there in the League Cup Final of 2010, relatives of mine at the game had no complaints whatsoever about the quality of the food and drink on sale; their only complaint was the cost of it.

On the positive side, Frosdick was clearly impressed with the scale of and deployment of stewards, their supervisors and managers. Other sources had also commented on this, and it is to the credit of the Wembley safety team, since they have to mount a major safety and security operation for every event held at the stadium. It is not enough to simply be safe; it is equally important to feel safe. Frosdick sums up the success of the safety operation at Wembley, because that is how he, his daughter and her friends felt during their visit.

At the end of the concert, egress was as straightforward as the ingress. This is an indicator of good exit design, including exit widths and spectator flow rates.

It is a pity that the day was let down by the poor sound quality and catering standards. The experience of my relatives in 2010 showed that the catering quality had improved – although not the cost. When Wembley's suitability to host music events is questioned, it is a clear indicator that changes need to be made. I hope that the Wembley management company also read the article and acted upon his 'mystery spectator' critique.

4.4. Wembley Progress

After his pop concert experience in 2007, Frosdick re-visited Wembley with his two sons, this time for a football experience. Had this been a music event, it would have been interesting to note whether the sound quality of the event had improved since his last visit. That may be something he will factor into a future 'mystery spectator' trip.

I am pleased he chose a match involving such a high profile club as Millwall FC, given their fans reputation for anti-social behaviour at both their home and away matches. I try to avoid using the term 'football hooliganism' if I can help it, since the term means very little other than as a newspaper headline to describe football fans engaged in violence or disorder.

It is disappointing that the British Transport Police and the Metropolitan Police appeared to have drawn up demarcation lines in the 'footprint' for their specific areas of operation. No doubt these were directly related to the provision of 'special police services', and what the police can or cannot charge Wembley for providing. This is not a unique situation. Up and down the country, the 'footprint' relating to police charges is a constant source of contention and disagreement between the police and football clubs. At the Football Safety Officers' Conference in October 2010 an Association of Chief Police Officers (ACPO) speaker said that ACPO was in discussion with the Home Office to have the current guidance on police charges changed. My understanding of this is that the police would like to have sole discretion in deciding the 'footprint' in which they could charge for their services. This would mean an astronomical increase in charges for the provision of 'special police services'. It also hints at the possibility of a 'police state', whereby the police can impose a financial penalty on any event organiser without any negotiation or level of agreement.

There are obviously differences of opinion with regard to the searching of young people at a stadium. I agree that the searching of any young person must be conducted with sensitivity and the consent of the young person and their parent and guardian. Sadly, age is no barrier to anti-social behaviour, and even includes the smuggling of prohibited items which could cause injury. I know of searches on young people detecting Stanley knives, screwdrivers, drugs, air horns, alcohol in pop bottles and even billiard balls to be thrown as missiles. At my own ground we operate a selective searching procedure and any young person acting suspiciously or suspected of having anything offensive on their person will be asked for permission to search them in the presence of their parent or guardian. If they refuse they will not be allowed into the ground. Given the present threat of terrorist attack, I would suggest that our national stadium presents a high risk as a potential target. If it is still the case that young people will not be searched, this could present an open door for the terrorist. If I was in charge of safety at the venue, this is a door I would close overnight.

With regard to the stadium seating and viewing, Frosdick had no complaints on these important aspects of the spectator experience. He found the catering service had improved dramatically since his 2007 pop concert experience.

Sadly, some of the Millwall fans lived up to their reputation for poor behaviour, in particular their anti-authority attitude. This is something which I experienced time and time again at many away matches involving Millwall supporters, who seemed to think that the normal rules of behaviour and conduct did not apply to them. During my time with the FLA, I likened the atmosphere at some of the matches involving this group of supporters with that of a war front in a militarised zone, with parts of the city closed due to the threat of high levels of disorder and violence. At this match, Frosdick cites examples of their anti-authority behaviour, flouting the no smoking rules and persistently standing throughout the game. This was made even worse when they blocked gangways and reacted aggressively towards the poor stewards who had the courage to ask them to move for safety reasons.

Frosdick could see for himself the dilemma facing the match day commander; if thousands of fans are determined to stand, then no force of stewards and/or police will resolve the problem. Any use of force by the stewards or police in this scenario would undoubtedly have led to resistance and retaliation, resulting in possible riot conditions with spectators, stewards and police suffering injuries. It appears that common sense prevailed in the best interests of public safety. Doing nothing was, without doubt, the best tactic.

If I were to be critical of the planning for this event, I would have expected the ground management to have taken out of use at least two seats either side of the lateral gangways. This is to ensure that fans who persistently stand do not encroach into the crucial ingress/egress route. Where persistent standing is a particular problem, I am aware that some certifying authorities have reduced the stand capacities. This has proved very effective, not in resolving the persistent standing issue, but in keeping the gangways clear. This is a tactic which could be usefully considered by the Wembley safety advisory group.

Frosdick also highlights the issue of the segregation arrangements and the constant dilemma of setting commercial or spectacle considerations against customer care and safety. Safety should always prevail, but despite this I know of many occasions where the safety officer's arguments have been overridden by commercial or television concerns.

Despite the aggression and the anti-authority behaviour by the Millwall fans, Frosdick and his sons felt safe amongst them. He was, of course, never likely to be at risk of threatening behaviour and abuse; he was accompanied by his two sons, and was on their side. I am not sure that the Scunthorpe fans will have felt the same way about their opponents.

4.5. Estadio de Luz

Frosdick next takes us to Lisbon's Estadio de Luz in 2009. This time he focuses on stewarding and policing, and how this had developed since Portugal hosted the 2004 European Football Championships.

I found it interesting that the command and control systems and arrangements at the stadium reflected what you would find at most Premier and Football League grounds in England. There were facilities for the ground management, police, fire/paramedic support and the local authority. The various safety systems were also similar. Overall the command and control environment compared very favourably, but perhaps this is no surprise given the involvement of English advisors in the lead up to the 2004 competition.

It would appear that in Portugal, the authorities have gone down the path that the Security Industry Authority (SIA) wanted to introduce in England and Wales; stewards are required to be licensed security guards as well as licensed sports stewards. It would have been interesting to note the extent of the training requirements to achieve both licenses, and the costs involved. This part of the article left me anxious to know more about how this is achieved in Portugal.

I have seen the 'volcano' filter cordon in operation at other European venues I have visited, and I can see how it is a very effective control mechanism. It can prevent a build-up of crowd pressure, assist in preventing prohibited articles entering the venue, and can aid in ticket control. Security is obviously a priority at the access points, with three distinct control stages which have to be passed before the fan can enter the stadium. Technology also plays an important part, with an automatic turnstile operation activated by the ticket. Given some of the problems experienced with some automatic ticket entry systems introduced in English stadia, I would have welcomed some comment on how effective and foolproof this system was. I would also have been interested to know the back-up system in the event of failure, together with some detail on the number of stewards required to assist at the access points to resolve any entry problems.

What was gratifying was Frosdick's explanation of how the Portuguese policing strategy for the event appeared to be modelled on the English approach; the ground management deal with any problems, and the police only intervene if the stewards cannot manage the incident. It would appear that the 'friendly but firm' police tactic adopted in 2004 has been maintained over the intervening years, and this does the Portuguese police and civil authorities great credit.

In his conclusion Frosdick is very complimentary about the stadium safety and security arrangements, but the article left me wishing he had written a longer piece. It would have been interesting to have some comment on the planning phase of the event, including an overview of the stadium preparation, i.e. the arrangements for the stewards briefing/de-briefing and their communication methods. I would also have welcomed more information on the steward training/assessment/qualification requirements for both licences and their costs. It would have been nice to know just how effective the multi-agency approach was in the control suite - particularly who was actually in charge. Was it the ground management or the police? Perhaps the event was incident free, but it would have been interesting to know if there were any problems for the 150 stewards and 150 police who were on duty to deal with. In my experience, even in the smaller English grounds, it is rare for any event to be totally incident free and yet, by virtue of his role, the 'mystery spectator' was unable to deal with these matters.

4.6. Nou Camp Night

On this occasion, Frosdick and his son travel to the Nou Camp Stadium in Barcelona in 2010 – a stadium which any football fan would love to visit. Anyone who visits Barcelona will generally put the Nou Camp stadium on their itinerary. I have only visited the stadium when it was empty, and to say it was impressive is an understatement. Mind blowing in size and scale would be a more apt description! I therefore read the article in hope that Frosdick would fill a gap in my understanding and knowledge of this stadium, describing the event experience when a match was being played. In this regard, I was not disappointed.

I was intrigued by the ticket purchasing procedure, with no knowledge of the day or time of the match. In England, the dates and times for many matches are controlled by television interests, although (thankfully) the television companies do not have the final say in the scheduling of fixtures. Frosdick relates the practical problems which this system of television control brings for the police, stewards and other club and stadium staff, since none of them knows when they will be needed for an event until a few days beforehand. It would also be unsettling for the managers and teams, with so much uncertainty as to the dates and times of the fixtures. It must therefore present a logistical nightmare for everyone involved in staging the event to get their systems and procedures into place when the television company press the 'go' button.

Frosdick's game kicked off at 9 pm on a Sunday evening, and he clearly had no problems finding his way to his seat as the access routes were well sign posted. The angle of the seating deck is steep, which explains the provision of barriers in front of the rows of seats, not uncommon in the upper tiers of major European stadia. From a spectator perspective, what is important is that the barriers do not give obstructed or restricted views of the game. This was not a problem for Frosdick, which again indicates good stadium design. It was interesting that the spectators did not persistently stand and lean on these barriers, as I fear they would in England, but this was due to a different culture of supporting and the steep rake of the stand.

It was disappointing to read that the stewards' dress code and appearance did not match the magnificence of their surroundings. This also begs the question of the standards of steward training, assessment and qualifications. When you consider the millions of Euros paid to the Barcelona players, it is a sad indictment on the stadium management that they have not invested in making the stewards the ambassadors they should be. A smart dress code and the provision of good quality, high visibility personal protective clothing – both standard in England – would present a totally different image of the stewards and their abilities. In my experience, the steward who looks the part will generally act the part. As it is, I would suggest that the concept of professional stewarding may not be high on the priority list of senior management.

Frosdick's observations on the stewards would indicate an apparent lack of risk assessment in providing the correct steward deployment to meet the needs. The standards of appearance and the lack of safety stewards at key points in the stadium would indicate that the principles of safety management which we take for granted in the UK may still need working on at the Nou Camp. Perhaps the Spanish authorities would benefit from having sight of the FLA guidance on safety management including how to prepare a stewarding plan?

I was surprised with the comments on a lack of atmosphere in the ground, since I always imagined that this venue would be a cauldron of sound during a game. Perhaps, as Frosdick notes, this is a reflection on the fact that he chose a day where there were more tourists present than fans. However, Frosdick and his son enjoyed the experience, and gave me a better insight in to how the Nou Camp stadium operates on a match day. It appears there are no lessons for the UK to learn from the experience; rather, perhaps the Spanish authorities could learn from the English stewarding experience.

4.7. O-Rena Orlando

In the final part of his journeys around sporting venues of the world, Frosdick pays a nostalgic 2010 visit to the Orlando O-Rena. Having seen pictures of the old venue, I was amazed that it was being demolished after only a life span of 21 years, which is very young in venue construction terms. It seems that American sports have not been so adversely affected by the current world recession!

I think anyone who has visited America will recognize the value they place on customer service – something which is now beginning to creep into English football. It is difficult to imagine a scenario in an English football ground, where sellers are able to dispense food and drink from the gangways, with money and goods being passed hand to hand along the seating decks by the spectators. I think we are still light years away from the customer service which is so common in American sporting venues. At football events, we are also a long way off from allowing alcohol consumption in the stadium bowl. This is, of course, only a football restriction which does not apply to other sports such as cricket and rugby. The example of the type of disorder experienced at the local football derby fixture between Birmingham City FC and Aston Villa FC in December 2010 means that any relaxation of the liquor licensing laws at our football games remains very unlikely.

This is not an occasion to start comparing societies or the differences between American and English spectators. However in my experience, the geographic distances between the home and away teams mean that there is rarely any travelling support at American home games. One only has to consider the fixture that Frosdick attended, with the distance between Orlando and the visiting team from Alabama. I doubt if there will have been many visiting supporters present. The fact that the ground management and police generally only have to manage the home fans makes life so much easier. Imagine how much more straightforward it would be to police Manchester United home games if there was never any visiting support present. That is why a like for like comparison between the American and English team sports experience is impossible.

I am sure the climate and the proximity to the Florida holiday attractions all contributed to the visit being enjoyable. I am not certain that a freezing winter's day in England would provide the same enjoyable opportunity! This was something which I used to think about in the 1980s, sat in the control room at Villa Park in Birmingham; will the American ethos of spectacle and customer service ever arrive at our football grounds in the UK? In many respects, I am still wondering and waiting.

Summary

I have enjoyed being able to travel around the world with Frosdick and to share in his visits. The venues have all varied, and his experiences too have differed, from the excellent to the disappointing.

The one thing that struck me as a common thread throughout the article is that, in terms of the safe management of events, there is little which the UK could learn from Frosdick's visits. His experiences would tend to show that, particularly in Europe, it is they who have learned from the English experiences in stewarding and policing, not the other way round. I therefore feel that the English football and police authorities can take some comfort in the fact that the lessons we have learned over the years are being shared and acted upon in an international context. We may not have won the opportunity to host the 2018 World Cup, but I believe we will continue to lead the way in safe management and policing of football grounds.

PART V – VENUE SECURITY CONFERENCES

Introduction

Part V comprises two short magazine features in which Steve Frosdick reports on two venue security conferences in 2005 (prior to the July 7 bombings in London) and then in 2008. The accompanying commentaries note the change in the terrorist threat, outline the forthcoming demise of the Security Industry Authority and give a 2011 update on the preparations for London 2012.

5.1. Event and Venue Security

This *Stadium and Arena Management* article from 2005 reports on the inaugural Event and Venue Security Conference held in London in April 2005. Twin themes for the event were the challenges of effectively managing the latest security threats whilst complying with recent industry legislation. Nobody knew that just a few weeks later, London's transport system would experience four simultaneous suicide bombings, the shooting of a civilian mistaken for a terrorist and four further attempted bombings.

The accompanying commentary notes how the 2005 bombings necessitated a change in security planning to include the suicide bomber as well as the deposit of improvised explosive devices. The commentary also notes that the Security Industry Authority is to be wound up and replaced with a new regulatory regime for the private security industry.

5.2. Optimising Venue Security

This short *Stadium and Arena Management* feature on the International Fire and Security Exhibition and Conference in Birmingham on in May 2008 is the catalyst for a detailed 2011 update by Jim Chalmers on the safety and security preparations for the London 2012 Olympic Games.

5.1. EVENT AND VENUE SECURITY

The original citation for this article is Frosdick, S. (2005) 'Basis for Security', *Stadium and Arena Management*, June 2005, pp. 8-10.

Steve Frosdick reports on the inaugural public venue, sport and live entertainment security conference and exhibition.

The inaugural Event and Venue Security (EVS) event was held at the prestigious QEII Conference Centre in London on 18 and 19 April 2005. EVS was organised by International Business Events Ltd and was supported by Group 4 Securicor and L3 Security and Detection Systems. Twin themes for the event were the challenges of effectively managing the latest security threats whilst complying with recent industry legislation.

The event had three components. First was a high level conference. The morning plenaries featured presentations by distinguished international speakers. Picking up on the two themes, the afternoon sessions were split into two streams. These covered live music and sports events and venues; and security guarding and security legislation. The second component was a short programme of workshops hosted by the UK Crowd Management Association and the National Outdoor Events Association. Third was the exhibition, which was supported by 19 different private and public sector organisations.

The conference twin themes were very comprehensively addressed. There were no less than 37 speakers listed in the programme, only two of whom did not attend as planned. The overall quality of the speakers was mixed. Some of the expert keynote speeches were quite brilliant, providing delegates with fresh and illuminating insights. Some of the commercial presentations were sales pitches, made worse by running over their allotted time. The afternoon sessions had been timed so that delegates were able to follow either their chosen stream or else 'pick and mix' between the two streams. Clearly I was not able to attend every session, so this article will focus on the more insightful speakers from my own 'pick and mix'.

The drivers behind EVS were the fundamental changes in the security environment following the September 11 attacks in New York, together with the introduction of the UK Security Industry Authority (SIA) and the legal requirements for licensing within certain sectors of the industry. Over 100 delegates were present to hear the first two keynote speeches, which were very clearly focused on the terrorist threat.

Professor Michael Clarke of Kings College London is a specialist government advisor on terrorism and was the undoubted star of EVS. His presentation covered the principles of counter-terrorism and highlighted the strengths and weaknesses of both the international terrorists and their targeted societies. Professor Clarke explained how the term 'Al-Qaida' had become a 'terrorist franchise', adopted by a 'network of networks' across the globe. Al-Qaida had about 30 individuals at its core, supported by about 200 messengers. These linked with various networks comprising about 5,000 to 10,000 active individuals, with a further 40,000 potential but inactive recruits. Internet technologies provided for easy communication. Al-Qaida thus had good tradecraft at its minimalist top; and clean recruits prepared to die for the cause at its extensive base. Al-Qaida was capable of exploiting anti-westernism wherever it occurred. This all stretched the resources of disparate security services.

However the franchise threatened the discipline and coherence of the Al-Qaida brand. The different networks had different purposes and 'with diversity comes disunity'. Links to separatist terrorist groups and international criminals were also dangerous. More fundamentally, the terrorists' analysis of the West was very poor. Of course we have weaknesses – we are an open and risk averse society, our security services have been slow to re-orientate and we have the democratic tendency to over-react to minor events – but 'we are orders of magnitude stronger than they think we are'. Moreover we understand and practise the '3-Ps' principles of counter-terrorism – protection, penetration and political dialogue.

Professor Clarke concluded by expanding on these principles. Operational action should be based on measures which added high value to the normal functioning of society. People should become habituated to a reasonable level of risk. We should reinforce our own social values and seek to divorce terrorists from their potential supporters. Vigilance should be flexible, avoiding systematic routines and checklists but mobilising the widest possible variety of services and functions. Above all, the rule of law should be maintained at all times.

Former Metropolitan Police Commissioner Lord Stevens spoke passionately in support of the maintenance of the rule of law 'or we will have lost the plot'. He highlighted the UK's extraordinary successes in dealing with terrorism over the years. The world had changed, but a balance had to be struck between making people alert and terrifying them. Lord Stevens argued for a 'grand alliance' to counter terrorism, pointing out that at the 2005 Interpol Conference, the police chiefs of the world had shown unanimity in understanding the global nature of the terrorist threat and the action needed to counter it. Lord Stevens remained quietly confident. 'Threats can, have been, and will continue to be thwarted', he said. 'Let's not create alarm and despondency when we don't need to. Democracy will win'.

The question and answer session picked up on the issues of the rule of law and the vulnerability of stadia and large-scale events. Both speakers agreed the need for a mature debate about the suitability of the current legal framework, but emphasised that we must avoid headline-grabbing initiatives and draconian laws which have a disproportionate effect. They also talked of the need to guard symbolic buildings and events with 'balanced normality', i.e. with vigilance but without over-reaction.

Following a break, the plenary turned its attention to the second conference theme. Private security expert Mark Button of the University of Portsmouth outlined the long road to regulation of the UK private security industry and the main provisions of the Private Security Industry Act 2001. This had set up a new regulatory body – the Security Industry Authority – and introduced a licensing scheme for staff in certain sectors. A voluntary approved contractors scheme had also been established. Using examples of poor practice, such as guards falling asleep due to long hours on low pay and exposés of airport security breaches, Button illustrated the need for standards to be raised. There were considerable challenges to be faced in overcoming such problems as poor pay and conditions, lack of career structure and required qualifications, management competence and the limited scope of the approved contractors scheme.

The fourth keynote speaker was scheduled to be John Saunders, Chief Executive of the Security Industry Authority (SIA), but he had pulled out at the last minute, citing the UK general election as making it inappropriate for him to speak. Many delegates felt this was a convenient excuse, since there was widespread bad feeling about the SIA's approach to its regulatory role and it was likely Saunders would have been given a rough ride – indeed one delegate took the microphone to call for his resignation, stating, 'the SIA has failed. I started as a fan, now I'm resentful'.

In Saunders' absence, a replacement presentation was given by David Dickinson, Chief Executive of the British Security Industry Association (BSIA). He recognised Mark Button's picture of low standards in parts of the industry and argued for a transformation. This should be driven by both regulatory requirements and by a changed business view. The costs of regulation had been estimated at £400 million, and security companies would require a return on that investment. Security must no longer be seen as a commodity, to be bought and sold as cheaply as possible, but as an essential business requirement which required significant cost investment. 'Budgets will have to change', he said.

Despite the comments about the SIA coming from the floor of the conference, Dickinson said. 'I will not criticise the SIA'. Given his position as head of a trade association, this stance caused some raised eyebrows.

There had been a long and difficult political battle about whether football and event stewards would require licences. The SIA had finally been forced to concede the football industry's case that the vast majority of stewards did not. Other sports and events would be seeking to follow the football precedent. Dickinson surprised the conference by threatening that, unless standards in stewarding were equivalent or better, he would seek a judicial review of this outcome on behalf of the wider security industry. This sounded like sour grapes. As Mark Button pointed out, event stewarding has always been regarded as a different sector – its primary purpose is safety not security and the work is often short-term and temporary.

In the live music and sports events and venues stream, Malcolm Millichap of Staffordshire Fire and Rescue Service set out the responses required in the case of a chemical, biological, radioactive or nuclear (CBRN) terrorist attack. He showed a fascinating film clip of a decontamination exercise and it was clear to delegates that there would be massive logistical difficulties and very long timescales if such decontamination proved necessary at a stadium or other large scale public event.

Next up was Daniel Ostergaard from the United States Department of Homeland Security. In a keynote address, he argued that terrorism was a real threat. Preparedness would both save lives and enable business continuity. This was becoming Darwinesque – only the strongest would survive. Preparedness was not a luxury but an integral part of doing business. Security was not a cost, but an investment in business continuity.

In the parallel security guarding and legislation stream, Jim Batty of Group 4 set out a risk management approach to event security. This mirrored risk management approaches in general and covered an assessment of assets, threats, vulnerabilities, existing safeguards, residual risks and additional necessary control measures. Batty also emphasised it was a mistake for business to see security as a commodity – you get what you pay for.

The attendance on day two was a little lower, with some 60 delegates present to hear Assistant Chief Constable Nigel Yeo give a detailed case study of the security arrangements for the 2004 UK Labour Party political conference. The complex array of stakeholder interests and their different views of success created a challenging environment. The police and their private security partners had to deliver security which was effective without being overbearing to delegates, damaging to commerce or disruptive to the local community.

In the next presentation, Ian Brook of Siebel Systems explained how CRM (customer relationship management) software could be used to support intelligence profiling. Software developments such as data mining could allow ticket sellers to filter out known hooligans, ticket touts, multiple purchasers and terrorist suspects. I thought this was a frightening prospect. These kinds of developments in airline security are already raising serious questions about civil liberties. I felt that Brook's sales pitch did not sufficiently emphasise that such software does not provide answers, rather it only raises questions for investigation. As an example of what might happen, do we really want to go down the road of refusing to sell a patron a ticket because he has a Moslem name?

Continuing the morning plenary, delegates were disappointed with Walter Gagg, Director of Stadiums and Security for FIFA (the world football organisation). Although people valued the opportunity to network with him, Gagg's presentation was weak, his content was puerile and some of his argument was plain wrong. For example, Gagg equated football hooliganism with terrorism. This was disturbing. In the subsequent coffee break, several delegates were visibly angry and voiced concerns about FIFA's capability to lead on counter terrorism for the 2006 World Cup in Germany.

In the afternoon, Bill Fox of Maybo Ltd dealt with staff training for conflict management, emphasising that such training had value only as part of a blended and integrated security strategy for dealing with violence. Stefan Hay of the Security Industry Training Organisation then explained the efforts being made to move from a plethora of largely similar security qualifications to a more standardised qualifications framework.

The highlight of the afternoon streams was the final session, which, with hindsight, the organisers might have wished they had timetabled earlier in the day. Before the crowd disasters of the 1980s, the needs of safety had been overshadowed by public order security issues. Safety had then become paramount, but was there now a danger that a focus on counter terrorism security would again put safety in the shade? So it was timely that John de Quidt of the UK Football Licensing Authority gave a reminder of the need for an integrated approach to stadium safety. Rico Hawkes of Clear Channel Entertainment then gave an insightful promoter's perspective on the implementation of safety and security practices in United States motor sports. Professor Chris Kemp of Buckinghamshire Chilterns reported the results of his fascinating research on audience perceptions of safety at live events. He concluded that there were three key factors for success: large, clear signage; crowd facilitation rather than control; and dynamic risk assessment from before, through during, to after the event. Finally, lawyer Ben Challis gave a succinct overview of legal obligations and liabilities at live events.

Overall, the inaugural EVS was a well-organised and well-marketed event held in a very comfortable venue with excellent catering and other facilities. The exhibition was well supported and conference programme generally a success, with a number of controversial issues debated. As David Wood (Managing Director of International Business Events) concluded, the event 'provided a much-needed forum for security industry professionals from across the sports and entertainment sectors to meet and share case studies and best practice approaches to safety and security. We are looking forward to an even more successful event in 2006.'

5.1 COMMENTARY BY JIM CHALMERS – EVENT AND VENUE SECURITY CONFERENCE

The article written by Frosdick on the subject of event and venue security stemmed from his attendance at the inaugural Event and Venue Security Conference held in London in April 2005. The article was published in June 2005, just a few weeks prior to the horrific suicide bombing events in London on 7 July of that year. I am sure that no one who was at the conference, including all the knowledgeable and eminent speakers, would have contemplated the atrocities in our capital city when human bodies were used as weapons of terrorism to such devastating effect.

The history of the UK has shown us to expect the use of conventional terrorist tactics, such as vehicle borne improvised explosive devices or packages left in streets or buildings, with very often a recognised warning. In the contingency plans for my small football club, we plan for the suspect vehicle or the suspect package, but the not the suspect suicide bomber. I would imagine that the contingency plans for the majority of football clubs are the same in this respect. All of this changed, however, on 7 July 2005. In the space of a few months, the 2005 conference was in many respects out of date. We suddenly had to change our thinking in the UK security environment, in a very similar way that the 11 September attacks in New York changed attitudes towards civilian aircraft being used as a terrorist weapon.

Our world did change after 7 July, and this is reflected to a degree in the fifth edition of the *Guide to Safety at Sports Grounds* published in 2008, when for the first time, acts of terrorism are referred to as events which should be planned for at our sports grounds. This is then supported by guidance on how to combat acts of terrorism, including suicide bombs, and in particular the guidance issued by the National Counter Terrorism Security Office (NaCTSO) in their *Counter Terrorism Protective Security Advice for Stadia and Arenas*.

In the ever changing world in which we live, the conference of 2005 has been superseded by events both nationally and internationally. These events affect event and venue security, and the Frosdick article presents merely a snap shot of opinion and beliefs in 2005, some of which may not be all that relevant in the present day.

A major part of the conference concentrated on debate surrounding the Security Industry Authority (SIA), and this is certainly one area which has been overtaken by events. Despite a threat by one the speakers in 2005 to seek a judicial review concerning the dispensation of sports ground stewards from the SIA licensing remit, this never materialised, and the situation remains the same. The most significant issue relating to the SIA is the government decision in October 2010 which stated that the SIA would no longer be a non-departmental public body (or 'quango'), and that there would be a phased transition towards a new regulatory regime for the private security industry. The exact nature of the new regime is yet to be determined. During the transition phase, the existing laws and regulations will remain in place and will continue to be enforced. Whatever the changes made in the future, it is clear that the government will still wish the private security industry to be regulated. To that end, the SIA is working with the security industry to determine how best to set up a new system of regulation. For the future, therefore, it is clear that the revised role of the SIA will have more to concentrate its mind on than sports ground stewards, and that will not be a bad thing for the sports industry.

5.2. OPTIMISING VENUE SECURITY

The original citation for this article is Frosdick, S. (2008) 'Optimising Venue Security', *Stadium and Arena Management*, June 2008, p. 8.

Steve Frosdick reports from IFSEC 2008.

Venue safety and security featured at the International Fire and Security Exhibition and Conference in Birmingham on 14 May 2008. Delegates heard from an international panel chaired by Chris Patzelt, General Secretary of the Football Safety Officers' Association. The four presentations took different angles but collectively drew out the key success factors, namely: multi-agency planning; resourcing the workforce; exhaustive communications; and proper training and equipment.

Terry Scallan and Errol Peace from the South African Institute of Security are involved in training the 45,000 event security officers (South Africa does not have 'stewards') needed for the World Cup 2010. South Africa has over 300,000 registered private security officers, so the staff resources are available. The need is for a new Specialised Events Security programme to provide the competent staff needed to help the police in the stadia, concourses and fan parks. Having prepared the new unit standard, the next steps are to develop the materials and appoint accredited providers to deliver the training. Scallan and Peace also gave a confident message about progress with the ten stadium developments.

Former Police Commander Mick Messinger highlighted the universal requirement to counter the terrorist threat, opportunistic criminality and crowd-related disasters. Standards had to balance safety and security with a welcoming environment to which customers would return. This meant understanding the customer's legitimate desires and maximum use of non-impacting measures such as scanners and crowd monitoring. Careful multi-agency planning was essential but the plans must be clear and easily understood. Effective and continual communication was needed between agencies, staff and visitors. Staff must look the part and had to be properly trained, briefed and equipped for both their ordinary and emergency roles.

The terrorist killings in Munich (1972), the lone bomber in Atlanta (1996) and the demonstrators in Torino (2006) were stark reminders of the threats to the Olympic Games. For London 2012, British Security Industry Association Project Director David Evans is acting as the lead voice for the private security industry. He referred to previous Games and outlined the failings. Most debriefs had noted poor training, poor command and control, lack of co-operation with the police, staff not turning up, poor communications, poor planning and confusion over budgets. London was determined to get it right and had made an early start on establishing the requirements, researching the current position and closing the gaps. A key feature was partnership between the police and the industry.

In contrast to South Africa where the required staff numbers are available, London has realised that the competing demands for labour – there are 160 other events in parallel with the Olympics – mean that the private security industry can only supply about one sixth of the staff needed. Innovative ideas to close the gap include an initiative with colleges for 14 to 19 year-olds.

The Millennium Stadium in Cardiff, Wales, is used for everything from ball games to concerts to motor sports. The international profile, city centre location and mass audience evidenced the security risks and the multi-event usage meant that there could be no standard security plan. Gerry Toms outlined his security menu, including roles for all staff, pre-event searches, ticketing, accreditation, access control, vehicle and spectator searches, bomb disposal and CCTV. He explained how risk assessment based on the nature and history of the event, the national threat assessment and local intelligence would result in different security mixes for different events. These differences could help confuse any hostile reconnaissance.

Delegates were clearly impressed with the quality of this excellent session and must have benefited from the expert insights on offer.

5.2. COMMENTARY BY JIM CHALMERS – OPTIMISING VENUE SECURITY

In the 2008 article Frosdick gives his account of a plenary session held during the International Fire and Security Exhibition and Conference held in Birmingham in May 2008, when four different speakers gave their perspectives on how to optimise venue security. This session was chaired by the general secretary of the FSOA. To be recognised in this way, in a forum of national and international dimensions, was in many respects, a feather in the cap of the association.

This session appeared to be taken up almost entirely on predictions of issues likely to affect safety and security at the 2012 London Olympic Games. In particular, the terrorist threat and the staffing implications for the sporting venues featured very highly in the debate. Even at this early stage in the Olympic Games planning, a senior police officer spoke of the need for a multi-agency approach to the games, with a clear understanding by everyone involved of their specific roles and responsibilities. This of course is nothing new, since success in any sporting event requires an attitude of 'we are all in this together' if successful planning and operations are to be achieved. No single agency, including the police, can operate on a standalone basis in this environment. From what I understand, the multi-agency approach and co-operation is regarded as a keystone in the games planning processes.

The balance between safety and security has already been debated in Part I of this book, but in the build up to and during the games, it is imperative that the perceived security needs do not get out of balance with the safety and enjoyment perspectives. If the sporting venues are turned into impregnable fortresses on the back of the terrorist threat, then the terrorists will have won. The balance therefore, has to be struck through the use of intelligence, technology, and an adequate number of properly trained staff and police, to minimise the terrorist threat and maximise the customer enjoyment and overall games experience. The eyes of the world will be on London for a few weeks in the summer of 2012. Get it right and we shall be the envy of the world. Get it wrong, and the recriminations will reverberate around the globe for generations to come.

The conference debate of 2008 relating to the South Africa 2010 World Cup has been taken over by actual events. However, it is interesting to compare their staffing prediction levels two years in advance of their event, and the staffing predictions at the same period prior to the London Olympic Games. At the conference the speakers from the South African Institute of Security were predicting a requirement of 45,000 security officers to manage safety and security at the World Cup venues. It was also interesting to note that they had 300,000 registered private security officers (stewards), so they did not predict any problems with the resources needed to manage their safety and security operations. Please see my later comments regarding the personnel requirements to manage safety, security and customer care at the London Olympics.

At the conference, one of the speakers mentioned how the private security industry in the UK was only able to provide one sixth of the staff needed for the 2012 Olympic Games. Some innovative ideas were going to be necessary if the staffing levels were going to be reached. One of these innovative ideas has already materialised; the Bridging the Gap project, which will seek to increase the number of trained security personnel who will be available for the games.

Representatives of the London Organising Committee for the Olympic Games (LOCOG) gave a presentation at the FSOA bi-annual conference in October 2010, where they gave some indication of the stewarding levels required for the Olympic venues. If my understanding is correct, there will be a need for 15,000 stewards (both paid and unpaid) to manage all of the venues. My belief is that the number of static and mobile stewards will be greater than the ratio advised in the *Guide to Safety at Sports Grounds.* There will also be a requirement for a higher number of supervisor stewards than would normally be necessary. This is in no doubt due to the temporary nature of the games, and the temporary nature of the stewards performing duty at the events compared to normal sporting events which regularly occur and are staffed by the same personnel all year round. My understanding is that the ratios will be along the lines of six stewards to one team leader and six team leaders to one Level Three qualified area supervisor.

The number of static posts will vary from venue to venue, but these can generally be determined well in advance of the games, once the venue structure and operation have been finalised. These locations will be identified in the venue stewarding plan. With regard to mobile posts, the Guide recommends a ratio of one steward per 250 anticipated spectators. This ratio can be increased if there is a need for a higher level of safety management, and my understanding is that the ratio will be one steward per 100 spectators. Indeed for the Paralympics, at which the audience profile is significantly different in terms of children and spectators with access assistance needs, the number of stewards will be higher at each venue. It is anticipated that the static and mobile stewards will comprise the unpaid volunteer stewards who will receive a lower level of training and qualification.

An additional category of steward will be created over and above the static/mobile definitions in the Guide, and this will be a 'key position' steward. Each venue will be required to identify the locations for these stewards and these posts will be covered by paid, qualified stewards.

It is too early to put numbers on the breakdown of static/mobile/key position stewards, but it is known that LOCOG have a dedicated team to assist in identifying the personnel requirements in each category.

The training requirements for the stewards will also vary depending on whether they are paid or unpaid volunteers. As far as the supervisors are concerned, there will be no change in the present requirement for all supervisors to hold a Level Three safety qualification. Until the required number of supervisors is determined, it is difficult to judge whether there will be a sufficient number of qualified personnel to meet the needs given the ongoing sporting events in the country at the time of the Games. This may mean that qualified supervisors will not be released by their employers. It is currently being debated how far it will affect normal football matches being staged at the same time as the Games. Even if the correct number of qualified supervisors is available, it will still present a problem for LOCOG if they cannot perform duties at the games due to other commitments.

Paid stewards who will staff the 'key position' posts will all be expected to hold a Level Two qualification on the relevant qualification framework. Again, until this number is established it is difficult to predict whether there will be a sufficient number of qualified stewards available to staff the key venue positions. Whilst the stewards may well be willing to volunteer for paid Olympic duties, there may again be the stumbling block of employers not wishing to release them for the games due to their local commitments. I again use the football match example where clubs will require their qualified stewards to safely manage their events, and if they defect en masse to the Games, this will place the football club in severe quandary. It could even result in severe sanctions being imposed on the club by the certifying authority if the number of stewards required by the safety certificate is not present at a match.

Unpaid stewards who are expected to make up the majority of the stewarding personnel for the games will be expected to have completed the training which provides the underlying knowledge to the occupational standards for spectator safety. This will include:

- Preparing for spectator events.
- How to deal with accidents and emergencies.
- Controlling the entry, exit and movement of people at spectator events.

An additional requirement is for the new steward to have attended four events before being allowed to work alone. I understand the LOCOG stewarding plan will allow for this.

This will present a significant training requirement when you consider how it will extend to several thousand unpaid volunteers at venues across the country. The questions that must be posed include:

- Who will undertake the training of the stewards, since this can only be done by competent trainers?
- When will the training be done and what are the timescales for completion?
- Where will the training be done?

- Who will assess the standard and consistency in the training?

- Who will assess whether the stewards have properly assimilated their training?

- Will the stewards receive any form of qualification?

My understanding is that LOCOG only intend to use competent trainers and are in talks with training providers. I believe the training will take place from the spring of 2012, and this will include test events at all of the venues being used for the Games. It is anticipated that most of the training will take place across the south east of the country and close to the main London venues. A process of assessment and accreditation will be in place and on completion of the training, unpaid stewards will be able to use this training as approved prior learning for the award of a Level Two qualification. I am therefore very confident that LOCOG understand the importance of training for all the safety personnel being employed for the Games and are dedicated to this provision.

LOCOG is already inundated by applicants to be an unpaid static/mobile volunteer steward and I am confident that thousands will wish to play even a small part in this unique event in our country's history. With regard to the provision of unpaid stewards, I do not consider there will be a problem in meeting these staffing requirements. If nothing else, it will be quite the tale to tell your grandchildren; you were part of the 2012 London Olympic Games.

Another issue which I believe will have to be resolved soon is the role of the Security Industry Authority (SIA) in respect of the stewards performing 'licensable' duties at the Games sporting venues. It is well documented how the SIA tried to bring sports grounds stewards under their licensing remit but failed in the attempt. Providing certain criteria are met within their training and qualifications, and whether stewards are carrying out licensable or non-licensable activities in certified sports grounds, then in house sports ground stewards are exempt from the SIA licensing requirements.

It is clear that, given the variety of venues being used for the Games, there will be a variety of legislation governing their certification, regulation and licensing. Some of the venues will meet the criteria for dispensation from SIA licensing, but many others will not, and in the absence of any dispensation, thousands of games stewards could technically fall within the licensing requirements of the SIA. Unless this issue is resolved, it will present LOCOG with a major problem in terms of training, registration and licensing costs. I would suggest that unless government adopts a common sense approach to granting dispensation from SIA licensing to the games stewards, this will seriously damage the availability and preparedness of stewards to participate in the games.

The 2008 conference only touched upon issues surrounding how best to optimise venue security. It is an issue which faces every venue manager, and in particular the person responsible for safety and security at the venue. The London Olympics will present many headaches and many challenges for all the agencies involved in making the games the successful event it deserves to be. Assembling the safety and security personnel required for every venue will present LOCOG with challenges in its own right, such as selecting the right personnel, acquiring the correct number of personnel, training them, accommodating them and managing them at each venue. They will also have to resolve with government the issue of SIA licensing. However, I am confident that given the history of the development of safety management and stewarding in the UK, this will present the opportunity to write another page in history, with the staging of a memorable Olympic Games.

PART VI – THE FOOTBALL SAFETY OFFICERS ASSOCIATION

Introduction

Part VI focuses on the Football Safety Officers' Association of England and Wales (the FSOA). Jim Chalmers is the FSOA President and both he and Steve Frosdick are founder members from 1992. The two articles give an overview of the FSOA and its work. The commentary by Jim Chalmers then looks forward at likely developments in the run-up to the FSOA's 25th anniversary in 2017.

6.1. The Football Safety Officers Association of England and Wales

This article appears on the website of the Football Safety Officers Association (FSOA). It explains the FSOA's post-Hillsborough origins in 1992 and its work over the subsequent eighteen years.

6.2. 15 Years of the FSOA

Following the 15th anniversary celebrations of the Football Safety Officers' Association in 2007, General Secretary Chris Patzelt discussed developments with Steve Frosdick in the Winter 2007/2008 edition of *Panstadia* magazine.

6.1-6.2. Commentary by Jim Chalmers – Looking Forward

In an impassioned and almost valedictory commentary, FSOA President Jim Chalmers brings the two articles in Part VI up to date and then offers a forward look to the FSOA's 25th anniversary. Chalmers comments on the parlous financial status of the FSOA, its use of technology, stewards training, safety officer qualifications, safety officer training courses, steward supervisor training courses, Institute status, new Football Licensing Authority guidance on safety management and safety certification, new Football Association crowd management guidance, the FSOA and major sporting events, the FSOA and Europe, and the future of the Football Licensing Authority.

6.1. THE FOOTBALL SAFETY OFFICERS' ASSOCIATION OF ENGLAND AND WALES

This article by Jim Chalmers was originally written in 2005 for the Football Safety Officers Association website at *http://www.fsoa.org.uk*. The article was then updated in 2009.

> Responsibility for the safety of spectators lies at all times with ground management

This principle was established with the publication of the first Green Guide in 1973 and repeated in subsequent editions including the most recent in 2008. However the debate and controversy on crowd safety can be traced back to the 1924 Shortt Report into the near disaster which occurred at the opening of Wembley Stadium. Yet despite a long history of tragedies at football grounds, with numerous inquiries and reports all agreeing that the safety of spectators was the responsibility of the sports ground management, the older football supporter will remember how football grounds in the 70s and 80s resembled secure fortresses guarded by hundreds of police officers. This however was not enough to prevent the 1989 Hillsborough stadium disaster when 96 football fans tragically died.

It could be argued that at that time the needs of safety and security were out of balance and that this was a fundamental reason for the disaster. Many of our current members, including Jim Chalmers, our president, were senior police officers in those days. They can tell you from first-hand experience how the police were obliged to fill the void in controlling and managing football grounds due to the absence of safety officers and competent stewards.

All of this however changed in the flurry of activities which followed Lord Justice Taylor's report into the Hillsborough disaster. The police had to seriously examine their role in sports grounds and the football authorities were forced to face up to their responsibilities for ensuring the care, safety and well being of their customers. In particular they were forced to look at how their grounds were managed with one of the main concerns being the variance in safety management performance around football grounds in England and Wales. Safety systems and practices were being evolved locally but in a piecemeal fashion and with very little consistency or uniformity of purpose. This included the appointment of safety officers, which before Hillsborough was not an established post at the majority of clubs. Even in the immediate post Hillsborough era there were many clubs who felt that ageing club secretaries with no knowledge or experience of safety management could discharge the role of a safety officer. This was unacceptable to the few capable and competent safety officers at the time and so created the climate which helped bring about the Football Safety Officers Association of England and Wales (the FSOA).

The birth of the FSOA was the brainchild of Mike Holford QPM, the then safety officer at Nottingham Forest. Mike later became the first president of the association but is sadly no longer with us. The inaugural meeting of the FSOA took place in Nottingham on 29 October 1992 and was attended by 28 safety officers. The aims of the association then and now can be summarised as,

> Improving safety at football grounds by enhancing the role of safety management and the status of the safety officer within the football industry. The association intends to achieve this by promulgating best safety management practices, enhancing the role of stewards and continually developing the expertise of safety officers.

From that inaugural meeting the FSOA membership now stands at over 300 members. English and Welsh Premier and Football League Clubs are represented, as are many of the lower football leagues. Full membership is open to safety officers, deputy and assistant safety officers who have successfully completed the FSOA six day event and match day safety management course. Associate membership is open to those same levels of safety officers who have still to complete the course.

Affiliate membership is open to anyone associated with the responsibility for safety at sports grounds. This could include officials of the Premier League, Football Association, Football League, Football Licensing Authority, rugby league, cricket, racecourses, local authorities, safety consultants and academics. Corporate membership is available to companies involved in safety at sports grounds i.e. those who provide relevant products and services to football clubs.

The success of the FSOA is well evidenced by other sporting bodies creating their own safety officers associations in Scotland and Northern Ireland and in sports such as rugby league, rugby union and cricket. All of these separate associations have as their aims the same principles established by the FSOA.

As membership of the FSOA has grown so has its influence in the wider sports industry. Over the years the FSOA has led the way in the development of the professional competencies of its members. This has principally been achieved by the introduction in 2002 of the six day FSOA event and match day safety management course. Up until May 2009, over 200 safety practitioners from all sports, including representatives from overseas, had successfully completed the course.

The association is committed to doing all it can to promote the development of professional safety qualifications for our members, many of whom possess various qualifications in sectors such a risk and security, health and safety, environmental health and in safety management. This commitment by the FSOA became even more relevant in 2008 when the fifth edition of the Green Guide recommended:

> That a Safety Officer should as a minimum have, or be working towards, a Level Four spectator safety qualification on the relevant qualification framework.

As a member of the joint football authorities safety management focus group, the FSOA has also been a major player in the development of stewards training and assessment and at a practical level our members are the key to ensuring that their stewards achieve the necessary training and assessment qualifications required throughout the football leagues. Our members are represented on various working groups related to all aspects of improving stadium facilities and management and are regular speakers at various safety and security seminars both here and abroad.

Coordination of the association activities is directed through the FSOA chair, supported by the six regional chairs. These persons comprise the national executive committee. It was however recognised in 2002 that the work of managing the association had outgrown this being done on a part time basis by full time safety officers who already had a demanding and time consuming post. In that year therefore the association appointed a full time general secretary. This person acts for and reports to the national executive committee on all aspects of the association's functions including the organisation and management of two national conferences each year.

Another key development was the establishment of the FSOA website in 2000. This enables members to exchange information and access all current documentation relevant to their role. The website also includes a facility for members to upload and download post match reports. These reports allow safety officers to exchange match day information such as attendances, methods of travel, visiting supporters, particular problems including any arrests or ejections and the reasons for these. This information enables members to plan their events use of resources more accurately without relying solely on police intelligence. Such achievements could only have been dreamed of when the association was formed in 1992.

Another valuable function of the website is the forum where members can seek advice or exchange information on any problems they might face in their day to day safety management operations. There is an old saying that there is never any need to re-invent the wheel and the vast experience of our members is available to any member of the association either through the forum or through personal contact.

The FSOA has certainly come a long way since 1992 but safety management is never a one-off concept. It has to be constantly worked at to avoid any suggestion of complacency creeping in. Our members are at the forefront of every football match day operation when supporters can and should expect that every effort will be made to ensure their reasonable care, comfort and safety when following their team and the sport they enjoy from the moment they enter the football ground. The person who has to ensure this, the safety officer, carries a tremendous responsibility on their shoulders, which can take its toll. That is why our association is committed to supporting members in any way it can and to ensuring they have the competencies, status and authority to effectively discharge the onerous demands of their role.

The future will continue to present many challenges both to the association and our members but experience has shown our ability to respond effectively to whatever issues have arisen. Stadium and spectator safety is a dynamic and ongoing concept, thus we must be alert, active and energetic in staying at the forefront of professional stewarding and safety management in the years ahead.

6.2. 15 YEARS OF THE FSOA

The original citation for this article is Frosdick, S. (2008) 'Safety First', *Panstadia*. Winter 2007/2008, pp. 112-114.

Following the 15ᵗʰ anniversary celebrations of the Football Safety Officers' Association, new General Secretary Chris Patzelt discussed recent developments with Steve Frosdick.

The English football disasters of the late 1980s were followed by a flurry of safety management activities. New systems developed ad hoc rather than in a co-ordinated way and there were soon concerns at the variations in standards and practices at different grounds. So in October 1992, safety practitioners got together to form the Football Safety Officers' Association (FSOA). The FSOA aims to improve safety at grounds; to promulgate best practice; to enhance the role of stewards and to continually develop safety officers' expertise. Over the last fifteen years, the FSOA has grown from 28 to over 300 members. Full and associate members are drawn from English and Welsh football grounds, whilst affiliate and corporate members come from the football authorities, stewarding companies, commercial suppliers, other sports and academe. The FSOA holds two national conferences each year, supported by other meetings at regional level. There is a monthly newsletter and day-to-day communication via a secure website.

The FSOA's fifteenth anniversary dinner and conference in October 2007 coincided with the appointment of Chris Patzelt as the new full-time general secretary. Patzelt's combination of commercial and safety experience in football made him the ideal candidate. He is aged 47 and has worked in football administration for over 25 years – as a ticket office manager, company secretary and safety officer. His interest in safety stems from 1991, when as company secretary at Huddersfield Town he found himself named as the responsible person on the safety certificate! In 1993, he moved to Barnsley where he combined the roles of assistant secretary and safety officer. This was unusual since most safety officers at that time were retired police officers. He joined Bradford City as safety officer in 2004 and was elected FSOA vice chairman in March 2007.

Patzelt is rightly proud of the FSOA's achievements over its first 15 years. As previously reported in *Panstadia* (September 1996, pp. 34-36), FSOA members (with Steve Frosdick as editor) worked with the football authorities during 1995/96 to develop a multi-media training package for stewarding at football grounds. The training covers general responsibilities, maintaining a safe environment, response to spectators, emergency aid, fire safety and evacuations. Additional modules on dealing with racism and disability discrimination and on conflict management were added when the training was revised in 2003 and 2005.

The training package became the industry standard for stewarding and has been used by various sports as well as in other countries, such as the 1998 World Cup in France. Still today, the package remains the recognised learning platform for a variety of level two stewarding qualifications.

Writing in *Panstadia* in July 2000 (pp. 70-71), Pat Carr questioned whether being a retired police officer was sufficient qualification for the demanding safety officer role. The FSOA had already seen the need and from 2002 began to deliver its own event and matchday safety management course. Delivered in three two-day modules, the course equips safety officers to manage the matchday operation; to assess and act on stadium risks; to create the required paper audit trail and to plan for and respond to emergencies. The course provides 70% of the requirement for a level four national vocational qualification and many attendees have gone on to achieve this. A few have progressed to higher education (see *Panstadia* January 2001, pp. 71-72) with FSOA president Jim Chalmers even obtaining a degree in risk and security management.

Patzelt does not think it will be long before all certifying authorities make it a requirement for the safety officer at a designated sports ground to hold or be working towards at least a level four qualification. This can only strengthen the popularity of the FSOA course.

Given the absence of anything similar, the FSOA course has extended its reach both beyond football and outside England and Wales. Delegates have attended from various spectator sports and courses have been run in Scotland and the Republic of Ireland. Patzelt would like to see the course exported further. He recognises that the safety culture in some European nations focuses more on security and policing than on safety in the round. Nevertheless, he comments that the FSOA would 'welcome the opportunity to discuss with UEFA and FIFA how the FSOA course could help them with training safety officers both in domestic leagues and for international tournaments.'

It is five years since the first safety officers attended the FSOA course. There have been legislative and other changes, for example the more frequent use of football grounds for other events such as pop concerts. Thus a two-day refresher programme has been piloted for delivery in 2008.

Reflecting on the key issues in football safety over the last couple of years, Patzelt highlighted two matters: the attempts by the Security Industry Authority (SIA) to regulate stewarding; and the ongoing problem of persistent standing in seated areas. Rebutting the SIA's argument that all stewards performed a security function and so needed to be licensed had been a Herculean effort. The eventual outcome had excluded in-house stewards who were fully trained; but required private stewarding companies to triple-train and double-licence many of their staff – as stewards, door supervisors and manned guards. All this for casual staff earning perhaps £30 a game!

Panstadia feature-writer Steve Menary dealt with the 'safe standing' issue in Summer 2007 (pp. 54-59). Although most fans are happy to sit in their seats, a sizeable minority stand up all through the match. There have been two supporter campaigns to allow standing. 'Stand Up Sit Down' fans argue that they should be allowed to stand in seated areas (see *http://www.standupsitdown.co.uk*). Meanwhile the Football Supporters Federation has argued for clubs to be allowed to choose to reintroduce standing terraces (see *http://www.fsf.org.uk/ media/pdfs/safe-standing-report-web.pdf*). Subsequent to Menary's article, a debate in the House of Commons on 24 October 2007 concluded with the Minister saying that there would be no changes to the current requirements, i.e. fans in all-seated grounds are expected to sit down. This is all very well at the policy level, however safety officers are still faced with the practical problem of managing persistent standing week in and week out.

Turning to the future, and drawing on his commercial football experience, Patzelt outlined his plans for the FSOA's further development. Now that funding from the Football Foundation has ended, the first priority will be to secure the FSOA's running costs. Membership and exhibitor fees will be reviewed and continued partnerships with small specialist companies are most welcome. However Patzelt is also thinking blue-chip and is 'looking for a significant commercial partner'. In parallel with increasing revenue, Patzelt is keen to improve the package of benefits offered to both members and sponsors. The website needs attention and other ideas could include merchandise and publications, help packs for new members and access to legal advice. According to FSOA President Jim Chalmers, 'the objective must be for the FSOA to become the leading authority on the practice of safety at sports grounds'.

Whilst representatives from other sports hold affiliate membership of the FSOA, Patzelt and the FSOA national executive committee do not wish to evolve into a sports safety officers' association. There are already safety officer associations for rugby union, rugby league, cricket, horse racing and motor racing as well as an FSOA Scotland. The vision, therefore, is to create an Institute of Sports Safety to act as an umbrella body for the existing associations. Such an Institute could be more influential than its constituent organisations and thus lobby more effectively with government on overarching safety issues such as the regulation of stewarding.

Patzelt can see two future training developments. One will be the further revision of the training package for stewarding at football grounds. Modern technology means that the modular approach could be superseded by individual topics delivered in any preferred order. Some private stewarding companies have adapted the training to provide e-learning materials for staff to use for distance learning with only the assessment provided on site. Patzelt agrees this approach can work for most of the underpinning knowledge, but believes that face-to-face training will remain essential for the more practical aspects. Accordingly, he would like to see the package revised to provide a 'blended learning' platform.

Given that there are level two qualifications for stewards and level four for safety officers, the obvious gap is at level three for supervisors. Patzelt anticipates that FSOA members will once again be heavily involved in the development of the relevant learning materials and that such a qualification will be mandated by certifying authorities by about 2010.

UK safety officers have an international reputation as experts in their field and continue to be called on for help by other countries. For example, earlier in 2007 FSOA chairman John Beattie was invited to address an Italian conference convened to discuss the problems with spectator behaviour in *Serie A*. 'These are exciting times for safety officers,' concluded Patzelt. 'We have the 2012 Olympic Games in London, the 2014 Commonwealth Games in Glasgow and a possible 2018 World Cup bid by England. Elsewhere are the 2010 World Cup in South Africa, the 2012 Euro in Poland and Ukraine and the 2014 World Cup in Brazil. UK football safety officers stand ready to lend their expertise to all these events.'

6.1-6.2. COMMENTARY BY JIM CHALMERS – LOOKING FORWARD

When asked to write about 'looking forward' in the context of the FSOA, I could only do so by looking at the articles 6.1 and 6.2, written in 2005 and 2008, and which look at the history of the association. Whilst it would be wrong to dwell on the past, it is the past which has shaped the present of the FSOA, and will have a significant bearing on the future. Looking forward, I then had the dilemma of just how far forward I should look. Since the FSOA was formed in 1992, much has changed in the football environment and I am certain there will be many more changes in the years ahead. I consider it sensible, therefore, to look at the likely challenges which will face the association in the seven years which lead up to the 25th anniversary of the FSOA.

In considering further the history of the development of FSOA, the reader should refer to Part 2.1 of *Safety and Security at Sports Grounds*, published in 2005. This was a significant year for me since 2005 was the year I was honoured by my peers and elected president of the association. When I accepted the honour I made it very clear to the membership that I would not just be a 'figure head', but would instead play an active role in assisting and developing the association for the benefit of not only the members, but of the game of football. I leave it to others to judge how successful or otherwise I have been in that context.

The Article for the FSOA Website

My article about the FSOA, which I originally wrote in 2005, was principally intended to summarise the history, roles and purpose of the FSOA. Since then, the article has been updated but it continues to be an introduction to anyone interested in finding out about the FSOA, and hopefully answers a few basic questions about the association. I saw the article as an open door leading into the association, and judging from the number of hits on the website, I believe it continues to achieve that objective.

In 2005 I said in the article:

The future will continue to present many challenges both to the association and our members but experience has shown our ability to respond effectively to whatever issues have arisen. Stadium and spectator safety is a dynamic and ongoing concept, thus we must be alert, active and energetic in staying at the forefront of professional stewarding and safety management in the years ahead.

My belief in this respect was expanded upon in the 2008 article by Frosdick, following his interview with Chris Patzelt, general secretary of the FSOA, on the 15th anniversary of the association. As one of the few surviving members of the FSOA who witnessed its birth in 1992, I can personally reflect on the many achievements of the association leading up to this anniversary, some of which are referred to in the article. However, the article focuses very much on Patzelt's vision for the future, including some of the challenges which he predicts the association and the membership would face in the years ahead. In 2008, Patzelt was also looking forward, and I will be commenting upon the extent to which his vision has been realised, and relating his vision to mine as I also look forward. In the article, Patzelt touches upon his vision of safety management challenges, such as:

- Steward training programme.

- Qualifications for safety officers and supervisors.

- The FSOA safety officer training course.

- The role of the Security Industry Authority (SIA) in football event stewarding.

- Persistent standing in seating areas.

- FSOA funding and organisational developments.

- Institute status of the association.

- The role of the FSOA in major football and other sporting events such as the London Olympic games of 2012.

The Patzelt interview only highlights the comments I made in 2005 about the many challenges which the FSOA would face in the years ahead. Some of the issues are long-running, such as stewards training, safety officer qualifications, safety officer training courses and persistent standing in seated areas. By the very nature of these topics, I believe they will still be key issues for debate and development in the years ahead, and will always be at the forefront of challenges facing the FSOA and others in the future.

I am however grateful for the opportunity to reflect on Patzelt's vision, and in looking forward, to consider the extent to which that vision has come to fruition or been adjusted to reflect more realistic expectations. I will also take the opportunity to bring these issues up to date in 2011.

The principle aims of the FSOA which were established in 1992 and remain equally valid today are,

> Improving safety at football grounds by enhancing the role of safety management and the status of the safety officer within the football industry. The association intends to achieve this by promulgating best safety management practices, enhancing the role of the stewards and continually developing the expertise of the FSOA.

More on how the FSOA intend to achieve these aims can be found in the FSOA 2010 constitution which can be downloaded from the FSOA website at *http://www.fsoa.org.uk.*

My main future objective is for the FSOA to become regarded as the lead authority on the practice of safety at sports grounds. This is a crown which the Football Licensing Authority (FLA) would lay claim to and there are those in the England and Wales football authorities who would also lay claim to that crown. However, while those authorities may be able to write or preach about the subject of safety management, it is the FSOA membership which actually has to implement and enforce the various laws and guidance. The football authorities may have safety responsibilities, but not safety accountability. That onerous task falls on the association members, and that is why I argue that it is only the association which can lay claim to being the lead authority on the practice of safety at football grounds. However I am not certain this is a view currently held, or likely to be held, by our football authorities, unless there is a dramatic change in attitude towards the association by some of these bodies.

Looking Forward – the Financial Status of the FSOA

In 2008, Patzelt suggested that the top priority was to secure the funding that would ensure the FSOA can continue to function. I fully support that contention. Since being appointed president, I have witnessed the constant struggle by the association to provide a quality of service to its membership, whilst securing revenue to maintain its financial viability. The association can only afford one full time employee, (this being the post of general secretary) and our constant financial priority is to secure sufficient annual income to pay this person's salary and other operating costs.

It is a fact that the membership subscriptions alone cannot meet these costs, and much of the general secretary's time and energy is spent in securing sponsorship and revenue from other sources. This is to the detriment of the service provision to members, and the ability to fund development projects for the future, such as enhanced use of technology to support our membership. The present tension between service to our members and revenue generation will continue into the years ahead, unless a guaranteed source of income can be found.

I am constantly frustrated that, whilst the FSOA is regarded as a partner with the Premier League, Football Association and the Football League when it comes to major projects such as the development of steward training, we are certainly the paupers in that relationship. Since the association was formed we have received no contributions from these authorities to assist in maintaining the support and services which our membership need to undertake the onerous duties of a safety officer, irrespective of the league which their club happens to be playing in. When I consider the level of income which these authorities have I find it scandalous that not until 2011 was one football authority prepared to provide any financial assistance to the association. These same authorities are prepared to give financial support to organisations such as the National Association of Disabled Supporters and the Football Supporters Federation and I do not begrudge the financial support they receive. But when you consider that it is the FSOA membership who are tasked week in and week out with keeping our football grounds safe and secure for all the fans, this lack of financial support in the past has been lamentable.

In 2010 the FSOA sought a miserly amount of £10,000 from each of the authorities – a total of £30,000 to assist in funding the day to day operating costs of the association. 2010 was of course the same year when these same football authorities spent millions of pounds in their failed bid for the 2018 World Cup. The request was also made at a time when some football players are enjoying a salary of over a quarter of a million pounds a week and I therefore find it obscene that our association has to scrape by each year wondering if we can survive as an entity.

In 2011, the Premier League kindly donated £15,000 to the FSOA. Regrettably neither the Football Association nor the Football League were prepared to offer any financial support. The Premier League donation will help the financial stability of the association in the short term. But it will not be enough to help the association develop in the way I would wish as I look forward.

In looking forward, therefore, unless the FSOA receives some long term major sponsorship or increased financial assistance from the football authorities, I have my doubts that the association will ever be able to develop in the future. At best the association will continue to struggle just to maintain the status quo whilst at worst we will go backwards. It therefore begs the question whether the football authorities really do mean it when they say their priority will always be stadium and spectator safety, since it is the FSOA whose membership delivers that priority for them.

Looking Forward – the FSOA and Technology

We are increasingly living in a technologically advanced society and it will be imperative that the association makes the maximum use of this in providing services to the membership. This will mean enhancing the association website so that members can have at their fingertips all the tools they need to meet the onerous and demanding responsibilities of a safety officer. Communication between the centre and the membership is equally vital, and again, technology should be used to greater advantage to improve this. Areas which I believe should be expanded upon are:

- The website should have a library section containing the main publications on safety and security at sports grounds.

- There should be a best practice document section containing examples of key documents such as operations manuals, stewarding plans, medical plans, dynamic risk assessments and contingency plans. These should relate to the League structures; there is no point expecting a Conference club to adapt the operations manual for Arsenal, or Arsenal adapting a Conference club medical plan to fit their match day operating procedures.

- Availability of a basic set of match day documentation which all clubs should be able to use to standardise their match day safety audit trails.

- The match reporting section should contain far more information than it presently does. For example, information on the number of arrests and ejections is recorded but there is no facility to record and subsequently analyse the reasons for the arrests or ejections. There is other data included on the match day report which would provide useful management information for all clubs, but this is never analysed or presented as an information base.

- There should be greater use of information technology in keeping safety officers up to date with safety developments and procedures. Ideally the FSOA newsletter should be electronically circulated on a fortnightly basis and should provide a summary of the forum discussion items which have featured in the preceding two weeks.

I am confident that the more technology orientated safety officers could recommend other ways in which technology can be used in the development of the association. However, this will ultimately require time and money, and only emphasises my concern that with only one full time employee and an absence of adequate funding, the association is prevented from expanding in the technological field as I and others might wish.

Looking Forward – Stewards Training

Since the 2008 Patzelt interview, a redesigned steward training resource, *On the Ball*, was introduced in October 2010 by the football authorities in conjunction with the FSOA. The new programme now has an introductory module and six training modules (the previous programme had eight). The modules provide the underpinning knowledge required for a Level Two qualification in spectator safety. The modules comprise:

- Module 0 – Introduction and familiarisation.

- Module 1 – Spectator safety and customer service.

- Module 2 – Preparing for stewards duties, searching and dealing with accidents.

- Module 3 – Monitoring and controlling spectators.

- Module 4 – Disability awareness and fire safety.

- Module 5 – Managing conflict.

- Module 6 – Contributing to the work of the team.

If I were to pick out the most significant difference between this and the previous steward training programmes, it would be that there is now a far greater emphasis on spectators being regarded as customers, with customer care now being the cornerstone for all of the modules.

As with the previous training programmes this is an essential training tool for all safety officers, irrespective of the league their club operates in. The new programme marked the culmination of a great deal of hard work by FSOA members, who carried out the review and brought the programme up to date, and Juice Learning, who were commissioned to produce the training package. The proof of the success of the new training resource will be if it is used as extensively and successfully as the previous programmes edited by Frosdick.

Looking Forward – Safety Officer Qualifications

Patzelt mentioned in 2008 how it would not be long before certifying authorities made it a requirement for safety officers at designated sports grounds to hold, or be working towards, a Level Four qualification. Since then, it has become generally accepted that all safety officers and their deputies must have at least a Level Four qualification in spectator safety management and that steward supervisors have a Level Three qualification in spectator safety. These measures were advocated in the fifth edition of the *Guide to Safety at Sports Grounds* and certifying authorities have started to introduce them as requirements within the general safety certificate.

I have supported this provision in the general safety certificate for a long time. For many years local authorities have included a condition that all stewards must have a Level Two qualification in spectator safety. So it always seemed an anomaly that there was no similar requirement to have the relevant qualifications made of the safety managers, their deputies and supervisors. It is therefore encouraging that this minimum professional qualification for the senior safety management at clubs is now being enforced by certifying authorities through the general safety certificate. The penalty is that, if the senior safety personnel do not have the relevant qualifications, the certifying authority can reduce the 'S' factor (their assessment of the quality of the safety management) and so cut the stadium capacity.

I would envisage that by the 25th anniversary of the FSOA, all senior safety personnel will have the relevant Level Three or Four qualifications. If the FSOA is ever to be regarded as a professional safety body, it is important that our members have the appropriate qualifications.

Looking Forward – Safety Officer Training Courses

Since the 2008 article, one of the FSOA success stories (the six day event and match day safety management course) is no longer being offered by the association. Having been a speaker on the course since its inception in 2002, and as someone who has attended and successfully completed the course, I was personally sad to witness its demise in 2010. From the outset, the course offered what no other course in the country could do; the chance to develop the knowledge, skills and expertise required to become an effective and efficient safety officer, deputy or assistant safety officer. Over the years, not only did club safety practitioners benefit from attending the course, but so did safety practitioners from overseas, emergency service officers and officers from certifying authorities. The course successfully filled a gap which existed in the safety management training market place for eight years.

In recent years, other training providers have introduced similar training courses. Perhaps the course most instrumental in the demise of the FSOA training course is the Level Four safety management course introduced in 2010 by the Emergency Planning College in Easingwold. This course was prepared in conjunction with, and supported by, the FLA. The course extends beyond the event and match day safety management concept of the FSOA course, and is targeted at a far wider safety officer audience. Having examined the courses which are now available, the association supports the Emergency Planning College course, since it seems to offer a more integrated safety management package than the association course could offer. Whilst the association supports the Emergency Planning College course, it is a matter for each safety officer to consider all the courses which are available, and to decide which one would best suit their training and assessment needs (and their budget).

Cost is obviously very much an influencing factor as to which course to attend and for the first three years of the FSOA course, the Football Foundation subsidised the cost to members attending. It has always been a wish of the association that if the funding had been, or was ever, available in the future, we would be able to offer financial assistance to safety officers, particularly those in the lower football leagues. This serves as yet another example of the how more funding for the association would be put to good use, in developing the safety officers of the future.

Looking Forward – Steward Supervisor Training Courses

In 2008, Patzelt spoke of the need to develop a specific national training course for steward supervisors, but this has not materialised. Some safety officers have developed their own Level Three training courses, but others such as myself have used a training college. Telford College of Arts and Technology provided my chief steward and four steward supervisors with all the help and support they needed to compile the portfolios of evidence required for the Level Three award. The message is very clear; if a small club such as Kidderminster Harriers can process its entire steward supervisory staff to the award of the appropriate qualifications without a national training course, there is no reason why other clubs cannot do the same.

This is another example of where, with the appropriate funding, the FSOA could develop and deliver a national Level Three training course, in much the same way as the association previously developed the course which provided all the underlying knowledge for the Level Four award.

Looking Forward – Institute Status for the FSOA

Alongside the training and development theme that has progressed considerably since 2008, we have been looking into the concept of Institute status for the association. The driving force behind this initiative has been John Newsham, the safety officer at Blackburn Rovers and a long time member of the FSOA national executive committee. John was also elected as chair of the FSOA in March 2011. The initial idea of Institute status for football safety officers has since been developed to include safety officers from other sports.

In July 2010, an inaugural meeting was held involving safety officers from football, rugby league, rugby union, cricket and horse racing. It was decided that the planning for Institute status would progress with the ultimate aim of introducing a new umbrella organisation. This would represent safety managers from various events, arenas and stadia under an Institute banner. The main objective of the organisation would be to have a body that would be consulted on safety legislative changes, safety policy changes and which could influence government policy makers on issues relating to event, arena, stadia and spectator safety.

At the FSOA bi-annual meeting in October 2010, the association was given a mandate by the membership to continue the debate with other safety officer organisations in the development of the Institute concept. The membership felt that belonging to a recognised Institute could only improve the status, recognition and professionalism of all safety officers. I am hopeful that, by the 25th anniversary of the association, its members will be able to also claim membership of an Institute of Safety Managers, and in doing so, further demonstrate their professionalism and competencies in their chosen field.

Looking Forward – New Safety Guidance Documents

In looking forward, new safety guidance publications will have a significant impact on the working practices of safety officers and in particular, the demands placed on them to produce various documentation and manuals in support of their safety management strategies and operating procedures.

New FLA Guidance on Safety Management

In 2009 the FLA produced the *Sports Grounds and Stadia Guide No4 – Safety Management*. This 116 page publication amplifies the sections on safety management in the *Guide to Safety at Sports Grounds*. From the outset, the FLA recognises that safety management at sports grounds has become more sophisticated and professional over the past 20 years. The new guide therefore identifies and draws together good practice with regard to safety personnel, safety management procedures, event management and preparing for incidents. It also brings together previous FLA guidance on topics such as spectator safety policies, contingency planning, exercise planning and the briefing and de-briefing of stewards. The most significant part of the new guide highlights the value of an operations manual prepared and owned by the ground management. In reality, this means it is the safety officer on whose shoulders this new burden will fall. The new guide also includes information on how to formulate stewarding plans, medical plans and dynamic ongoing risk assessments.

Not only does the safety officer have to fully understand and implement the safety management requirements in the *Guide to Safety at Sports Grounds*, they now have to have a full understanding of and implement the new FLA safety management guidance.

Having introduced documentation such as operations manuals, stewarding plans, medical plans and on-going risk assessments, I speak from personal experience on just how much time and effort is required to comply. The challenge for all safety officers over the next few years will be to demonstrate their compliance with the rigorous standards and procedures set out in the new FLA guidance, much of which is also now required as a condition of the general safety certificate.

New FA Crowd Management Guidance

If this new FLA guidance were not enough for safety officers to contend with, in 2010 the Football Association (FA) issued the publication *Crowd Management Procedures – FA Good Practice Guide for Football Clubs.* The 31 page document contains guidance on topics ranging through:

- Part 1 – General crowd management measures.
- Part 2 – Management of visiting supporters.
- Part 3 – Crowd management measures to discourage the throwing of objects.
- Part 4 – Crowd management measures to discourage pitch incursion by spectators.
- Part 5 – Crowd management measures against hate crime including racist or homophobic abuse by spectators.
- Part 6 – Crowd management measures to discourage offensive chanting by spectators.
- Part 7 – Ensuring the safety of players, match officials and personnel in the technical area.
- Appendix 1 – Protocol for dealing with racist abuse.
- Appendix 2 – Technical area dismissals and touchline bans.

In this publication, the FA describes how football clubs have a responsibility under FA rules to take appropriate measures to provide an environment that is as safe as reasonably practicable for spectators, players and match officials, and to encourage good conduct by the supporters of both teams. The guidance provides good practice recommendations to assist in achieving this responsibility.

When the FSOA was formed in 1992, the only knowledge that safety officers were required to have was based on the safety legislation, the *Guide to Safety at Sports Grounds* and the general safety certificate. Since then, safety officers have had to contend with a plethora of safety legislation, safety guidance and safety requirements. None of this has made the life of a safety officer any easier. In fact, when any new guidance is published, it adds to the burden of responsibilities and accountability which a safety officer has to face. The recent FLA and FA guidance are only examples in support of my argument.

The life of a safety officer has become more sophisticated, more complicated and more demanding with the passage of time, as they try to keep up to date and in step with current safety thinking, and in particular, show compliance with any safety guidance emanating from the football authorities. The penalty of course is that if they fail to show compliance with the guidance, and there is a serious safety failure resulting in death or serious injury, it will be the safety officer who will have to face the consequences, either criminal or civil.

I wonder therefore just how long it will be before clubs, particularly those in the Premier League, employ a match day tactical advisor to advise the safety officer of safety options in any particular circumstances. Using tactical advisers is already well tested and tried in the police service, and with all the demands being placed on a safety officer during a match, can they be absolutely sure that they have taken into account all the safety options available to them? There is always a possibility that they may have overlooked something which could lead to tragedy. It was the Hillsborough stadium disaster which caused the police to introduce the role of tactical advisor to assist the police commander in the decision making process. I would suggest that at our major clubs, this is something which can only benefit the hard pressed safety officer on a match day.

What the recent guidance does illustrate is the complexity of the knowledge now required by safety officers if they are to properly discharge their responsibilities. In 2011, the expectations of a safety officer are now far greater than at any time in the history of the FSOA. I would suggest that, for the future, those expectations will continue to grow. That is why the FSOA, in the service it provides to the membership, must be able to keep pace with change and the increasing demands and expectations of our membership.

New FLA Guidance on Safety Certification

Part of that change will relate to the current safety certification process of sports grounds. In December 2010, the FLA published a new *Guide to the Safety Certification of Sports Grounds*. This replaced the original FLA guidance of the same name published in 2001. At the same time, the London District Surveyors Association (LDSA) published a new model safety certificate which is in full accordance with the FLA guide. This replaced their previous specimen safety certificate and guide published in 1997. Both documents can be downloaded from the FLA website.

The FLA guidance offers two possible styles of safety certification, instead of the existing one model. This will have great significance for the FSOA membership, since it is generally safety officers who have the responsibility of ensuring compliance with the terms and conditions of the general safety certificate.

The FLA favours a new and less directive approach under which the ground management (normally the safety officer) uses risk assessments to identify the conditions which it considers are necessary to secure the reasonable safety of spectators. This is then recorded in an operations manual for scrutiny, acceptance and incorporation into a schedule to the safety certificate issued by the certifying authority. The FLA view is that this new style of safety certification is in line with the modern approach to public safety, whereby the operator of a sporting venue is responsible for identifying any risks and the steps to be taken to reduce those risks to an acceptable level. This approach leaves the initiative and the responsibility with the ground management, which is able to tailor the requirements more closely to the particular needs and circumstances of the sports ground. The FLA argues that the fifth edition of the *Guide to Safety at Sports Grounds* reflects this approach to safety certification. In effect, what the FLA is advocating is a process of self certification.

The less direct approach will not be mandatory and could mean that two local football grounds could be operating under two different styles of safety certification; one prescriptive, as at present, and one less directive, as favoured by the FLA. When I joined the FLA in 1991, one of the greatest complaints my colleagues and I received was that clubs separated in some instances by only four miles were issued with safety certificates from different certifying authorities, which dictated totally different terms, conditions and requirements for them to comply with.

One of the first guidance documents issued by the FLA was a *Guide on Safety Certificates* issued in 1992. This provided guidance to certifying authorities on the structure and contents of safety certificates. This proved to be one of the FLA success stories, with a degree of consistency being achieved in safety certificates issued by certifying authorities. During the rest of my FLA career and up to the present time, that degree of consistency has been sustained.

I have no concerns over a less directive approach to safety certification, but I believe it will be a step backwards to have two differing styles. If a less directive approach is considered the way forward, then it should be enforced by legislation. However, my understanding is that government will not make the new style of safety certification compulsory, and therein lies the weakness. It will be left to certifying authorities in consultation with clubs to determine which path they wish to go down, hence my concerns about a lack of consistency in the approach to safety certification.

Change will not occur overnight. The FLA acknowledges that clubs should be given sufficient notice of any proposed move by the certifying authority to the new style of safety certificate, to allow the club time to undertake the necessary risk assessments and produce the operations manual. I have no doubt that this will not present a problem for the larger sports grounds that will generally have the staff, time and competency to carry out these processes. From personal experience I would question whether the management of smaller sporting venues will have the knowledge, skill and competence to carry out the risk assessment processes and the production of the operations manual to the satisfaction of the certifying authority. As a consequence, it could result in the smaller sporting venues paying exorbitant consultancy fees to provide the certifying authority with the information it requires in the new style safety certification process. Of course, this is at a time when smaller sporting venues are struggling financially to survive.

Shifting the onus of safety certification from the certifying authority to the ground management will undoubtedly save the certifying authority a great deal of time and effort. It will however, in my opinion, place a greater burden on the ground management and in particular, the safety officer at a time when the majority are already overworked and underpaid.

Whether the less directive style will make our grounds any safer is also debateable. One thing I do believe is that smaller sporting venues will have to bear a substantial cost to produce the risk assessments and operations manual to support the new style of safety certificate. This leads me to conclude that in the future there will be a mixture of safety certificate styles up and down the country. This in itself may lead to confusion at best, and a reduction in safety standards at worst. Only time will tell whether my concerns will be realised.

Looking Forward – The FSOA and Major Sporting Events

It is encouraging that one of Patzelt's 2008 visions for the future has come to fruition, namely the role of the FSOA in the safe management of major sporting events. FSOA members have been involved in the training of stewards in South Africa, Greece, Poland and Ukraine. The number of FSOA members who have spread the safety management gospel at conferences throughout Europe and beyond is testimony to their individual knowledge and skills, and also to the regard in which the FSOA is held in other countries.

It is also encouraging that the FSOA has become involved at a very early stage with the local organising committee of the 2012 London Olympic Games. At the FSOA bi-annual conference in October 2010, representatives of the London Olympics spoke of their need to tap into FSOA members skills and expertise to find suitably qualified and competent safety personnel to manage safety at the venues. So Patzelt's wish has come to fruition, and in looking forward, I hope that the FSOA will be able to continue to play its part in the safe management of major sporting events wherever they are held. This can only further enhance the status and reputation of the association.

Looking Forward – the FSOA and Europe

In 2010 there was another milestone in the development of the FSOA, when after approaches by the Football Association of Ireland, this body (together with its club safety officers) became the seventh region of the FSOA. This enables us to share experiences with our colleagues across the Irish Sea, and I hope this will be just the start of a move towards a more European based safety officers association.

In fact there is already a European Stadium and Safety Management Association (ESSMA). It is interesting that its president is John Beattie, safety officer at Arsenal and a previous chair of the FSOA. ESSMA describes itself as a professional organisation that allows stadium and safety managers to exchange experience, and to develop a framework of best practices in the sports industry. In many respects, the aims and aspirations for their membership are much the same as those of the FSOA, but on a far wider scale than safety management. I look forward to seeing closer co-operation between our two organisations.

Looking Forward – the Football Licensing Authority

Over the next seven years, it is not just the FSOA that will face the challenges that change brings. It will also affect one of the association's closest friends and allies, the FLA. In 1997, FLA Chief Executive, John de Quidt, said in *Sport and Safety Management*,

> The FLA has taken great pleasure in the growing professionalism and expertise of club safety officers. It particularly welcomed the formation of the Football Safety Officers Association whose meetings it regularly attends. This body provides an invaluable forum where safety officers can share their experiences, learn from each other and foster their own commitment.

I know from personal experience of the close working relationship between the two bodies and how this has proved to be of a mutual benefit. The aims and aspirations of the FLA and the FSOA are almost identical, so it is no wonder that we constantly sing from the same hymn sheet. Over the years, many improvements in stadium and spectator safety have been very much due to the close bonds developed between both organisations.

However, the FLA suffered in the 2010 government cull of non departmental public bodies. It will cease to exist as an independent entity after the 2012 Olympic Games. In addition, due to budget cuts of 15%, the levels of staffing and the level of service to football, will also be affected. By 2010 the FLA Inspectorate staff had already reduced and it is likely to be further reduced in the coming years.

In addition to these changes, a private members bill was introduced in parliament in 2010, to change the name of the FLA to the 'Sports Grounds Safety Authority'. If the bill goes through, it would allow the organisation to provide advice on safety at sports grounds to any national or international organisation, person or body and to charge for these services in certain circumstances. This will undoubtedly help with the FLA's operating costs. It is expected that the renamed organisation would retain its football licensing remit and its monitoring role of certifying authorities for designated football grounds, but that this remit will not be extended into other sports.

In my opinion, these changes will mean the FLA influence in the football environment will gradually wane. As of 2010, this was already being experienced, with far less match visits being made by the Inspectorate, and attendance at meetings being drastically reduced. Through its Inspectorate, the FLA is currently heavily involved in advising on the safety management and stewarding requirements for the 2012 Olympic Games, and as the Games draw closer, this involvement will become even greater. This change in emphasis, together with the cuts in budget, will mean that the support, encouragement, counsel and advice which traditionally the FSOA membership has enjoyed from the FLA, will be substantially reduced.

With the support of the FLA, clubs have demonstrated their ability to take charge of safety, and the reduced role of the FLA in football should not have a detrimental effect, providing clubs and certifying authorities fully accept and discharge their safety responsibilities. However, over the years it has been demonstrated that not all clubs and certifying authorities are prepared to accept their safety obligations. There is a danger that because we have not had a disaster at one of our football grounds since 1989, that complacency might creep back. It bears repeating that safety is not a one off concept, but something that has to be constantly worked at.

The FLA is the ultimate insurance policy at designated football grounds, ensuring that if complacency or disregard for safety is evident, positive action is taken to address this. I hope the reduced role of the FLA in football is not taken as an excuse by some to reduce safety standards, and thus undo all the hard work and achievements of both the FLA and the FSOA.

Looking Forward – Summary

I have no doubt that as the FSOA moves towards its 25th anniversary, there will be many other challenges and changes for the association membership. Experience has shown just how resilient the membership is in addressing change, whether it is new legislation, guidance, technology, training or qualification requirements. Over the years the association has been the driving force in improving safety and security standards at our football grounds, and in looking forward I have no doubt that this will continue.

However, I am not at all optimistic that as demands on the membership increase, the funding required by the association will be there to support their needs and aspirations. I certainly have grave doubts that the association will be able to play as full a part as it would wish in the development of safety management practices and procedures, due to the lack of funding. Whilst I accept that we live in a harsh economic climate, compared to the wages of some players, and the funding and resources available to other football authorities, the funding needed to provide a secure and stable future for the FSOA is merely a drop in their financial ocean. In looking forward I would hope that old attitudes would change and that all three football authorities will recognise the benefits of having an adequately funded Football Safety Officers' Association.

I have deemed it an honour and a privilege to be a member and president of the FSOA since 2005, and to have been able to share my life with a group of men and women who rarely, if ever, receive the credit they deserve in making our grounds the safe and secure environment they continue to be. It is they who have put the word 'professionalism' into the safety management arena, and it is they who will shape the future of safety management at our grounds, under the leadership of the association. It is also they who will provide the leadership, skill and expertise to spread the English concept and standards of safety management and stewarding to Europe and beyond. In looking forward, I hope in my lifetime to see a stronger and more financially secure association, because the other option – of a weak and insecure FSOA – does not bear thinking about.

APPENDIX – MANAGEMENT RESOURCES

Books

Frosdick, S. and Chalmers, J. (2005) *Safety and Security at Sports Grounds*. Rothersthorpe: Paragon Publishing (ISBN 1-899820-14-0).

Frosdick. S. and Marsh, P. (2005) *Football Hooliganism.* Cullompton: Willan Publishing (ISBN 1-84392-065-4).

Frosdick, S. and Walley L (Eds.) (1997) *Sport and Safety Management*, Oxford: Butterworth-Heinemann (ISBN 0-7506-3281-X).

These three books are in print and available from Amazon.

Official Guidance and Reports

Football Licensing Authority (2011) *Guidance Regarding the Handling of Flares and Fireworks in Sports Grounds*. London: Football Licensing Authority.

Council of the European Union (2010) *Council Conclusions Adopting the 2011-2013 EU Work Programme on Minimising Safety, Security and Public Order Risks in Connection With Sports Events, in Particular Football Matches, With an International Dimension.* Brussels: Council of the European Union.

Football Licensing Authority (2010) *Guide to the Safety Certification of Sports Grounds*. London: Football Licensing Authority.

National Policing Improvement Agency (2010) *Guidance on Policing Football Matches.* London: National Policing Improvement Agency on behalf of the Association of Chief Police Officers.

Premier League (2010) *Persistent Standing and Crowd Safety.* London: The Premier League.

Football Association (2010) *Crowd Management Measures: FA Good Practice Guide for Football Clubs.* London: The Football Association.

Official Journal of the European Union (2010) *Council Resolution of 12 May 2010 Concerning an Updated Handbook With Recommendations For International Police Cooperation and Measures to Prevent and Control Violence and Disturbances in Connection With Football Matches With an International Dimension, in Which at Least One Member State is Involved*. Brussels: Council of the European Union.

** Football Licensing Authority (2009) *Sports Grounds and Stadia Guide No. 4 – Safety Management*. London: Department for Culture, Media and Sport.

The Cabinet Office Emergency Planning College (2009) *Understanding Crowd Behaviours: Guidance and Lessons Identified*. York: The Cabinet Office Emergency Planning College.

House of Commons Home Affairs Committee (2009) *The Cost of Policing Football Matches*. London: The Stationery Office.

Security Industry Authority (2008) *Guidance on the Private Security Act 2001*. London: Security Industry Authority.

Department for Culture, Media and Sport (2008) *Guide to Safety at Sports Grounds (Fifth Edition).* London: The Stationery Office.

Council of Europe (2008) *Checklist of Measures to be Taken by the Organisers of Professional Sporting Events and by the Public Authorities*. Strasbourg: Council of Europe.

Football Against Racism in Europe (2008) *Racist and Neo-Nazi Symbols in Football: A Training Manual for Stewards and Security Staff. FARE.*

UEFA (2006) *UEFA Safety and Security Regulations*. Nyon: Union des associations européennes de football.

UEFA and Football Against Racism in Europe (2006) *Tackling Racism in Club Football: A Guide For Clubs.* Nyon: Union des associations européennes de football.

NaCTSO (2006) *Counter Terrorism Protective Security Advice for Stadia and Arenas*. London: National Counter Terrorism Security Office.

COT (2005) *Good Practices for Safe and Secure Major Sporting Events: Experiences and Lessons From UEFA EURO 2004*. Den Haag: COT Institute for Safety and Crisis Management.

UEFA (2004) *UEFA Delegate's Handbook*. Nyon: Union des associations européennes de football.

FIFA (2004) *Safety Guidelines*. Zurich: Fédération Internationale de Football Association.

IAAM (2002) *Safety and Security Task Force Best Practices Planning Guide – Arenas, Stadiums, Amphitheaters*. Coppell TX: Center for Venue Management Studies.

Home Office (2001) *Guidance Notes for the Procurement of CCTV for Public Safety at Football Grounds (Second Edition)*. Horsham: Home Office Police Scientific Development Branch.

Council of Europe (1985) *European Convention on Spectator Violence And Misbehaviour At Sports Events And In Particular At Football Matches*. Strasbourg: Council of Europe.

With the one exception of **, which is not available as an electronic document, these publications can be downloaded free of charge from Steve Frosdick's library pages at www.iwi-associates.co.uk/library.html

INDEX

T

U

V

Lightning Source UK Ltd.
Milton Keynes UK

174151UK00001B/3/P